MOTHERING
DAUGHTERS

MOTHERING DAUGHTERS

NOVELS *and the* POLITICS *of* FAMILY ROMANCE FRANCES BURNEY *to* JANE AUSTEN

SUSAN C. GREENFIELD

WAYNE STATE UNIVERSITY PRESS   DETROIT

A portion of chapter 1 (now much revised) appeared in
Eighteenth-Century Fiction 3 (1991): 301–20.
I thank *Eighteenth-Century Fiction* for permission to use it here.
Chapter 2 includes a portion of an article
(also much revised) that appeared in
The Eighteenth Century: Theory and Interpretation 33 (1992): 73–89.
I am grateful to the journal for allowing me to reprint this material.
An earlier version of chapter 4 appeared in *PMLA* 112 (1997): 214–28.

Library of Congress Cataloging-in-Publication Data

Greenfield, Susan C.
    Mothering daughters : novels and the politics of family romance : Frances
Burney to Jane Austen / Susan C. Greenfield.
        p. cm.
    Includes bibliographical references and index.
    ISBN 0-8143-2992-6 (cloth, alk. paper)
    1. English fiction—Women authors—History and criticism.   2. Moth-
ers and daughters in literature.   3. Women and literature—Great Britain—
History—18th century.   4. Women and literature—Great Britain—
History—19th century.   5. English fiction—18th century—History and
criticism.   6. English fiction—19th century—History and criticism.
7. Feminist fiction, English—History and criticism.   8. Domestic fiction,
English—History and criticism.   9. Motherhood in literature.   10. Mothers in literature.   11. Family in literature.   I. Title.
    PR858 .M69 G74 2001

823' .5093520431—dc21   2001004773

    ISBN 0-8143-3201-3 (pbk., alk. paper)

For my parents

JUDY *and* JAY GREENFIELD

CONTENTS

7

ACKNOWLEDGMENTS

There are those who have followed this book from its long eclipsed origin as a doctoral dissertation. Ellen Pollak introduced me to the eighteenth-century novel, and her work and friendship have been an enduring inspiration. John Richetti's teaching, writing, and unflagging support have sustained me at every stage of my career. I thank Stuart Curran for his early sponsorship and Daniel Traister for consistently fielding my questions about rare books.

Shortly after receiving my doctoral degree, I met Claudia L. Johnson, whose stunning work on women novelists influences so much of this book and whose generosity and faith gave me the courage to finish it. Deborah Rogers offered critical insights at a key moment. Ruth Perry's advice was essential. I'd like to thank Arthur Evans and Adela Garcia at Wayne State University Press for seeing the book to completion.

It is a pleasure to acknowledge the many friends and academic colleagues (all are both, in that order) who commented on portions of the book, informed its ideas, or helped me to prepare for publication: Carmen Birkle, Robin Bower, Saul Cornell, Kathy Eden, Mary Erler, Christopher Flint, Luis Gamez, Ellen Garvey, Richard Giannone, Christopher GoGwilt, Kim Hall, Constance Hassett, Stuart Sherman, Philip Sicker, and Michael Suarez. Lenny Cassuto was always forthcoming with comfort and excellent advice. With brilliant clarity, Eve Keller consistently sharpened my understanding. Frank Boyle's inimitable conversation has been an intellectual challenge and a joy.

I am proud and fortunate to have remained close with friends from my graduate school class: Jennifer Green, Laura Tanner, and Wendy Wall. James Krasner rescued me and this book at a very difficult time. Jules Law's careful reading made it better. Allyson Booth has talked to me on all subjects and at all hours. Although she views life as a series of pianos randomly falling out of windows onto people's heads, her own unfailing integrity and compassion prove that, even amid chaos, there is a certain good.

I thank Fordham University for the summer fellowship and the faculty fellowship that enabled me to write full-time. The librarians and clerks at both the Quinn and Walsh libraries have kindly tolerated my constant requests and my absurd accumulation of books. I am honored by the friendship of the university librarian, Jim McCabe. My students were an exacting audience for some of the ideas refined here, especially about Austen. Janice Cable's editorial assistance was invaluable.

There are so many whose interests, distractions, and good humor gave me the stamina to work in solitude. I thank all of you and am particularly indebted to: Joy Brownstein, Carmel Fratianni, Leslie Fuchs, Charles Gropper, Elizabeth Kolbert, Melissa Robbins, Melanie Rubin, and Lois Wedin. Laura Dukess has been unquestioningly generous with her wisdom, her sympathy, and her apartment. Stuart Smith provided me with a space to work in peace. In countless ways the members of the MSC book group retaught me how to read.

I was free to write about motherhood only because other women helped care for my home and family. I am grateful to Yvonne Brizan, Sharon Brown, and Sandra Mahase.

I am especially thankful to my mother-in-law, Thelma Weissman, who, during my first pregnancy, promised to come once a week to watch our child. Except for the time she suffered a broken arm on a kindergarten ice-skating trip, she has faithfully kept her promise for ten years and two children. While I wrote, she cooked, colored, and, on occasion, persuaded the bank not to charge us for bounced checks.

Barrie Weissman has inspired me with her own professional accomplishments. Mark Greenfield's avant-garde theater has reminded me that literature should be fun. For powers of attention and analysis (whether focused on ecology or emotions) Ben Greenfield is unmatched.

Matthew Weissman read much of this book. With characteristic wit, he also urged me to keep it in perspective. His love and warmth have enriched everything else beyond measure—beyond what I ever dared hope. Anna and Lenny are our comfort and delight.

In their different ways my parents taught me to love narrative. My father invented the family stories that made my brothers and me laugh. My mother read to me with the voice for which I still listen when I read. For their kindness, generosity, and love, this book can only be a token.

INTRODUCTION

Mothering Daughters
Novels and the Politics of Family Romance

By the end of the eighteenth century, novels by women about missing mothers and their suffering daughters were so common that Jane Austen parodied them in *Northanger Abbey*. Schooled in popular fiction, Catherine Morland cannot visit the Tilney family abbey without growing convinced that the late Mrs. Tilney was murdered by her husband. Catherine listens sympathetically as Mrs. Tilney's only daughter Eleanor describes her mother's absence as her "great and increasing [affliction]" (180). Austen, of course, debunks Catherine's literary expectations. Not only does the heroine discover that Mrs. Tilney was not murdered, but relatively little narrative attention is paid to Eleanor's plight. With pointed emphasis, Austen makes clear that neither a missing mother nor a mournful daughter is the subject of her own interest. And yet the very need to announce this testifies to Austen's investment in—and the centrality of—the mother-daughter plot.

In *Mothering Daughters* I analyze the literary, historical, and psychoanalytic significance of this plot, suggesting that its very predictability marks a growing cultural obsession with motherly duty and influence. In novel after novel, the mother's absence highlights her indispensability; the daughter's pain bears witness to her love. Many historians argue that the eighteenth century witnessed the idealization of maternity that gave rise to modern motherhood. Literary critics situate the consolidation (if not the creation) of the English novel in the same period. Viewing the prominence of the mother-daughter plot in the context of these concurrent developments, *Mothering Daughters* demonstrates the elaborate extent to which women's novels helped construct modern maternity, generating a literary tradition with politically complex and psychologically enduring effects.

I make two major claims. One is that even though it is tempting to emphasize the conservative impact of modern maternity, maternal standards were never ideologically static. Images of good motherhood and of mother-child bonding were deployed in remarkably diverse ways for progressive as well as conservative causes. Dispelling the possibility of a politically unified maternity, the novels studied here indicate the ambiguity and flexibility of the institution itself.[1] *Mothering Daughters* considers this variety from a range of historical vantage points: it examines the social understanding of female sexuality, the scientific and legal treatment of pregnancy, the contradictory debates about maternal breastfeeding, the gradual development of parliamentary support for women's rights to child custody, and the role of maternity in colonial and abolitionist discourses.

Even as the political implications of the novels vary, their models of kinship relations often overlap. My second claim is that the family romance popularized in women's novels was among the many cultural paradigms that laid the ground for the creation and acceptance of psychoanalytic theory. Psychoanalysis places the preoedipal mother-infant bond and its loss at the origin of psychological development, but the very idea of a preoedipal connection depends upon historically contingent assumptions about the mother's primary role in infant care and attachment. *Mothering Daughters* argues that women's novels helped construct the preoedipal period and thus influenced the psychoanalytic theories derived from it. Though the novels deviate from psychoanalysis in significant ways, they anticipate its fundamental premises about mother-child relations with a precision that suggests their own constitutive role.

Modern Maternity and Women's Novels

While there is considerable disagreement about when the nuclear family first materialized, most historians concede that the eighteenth century witnessed its entrenchment. The novelty of the maternal responsibilities on which the nuclear family depended has also been the subject of debate. What is clear is that regardless of whether maternal practice or feeling radically changed in the 1700s, motherhood was idealized with exceptional fervor by the century's end and commonly represented as a full-time occupation. Increasingly, women were defined by their maternity, and maternity was supposed to occupy a woman's perpetual interest. Motherhood became "a biologico-moral responsibility lasting through the entire period of the children's education," writes Michel Foucault (104); or as John Gillis puts it, "birth ceased to be something that happens to a woman and became the ultimate source of adult female identity" (*World* 174).[2]

There were many signs that the idealization of motherhood in England was, if not new, intensifying during this period. Perhaps the most frequently cited shift concerns maternal breastfeeding, which began to rival wet-nursing as a popular form of child feeding; an endless stream of medical tracts and conduct books urged mothers to exercise their "natural" duty to suckle, and the viability of maternal nursing became a widely recognized register of national health.[3]

Change was also evident in the legal arena. It became increasingly difficult to convict mothers of infanticide, for instance, because juries and judges grew unwilling to accept the possibility that a mother might not love her newborn. As long as an accused woman could demonstrate the most minimal signs of affection (even if only by showing that she had prepared linen in advance), she was apt to be acquitted of child murder.[4] By the third decade of the nineteenth century, the idealization of maternal love was pronounced enough to rattle centuries of exclusive paternal custody rights. The Infant Custody Bill, passed in 1839, was the first law in English history to grant women the right to retain or visit with their children in cases of separation or divorce.[5]

Scholars tend to associate the eighteenth-century investment in maternity with the rise of the middle class—the gradual replacement of an aristocratic society based on property and patronage with a bourgeois structure privileging capitalist individualism.[6] It is commonly argued that women were eventually domesticated in a capitalist society that defined the acquisition of money as a male pursuit while designating the home as a woman's special arena.[7] "The equation of women with domesticity came to be one of the fixed points of middle-class status" (Davidoff and Hall 275), and motherhood came to be one of the fixed points of domesticity. From one view, capitalist individualism and maternity appear to depend on antithetical ideals. The loving mother, celebrated for her removal from the economic world, was, as Toni Bowers argues, valued for her abnegation of self (*Politics* 96). At the same time, though, the unique subjectivity of her child was underscored by the requirement that she supply him with devoted attention.

The "rise" of the novel roughly corresponded with the idealization of full-time maternity, a parallel characteristic of the genre's general preoccupation with the problem of family, about which scholars often comment. Eighteenth-century texts so consistently concern what Patricia Spacks calls "the dynamics of affiliation" (115) or Homer Brown describes as questions about genealogical order, inheritance, legitimacy, and "proper names and naming" (*Institutions* xiv) that Christopher Flint suggests we identify a "coupling of family and fiction" during the period (20).

Of course, there is otherwise considerable debate about the novel's formal characteristics and its origin. Many have stressed that the novel was not new, not uniquely English, and not a recognizably coherent form in the eighteenth century.[8] *Mothering Daughters* ascribes to a few premises about which there is nevertheless some consensus: that the novel was seen as "palpably new" during the eighteenth century itself (Davis, "Reconsidering Origins" 481); that the period clearly witnessed the proliferation of the kind of fiction that influenced the genre's national consolidation; and that the novel's nomenclature was reasonably well established by the century's end, the period under examination here.

Critics also generally (if implicitly) agree on the novel's value as a resource for interpreting modern subjectivity. In his heuristic *The Rise of the Novel,* Ian Watt ascribes the novel's popularity to its realistic reflection of the new values of individualism. Adjusting Watt, more recent scholarship stresses the novel's role in producing and contesting (as well as registering) individualist values. Thus, John Richetti argues that "the ideology of individualism . . . is precisely what" the novel interrogates (*English Novel* 3; see also 16). Drawing attention to the national, racial, class, and gender differences on which modern notions of individuality depend, novel studies have to some extent shifted "from refining the definition of the novel as a literary type to understanding how novels produce social divisions" (Lynch and Warner, introduction 2). There is also significant interest in how commercialism and the commodification of print shaped the rhetoric about both individual identity and fiction, influenced especially by Catherine Gallagher's *Nobody's Story* (1994).[9]

It is symptomatic of the novel's reflection, production, and commercialization of social identity—as well as of its related preoccupation with family matters—that by the end of the eighteenth century, at precisely the moment the genre's nomenclature stabilized, female novelists appeared to have exceeded male novelists in importance. Novels by women did not actually outnumber those by men (Turner 31), but because there was an "unparalleled surge" in female literary productivity (Turner 38–39), common lore suggested otherwise.[10] As one writer for the *Monthly Review* memorably put it in 1790: "Of the various species of composition . . . there are none in which *our* writers of the male sex have less excelled, since the days of Richardson and Fielding, than in the arrangement of the novel. Ladies seem to appropriate to themselves an exclusive privilege in this kind of writing" (qtd. in Tompkins 120–21n).

There are a number of good full-length studies of the female novelist's general celebrity, including books by Terry Lovell, Rosalind Miles, Ruth Perry, Jane Spencer, Dale Spender, Janet Todd, and Cheryl Turner.[11] A few of their major points can be stressed here. Because the novel tended—like no previous form—to focus on domestic events rendered from a female character's perspective, female authors seemed naturally suited to the genre. So too, at a time when genteel women were discouraged from making money, writing novels offered a rare opportunity to earn an income without sacrificing femininity. The novel's dependence on vernacular prose also made it generally more accessible to relatively uneducated writers and readers, among whom women were inevitably included. It is likely that the prominent female audience that emerged by the end of the eighteenth century played a significant role in supporting women's novels.

Beginning with the fact that many of these novels concern problems of maternity and mother-daughter relationships, *Mothering Daughters* considers their complex role in the modernization of female kinship. I focus on specific novels by six authors: Frances Burney's *Evelina* (1778); Ann Radcliffe's *The Italian* (1797); Mary Wollstonecraft's *The Wrongs of Woman; or, Maria* (1798); Maria Edgeworth's *Belinda* (1801); Amelia Alderson Opie's *Adeline Mowbray* (1804); and Jane Austen's *Emma* (1816). Though the list could easily be expanded to include additional works by the same or different novelists (Elizabeth Inchbald's *A Simple Story* [1791], for instance—or even, with some qualification, Mary Shelley's *Frankenstein* [1818]), I believe a detailed study more effectively reveals the intricacies of familial relations. I offer *Mothering Daughters* as a work of close analysis, not a survey.

Politics and Psychoanalysis

The political variability I chart in the novels is characteristic of a broad range of late eighteenth- and early nineteenth-century maternal discourses. As maternity gained currency in conduct books, medical texts, and religious, philosophical, and political tracts, conservative and progressive writers generally agreed about the mother's basic responsibilities, but they invested her with different meaning. Thus, while most authors writing on the subject argued in favor of maternal breastfeeding, there are telling distinctions in how the politics of suckling are defined. English medical writers such as William Cadogan and William Buchan suggest that maternal breastfeeding will guarantee husbands control over their wives, the privileged control over the poor, and the European race control over "savages" and slaves. Yet in *A Vindication of the Rights of Woman* (1792), Mary Wollstonecraft claims that middle- and upper-class mothers will not successfully suckle their children until sexual, class, and racial hierarchies are dismantled. [12]

Even as the novels typify such political diversity, they tend to share at least one narrative similarity: either the mother figure is missing or the mother and daughter are separated. The novels endorse maternal practices like breastfeeding not by evidence of their successful enactment but rather by negative examples of their problematic unavailability. Whether she is dead, missing, emotionally detached, or present without the daughter's realizing it, the mother is conspicuous in her absence. [13] Admittedly, the same can often be said of the father (one symptom perhaps of the waning of the monarchy and the related dissociation of patriarchy and paternity in a modern civil society "not structured by . . . the power of fathers" [Pateman 3]). [14] Moreover, maternal absence itself is an old and persistent narrative problem—characteristic not just of earlier novels but of a wide variety of other literary forms as well.

Nevertheless, it is particularly striking that at a time when motherhood was becoming a major subject of public discussion and a key litmus test for femininity, representing its successful enactment remained a near narrative impossibility. One might argue that the novel's attention to the mother's absence captures the fallacy of contemporary maternal ideals—that successful motherhood does not exist in women's novels because it does not exist in real life, and that the authors are self-consciously rejecting the proliferating images that suggest otherwise. [15] Yet in many of the novels the absence also becomes the point around which maternal ideals are articulated and reinforced. As the family and social order collapse without the mother, the novels prove her fundamental importance.

What is most consistently significant about the mother's—or in some cases the daughter's—unavailability is its impact on desire. In several of the novels examined here the separation between mother and daughter shapes the protagonist's basic longings and thereby forms the basis of the narrative's structure. Although played out in different ways in the texts, absence produces the desire that is the subject of the novel. This desire, which can be loosely categorized as homoerotic and incestuous, becomes the center around which familial relations are configured.

Psychoanalysis plays an important role in this book precisely because it provides valuable discussions of mother-child separation and of the familial production of desire. Some chapters make use of Freud's account of mother-child kinship and incest, some of Lacan's theory of absence and language, and some of gender-inflected adaptations of both, especially those offered by Nancy Chodorow, Luce Irigaray, and Julia Kristeva. The hazard of using psychoanalysis to interpret pre-Freudian novels is that the theory can emerge as historically transcendent—as a register of universal truth applicable to all cultures and all times. But I mean to stress the historical contingency of psychoanalysis even as I depend on its well-known familial paradigms to help define those in the novels. My goal is not to show that the novels affirm psychoanalysis but rather to suggest that they anticipate and help shape it by popularizing the bourgeois family relations that, as Mary Jacobus puts it, arguably produced "the psychic formations and subjectivity associated with" Freud (209). If the novels share any one political effect it is this.

As a form, the early novel helped construct the interiorized individual subject, defined not by external aristocratic assets like birth and inherited property but by internal "middle-class" virtues like intelligence, industry, and character—a self defined especially by a Lockean process of thinking. Because the early novel tends to follow a protagonist's internal development both in relation to and in reaction against a nuclear family that is "dramatized . . . as both problem and solution" (Richetti, *English Novel* 7), it brings together some of the narrative features that were to become central elements in psychoanalytic theory. The novel's sustained interest in the protagonist's thoughts—epitomized by the number of early eighteenth-century texts written from a first person or epistolary perspective—offers the illusion of a uniquely interior view of the family's effect.

Granted, familial relations have always been a staple of literature, and Freud was especially indebted to Sophocles's *Oedipus the King*.[16] But even as Freud draws on the ancient drama, his story of the *pre*oedipal mother-child bond marks the promotion of a particularly popular (if not a uniquely) modern concept. Freud is famous for his narrative of oedipal father-son rivalry. But Freud's most original contribution may inhere in his invocation of the earlier maternal story, on which so many later theorists—including Lacan, Chodorow, Irigaray, and Kristeva—rely even when complicating or challenging Freud.[17]

The preoedipal bond describes a period before the onset of the oedipal crisis during which a child experiences a sensuous and symbiotic attachment to its mother; it is only after the child painfully separates from the mother at the onset of the incest taboo that he or she develops other family relationships, notably with the father. Sophocles's Oedipus is not raised by his mother, and thus the story of his incestuous love for her cannot include an earlier and potentially more innocent moment of mother-child symbiosis. By contrast, late eighteenth-century women's novels often implicitly evoke this moment, as do some of the most famous works they influenced, such as Dickens's *David Copperfield* (1850).[18] Of course, the visual iconography of the Virgin and Christ child long predates the "rise" of the novel, but I would suggest the genre played an important role in secularizing and universalizing the maternal bond by making it part of every child's story.[19]

In designating the preoedipal moment, psychoanalysis takes as given a method of mothering that did not fully evolve in the West until the eighteenth century. Although the eighteenth century was not the first time the mother-child bond was described as "natural," this was the period when the idea of its naturalness became entrenched throughout western Europe. The increasing emphasis on "forced close, daily contact between the mother . . . and her child" provided what E. Ann Kaplan describes as "the need for, and subsequent findings of, psychoanalytic theory" (*Motherhood* 27).[20] Along with other discourses, the early novel helped confirm the cultural consensus about the centrality of mother-child attachment and ultimate separation that psychoanalysis inherited. Psychoanalysis provides useful tools for interpreting mother-daughter relations in women's novels, I suggest, because the novels themselves participated in the popularization of the maternal models that gained currency in the next centuries and the beginnings of structural definition with Freud.

Mothering Daughters and Feminist Scholarship

My aim to situate women's novels in their historical context obviously
bears the mark of feminist academic history. Perhaps the single most
significant effect of feminist literary criticism has been the resurrection
of female authors who would have otherwise remained invisible. Yet
segregating authors by sex has run the risk of "isolat[ing] women as
a special and separate topic," as Joan Scott puts it in another context
(*Gender* 20). The publication of Nancy Armstrong's *Desire and Domestic
Fiction* (1987) was instrumental in transforming discussions of novels
by and for women because the book avoided such segregation. Adjusting truisms about the rising middle class's role in popularizing both
the novel and domestic womanhood, Armstrong reverses the order of
events and concludes that the endorsement of domestic womanhood in
women's fiction was instrumental in consolidating the modern middle
class. Her attention to the role women's literature plays in the development and political utility of sexual and social difference marked the
beginning of a critical perspective that continues in some of the most
influential books on eighteenth-century English women authors, such
as Claudia L. Johnson's *Equivocal Beings* (1995). It has clearly informed
the methodology here.

  Similarly, my interest in mother-daughter relationships is a
product of at least three decades of lively discussions of the topic
across a range of disciplines. There are, for instance, a number of
historical accounts of the rise of modern maternity.[21] And even when
it is not the explicit subject, motherhood is often a central topic in
feminist-inflected histories of the early modern period,[22] especially
those concerning the development of modern science.[23]

  Because psychoanalysis relies so heavily on family narrative,
it has been especially attractive to feminist theorists, many of whom
have drawn on Freud's account of the preoedipal period but have questioned his inattention to the mother's perspective and his unwillingness to investigate the daughter's enduring maternal attachment.[24] Two
schools of thought have become particularly prominent. One, based in
D. W. Winnicott's object-relations theory and energized by Nancy
Chodorow's pathbreaking and controversial *The Reproduction of Mothering* (1978), examines the material dynamics of mother-daughter attachment and the subject positions resulting from this bond. Chodorow
famously argues that the daughter never fully relinquishes her mother,
and that this makes individuation difficult.[25] The other approach, based

in Lacanian theory and associated with the French writers Hélène Cixous, Luce Irigaray, and Julia Kristeva, emphasizes the inevitable loss of the mother, linking her absence to the symbolic order of language; language itself is seen as the source of a subjectivity that is at once incoherent and particularly problematic for women.[26]

Literary treatments of maternity and the mother-daughter bond have tended to be quite interdisciplinary, drawing on psychoanalysis or history or both for interpretive support.[27] In integrating these fields, *Mothering Daughters* has many excellent precedents, including Margaret Homans's *Bearing the Word* (1986), Marianne Hirsch's *The Mother/Daughter Plot* (1989), Barbara Gelpi's *Shelley's Goddess* (1992), Felicity Nussbaum's *Torrid Zones* (1995), and Toni Bowers's *The Politics of Motherhood* (1996). What is new is my attention to both the political flexibility *and* the psychoanalytic consistency of novelistic models of female kinship. The ideological variances among the texts I study disprove the universality of women's interests, but their narrative similarities (like the treatment of the mother's absence) suggest that certain writers deliberately imitated each others' strategies, aiming to manufacture a sense of kinship and even of matrilineal descent.[28]

Earlier Mothers: Roxana and Mrs. Shandy

Some of the most prominent details about maternity appear in earlier and now canonical novels by male authors, including Daniel Defoe, Samuel Richardson, Henry Fielding, and Laurence Sterne. This is not to say that maternal paradigms originate with the "fathers of the novel." Margaret Doody has shown that many of the genre's familial conventions date back to the ancient novel. And Paula Backscheider and William Warner, among others, argue that the works of Defoe, Richardson, and Fielding were specifically influenced by and intertwined with the contemporary amatory fiction of Aphra Behn, Delariviere Manley, and Eliza Haywod.[29] But precisely because the male tradition has achieved such critical status, it is instructive to examine its unexpected attention to maternal problems. That motherhood provides part of the occasion for narrative in texts that helped classify the genre suggests just how pivotal it was to the novel's canonization.

Samuel Richardson's enormously influential *Clarissa* (1747–48), for instance, is punctuated by maternal absence; the heroine fruitlessly seeks to retain her mother's affection and loyalty when her father and brother force them apart.[30] A less melodramatic but equally popular account of maternal loss is available in Henry Fielding's *Joseph Andrews* (1742) and *Tom Jones* (1749), both of which record the missing mother's critical role in determining kinship relations; because only the mother knows the true origin of the hero, only she can resolve the identity questions that keep the plot in motion.[31]

Though women novelists inevitably incorporated earlier (and in some cases ancient) plots in their works, many also sought to "feminize" old patterns and say something new about female kinship in the process. Thus, in several women's novels maternal loss becomes a more central problem than it is in either Richardson's or Fielding's work, and the significance of the mother's powers of identification is heightened.

Like *Clarissa, Joseph Andrews,* and *Tom Jones,* Daniel Defoe's *Roxana* (1724) and Laurence Sterne's *Tristram Shandy* (1759–67) offer cogent examples of the paradigmatic features that women novelists regularly adopted and revised. I discuss them at some length below not to suggest that they have an exclusive relevance but because *Roxana* and *Tristram Shandy* are particularly useful in highlighting both the narrative constraints and the ideological flexibility of the mother-daughter story. The same could obviously be said of other novels.

Often defined as one of the earliest English novels, *Roxana* is notable, as Richetti puts it, for the precision with which it "anticipates . . . the affections and alliances" of the "interior life" that characterize the domestic novel (Richetti, *English Novel* 66). I would add that it is specifically maternal affection and the alliance between mother and daughter that become structurally critical in the book.[32] Abandoned by her "fool" of a husband in the early pages, Roxana responds by abandoning their five children. Disguising herself, she embarks on a life of profitable prostitution, during which she produces several more children. In the harrowing and suspenseful finale, she is discovered by one of her legitimate daughters and brought to the brink of insanity by the memory of her failed maternal obligations.

Like many of the novels studied in *Mothering Daughters, Roxana* explores the inevitable obstructions to maternity in a world where woman's sexual options and reproductive outlets are limited to either wifehood or prostitution. Marriage, to which maternity is legally bound, ironically provides no legal support for woman's role as caretaker; thus, Roxana's husband deserts her and she cannot maintain their children. Prostitution is incompatible with maternity because

although it generates children, a whore's sexual value depends on her removal of them. As much as any late eighteenth-century woman writer,
Defoe draws attention to the social conditions that make the mother
disappear.[33]

Granted, Defoe's text is distinguished by chronology. Written
when full-time motherhood was only beginning to be touted with
the gusto that characterized the century's end, *Roxana* registers an
ambiguity about maternal nature that later novels rarely share to the
same extent. When Roxana famously dismisses the death of her infant
by saying "nor . . . was I sorry the Child did not live, the necessary
Difficulties attending it . . . being consider'd" (142), her nonchalance
suggests not so much that she is resisting maternal ideals but that they
have not yet had a concrete impact on her.

At other times, however, Roxana waxes eloquent about her maternal sentiments with a certainty that anticipates later novels. Though
she nearly contemplates eating her children (51), she is also distraught
by their hunger: "I saw nothing but misery and the utmost distress
before me, even to have my Children starve before my Face; I leave
any one that is a mother of children . . . to consider and reflect, what
must be my condition" (46). Naturalizing maternal love, Roxana here
suggests that all mothers instinctively care for their children, that they
share a certain knowledge and set of feelings only other mothers can
understand.

When Roxana's daughter Susan returns in the last section of
the book, the ambiguity about motherhood is largely resolved as, to
her horror, Roxana learns that she cannot escape kinship. Whether she
disguises herself as a Turkish slave or a humble Quaker, her maternal
history emerges intact because it constitutes an identity so indelible that
it permeates any of the other selves she tries to fashion. The daughter,
Susan—who bears her real name, and whose narrative reintroduction
provides the only occasion upon which Roxana admits to that name—
eventually realizes that Roxana is her parent despite her mother's
elaborate schemes to prove otherwise. In the end, motherhood becomes
Roxana's only true identity, and as such it is irrepressible.[34]

Fittingly, Roxana is physically drawn to Susan even as she
tries to disengage herself. One of the most dramatic and oft-quoted
scenes in the novel recounts a time when Susan suspects but has not
yet confirmed the kinship of which Roxana is certain. The women kiss
and Roxana nearly faints with excitement: "it was a secret inconceivable
Pleasure to me when I kiss'd her, to know that I kiss'd my own Child;

my own Flesh and Blood, born of my Body; . . . much ado I had, not to abandon myself to an Excess of Passion at the first Sight of her, much more when my Lips touch'd her Face; I thought I must have taken her in my Arms, and kiss'd her again a thousand times" (323). Sexually intensified by years of separation, Roxana's love for her child confirms the sentiments of which she had formerly seemed free, becoming what seems irrefutable proof of the natural basis of maternal affection.

Yet the problem of Roxana's ever acting upon maternal love—of her ever actually playing the role of mother—remains as intractable as it was at the beginning of the novel. The more maternity emerges as the foundation of female identity, the more it comes into conflict with the roles of wife and whore that have long constituted the grounds of womanhood. After Roxana marries the merchant, Susan follows the clue of the pseudonym "Roxana" and uncovers the history of her mother's first marriage and later prostitution. The sexualized name that had, for Roxana, epitomized the disposal of her first marriage—and which she now wants to dispose of to protect her second—marks the collision of her roles as wife and mistress.

There is no place for a mother-daughter relationship amid the wreckage. Though Susan is so closely bonded to Roxana that she has uncanny insight into Roxana's identity, she cannot gain the acknowledgment for which she longs: Roxana calls herself Susan's "tender . . . Mother" (239) and fires her servant Amy when she threatens to harm her (361), but she flies from Susan's love. Her relationships with her surviving sons are much less intense, marked by neither the same attachment nor the same revulsion. Roxana raises none of her children, but she pays for her legitimate son's education and apprenticeship and pleads with the prince concerning the education of their illegitimate son, who becomes a military hero. If only from a distance, Roxana creates a mother-son tie.

But though she finances her daughters, Roxana can never make the same connection with them, in part because women have such limited social positions. In a world where women are identified exclusively in terms of their association with men there is no position from which they can relate to each other.[35] Luce Irigaray has developed an elegant theory about this obstruction, which I discuss in chapters 3 and 5. Here, I will simply suggest that Roxana's daughter is poised to replicate her mother's fate but cannot face her as another person. Indeed, Roxana imagines Susan as a degraded version of herself, who will either make a foolish marriage or conceive a bastard child—or do both (239). Later, when Roxana meets her other daughter, she is struck by "how the Girl was the very Counterpart of myself" (378).

Without difference, there are no grounds for interaction, and the mirroring mother and daughter are doomed to implode. By the end of *Roxana*, all distinctions between female characters collapse as Susan stalks the parent whose name she shares, armed with the same details about Roxana's past that Roxana herself relates in the novel. Desperate to separate Susan from Roxana, Amy offers to murder Susan, upon which Roxana threatens to kill Amy, only to realize that "to have fal'n upon *Amy*, had been to have murther'd myself" (350). When Amy finally does kill Susan, the violence stands as gruesome testament to the impossibility of sustaining a mother-daughter relationship in the living world, even as the power of the bond persists—in all its chaos—on an imaginative register. Susan is more present to Roxana in her absence: "She was ever before my Eyes. I saw her by-Night, and by-Day she haunted my Imagination. . . . Sometimes I thought I saw her with the Throat cut; sometimes with her Head cut, and her Brains knocke'd out" (374). The book ends with conflation as Roxana describes Amy's murder of Susan as "the Injury done the poor Girl, by both of us" (379).[36]

That the mother-daughter bond is just as emotionally dense and intractable in late eighteenth-century novels by women suggests the ironic fruitfulness of a relationship that cannot be represented. As both narrative subject and problem, the mother-daughter bond registers the simultaneous impetus for—and difficulty of—novel narrative itself. More concretely, key features of the problem in *Roxana* might be seen as paradigmatic: mother and daughter are separated, but separation breeds an urgent desire for reunion. The daughter's resemblance to the mother marks their transcendent connection, though it also signals the impossibility of their ever interacting. Too vexed to be negotiated by mother and daughter alone, the kinship requires the mediation of a third party, often a servant.

Yet the paradigm offers significant room for adjusting particularities. Perhaps the single most important difference between *Roxana* and the women's novels studied here is that none of the latter features mothers as evasive or as violent as Roxana.[37] In both *Belinda* and *Adeline Mowbray*, for instance, the mother character rejects the mirroring daughter, but her rejection is ultimately reversed, and she emerges a doting parent. More typically, in novels like *Evelina* and the many subsequent texts modeled upon it, it is the father, not the mother, who refuses to identify and reunite with the daughter. Susan says of Roxana, "She is my Mother; She is my Mother; and she does not own me" (352). But Evelina's father is the parent who will not "*properly* own her" (19). Such neglect would be as unthinkable of Evelina's mother as murder. In many women's novels, mother and daughter are innocent victims of a patriarchal figure who is largely responsible for their separation, often because he has tried—or actually managed—to kill one of them. Working within the structural boundaries of the mother-daughter plot, female authors make it even clearer than Defoe that women's separation is the consequence of social oppression, not of their volition.

Tristram Shandy draws attention to other narrative options and constraints in representations of maternity. In a novel that begins with the narrator's hilariously protracted and digressive description of his own conception and near death during childbirth, authorship itself is indivisible from pregnancy and parturition. Tristram can write only because he is conceived and delivered, neither of which is easy. His difficulty in ushering his character into the world invariably returns to his dependence on the maternal body and thus to the tenuousness of his own—and the novel's—existence. Although Mrs. Shandy is just as much at risk of dying during childbirth as Tristram, she ultimately emerges with a certain control over human origins that neither Tristram nor any other male character wields. *Roxana* naturalizes the mother by suggesting that the heroine's true identity is her maternal one. *Tristram Shandy* does the same by emphasizing the mother's privileged access to the secret of birth.

Tristram's near death in birth is just one of countless examples of the threat of absence around which the novel is loosely organized. Death hounds Tristram for the remainder of the book and eventually claims Yorick, Trim, Bobby, and Tom. Fear of castration, another version of loss, is the book's most comic preoccupation. Whether referring to Walter's frequent impotence, Toby's wounded groin, Dr. Slop's cut thumb, or Tristram's crushed nose, accidental circumcision, or shortened name, the novel rarely advances a page without invoking male anxiety about bodily or sexual deficiency.

Paternity, which cannot be physically guaranteed, is a related and especially vexing concern. No man can bridge the gap between himself and his son; no son can be sure of his father. With a wife so bored by their monthly lovemaking that she thinks only of whether he has remembered to wind the clock, Walter has particular reason for worry. Little wonder that the timing of Tristram's birth is suspicious, that Tristram does not bear any resemblance to Walter (422–23), that Yorick jokingly (or not) claims Tristram as kin (327), and that there is a bend-sinister (signifying bastardy) on the Shandy carriage's coat-of-arms (311).[38] Not so much literal proof of Tristram's illegitimacy, these details testify to the father's fundamental powerlessness over the circumstances of birth.

Never one easily to accept defeat, Walter compensates by trying to control his wife's fertility, only to exacerbate the threat of castration and death.[39] The consequence of his specifying the terms of Mrs. Shandy's lying-in and then opposing her will in asking Dr. Slop to oversee her delivery is that Slop crushes Tristram's nose after cutting his own thumb. As Arthur Cash so convincingly establishes, Dr. Slop is the agent of death, not birth. Except for the forceps, every instrument in his medical bag is designed to save the mother by destroying and extracting the fetus in a difficult delivery such as Tristram's.[40] Dr. Slop also appears willing to perform a cesarean section, which was invariably fatal for the mother. Walter favors a cesarean not only because he is convinced that the vaginal canal is the most dangerous place for a fetus's brain but also perhaps because his anxiety about his own fatherhood makes him hostile toward his wife.

The fallacy of paternity is linked to the novel's preoccupation with the fallacy of narrative, itself another version of castration. Because of the irrevocable gap between abstract word and material referent, human meaning is founded upon absence; loss constitutes the basis of representation. Though characteristically unable to capture the whole problem, male sexual anxiety and paternal uncertainty offer analogues for the ease with which words are deflated—for the infinite distance between what is said and what is actually known. As Dennis Allen describes it, language in *Tristram Shandy* "can only inadequately convey [what happens]. . . . The inability of language to reflect reality . . . is a form of impotence" (659).[41] Thus Tristram exclaims: "Well might Locke write a chapter upon the imperfections of words" (354), and "what little knowledge is got by mere words" (595). With its "bastardly digressions" (515), blank, marble, and black pages, skipped chapters, and countless ellipses, the novel's textual apparatus reinforces the message, drawing attention to the inefficacy of its own narrative purpose, the many moments when even the pretense of linguistic meaning fails.

With the possible exception of Tristram, the central male characters do not get the point. As if hoping that representation will overcome absence, they are driven to locate certainty in signs.[42] Uncle Toby's misguided belief that maps and fortifications can recount the moment he was nearly castrated during the siege of Namur is exemplary.[43] Similarly, Walter forces "every event in nature into an hypothesis" (613), often to compensate for the dubiousness of paternity. As Tristram explains of his father's fears of the vaginal canal: "It is the nature of an hypothesis, when once a man has conceived it, that it assimilates everything to itself, as proper nourishment; and, from the first moment of your begetting it, it generally grows the stronger by every thing you see, hear, read, or understand" (165). Pregnant with theories about the danger of the mother's body, Walter deflects his anxiety about his inability to control it.

Lest we miss the extent to which all representation derives in part from men's need to compensate for their material detachment from kinship, other signifying efforts are also rendered with mock maternal imagery.[44] Toby is, at one point, "two full months gone" in his efforts to recount the history of his injury and, with the help of military plans, made more eloquent "before the first year of his confinement" (109). And Yorick speaks of having undergone "unspeakable torments, in bringing forth [a] sermon" because "I was delivered of it at the wrong end of me" (314). With an exaggerated rhetoric that draws attention to his own dependence on birth metaphors, Tristram ridicules the tropes that have long characterized male creativity and is fittingly unable either swiftly or directly to render his birth.

The female characters in *Tristram Shandy* are spared such problems because they generally attach less importance to words, one consequence of which is that they repeatedly confound men's representational efforts. Thus, when Susannah rushes the ailing newborn Tristram to the curate for christening (as Walter struggles to put on his breeches), she shortens Walter's choice of name (287–88). Similarly, Mrs. Shandy has "such a head-piece, that [her husband] cannot hang up a single inference within side it" (161; see also 452, 584). When they do attend to language, women are apt to be more literal than men: believing in the material connection between body and word, the Widow Wadman expects to see Toby's groin when he promises to show her "the very place" he was wounded (594). But Toby, for whom signification has become an end in and of itself, alludes only to his map.

For Walter Shandy, it is precisely the difference between female materialism and male abstraction that is so dangerous to men. His theory about the threat his wife's vaginal canal poses to his son's brain pits female object against male intelligibility, the mother's pelvis against the unborn boy's capacity for "wit" and "eloquence" (163). If signification is Walter's comfort for the uncertainty of fatherhood, the female body marks the limits of his solace, becoming the place where language is thwarted. Although the novel can never say so directly while insisting on the immateriality of words, it suggests by negative example that woman is the bodily source from which language deviates. By logical extension, the gap between word and thing originates with the problem of birth—with the difference between the abstraction of fatherhood and the material assurance of motherhood. Women do not rely on language because they do not have to.

"Of all the riddles of a married life," an exasperated Walter complains to Toby:

> there is not one that has more intricacies in it than this—that from the very moment the mistress of the house is brought to bed, every female in it, from my lady's gentle-woman down to the cinder-wench, becomes an inch taller for it; and give themselves more airs upon that single inch, than all their other inches put together.
> I think rather, replied my uncle Toby, that 'tis we who sink an inch lower. (284–85)

The riddle is perhaps not so intricate as Walter need believe. Sinking an inch in the face of women's cross-class assurance about birth, men meet their inevitable impotence. As Walter well understands, a father's only recourse is to try to supervise the reproductive process, by insisting, for instance, that a doctor be present at his child's delivery: "I know not," he says, as he waits for Tristram to be born, "what we have left to give up, in lieu of who shall bring our children into the world,—unless that,—of who shall beget them" (159). But, of course, Walter may have already given up his power of begetting. Only Mrs. Shandy knows for sure, and she is not talking.

Of the abundant interpretations of *Tristram Shandy*, two are especially helpful here. J. Paul Hunter suggests that *Tristram Shandy* registers a growing cultural conviction "that men [are] holding their place only nominally and that women [are] beginning to control energy, vitality, and ultimately identity" ("Clocks" 194). Ross King argues that *Tristram Shandy* mirrors the Enlightenment dissolution between word and thing, the erosion of an earlier belief in their "divinely ordained bonds of resemblance or affinity" (304). Both explanations are based on the idea that Sterne's novel reflects a new challenge to the order of

things. What had once appeared inherently referential and valuable—
the word, the father, and, especially, the word of the father—was, in
the wake of socioeconomic change and the diminution of monarchal
and aristocratic authority, no longer so reliable. For Hunter, Tristram's
mother's assurance about birth stands for a new cultural moment:
She "is finally the figure of the novel's subversive creative imagination
that begets without regard to linear or patrilinear order" (Hunter,
"Clocks" 196).

Several late eighteenth-century women's novels are both similarly premised on the inherent paucity of patrilinear power and similarly preoccupied with the sexual dynamics and cultural implications
of language usage. Like *Tristram Shandy,* these novels often attribute
singular importance to the mother's biological certainty about birth
and, as Hunter suggests, link this certainty to the possibility of social
change.

But at least some women writers are more emphatic about
woman's advantages. Whereas Mrs. Shandy's body is an ever-receding
point before language—the space of origin that cannot be defined—in
a series of women's novels the mother's physical authority is repre-
sentable, and the mother herself skilled at representation. Indeed, the
mother's privileged materiality can constitute the basis of a linguistic truth inconceivable in *Tristram Shandy.* For Sterne, the difference
between father and mother corresponds to the irrevocable division
between word and thing. For popular female authors, the mother's
proximity to material origin affords her access to an imagined moment
before this division occurs. It is the combined impact of the mother's
assurance about kinship and her ability to speak the truth about its
bodily source that provides the basis for social reconstruction.

Frances Burney to Jane Austen

Along with the problem of mother-daughter separation and its impact
on desire, the connections among maternity, materiality, and language
constitute major preoccupations of late eighteenth-century women's
novels. In the chapters that follow, I explore these concerns in the
context of historically specific discussions about sexuality, pregnancy,
breastfeeding, child custody, and the generation of racial and colonial
difference and authority. Together the chapters consider the extent to
which women novelists helped produce both the modern mother—with

all her political power and pitfalls—and what have become psychological truisms about the mother-daughter bond.

Many of the chapters, for instance, document the insistence with which women novelists privilege the mother's imprint on her daughter, even when the mother herself is missing. In Frances Burney's first novel *Evelina,* the heroine looks so much like her dead mother that she seems to have been stamped with her image. Chapter 1 examines the linguistic, scientific, and legal implications of the astonishing moment when this resemblance becomes the means by which Evelina is legitimated. Such a resolution, I argue, adapts eighteenth-century medical theories about the mother's influence on fetal development to question the father's legal rights, especially that of naming. Extending the kind of association between pregnancy and materiality offered in *Tristram Shandy, Evelina* insists that the mother's physical impression on her child makes her the actual author of identity. Several later women writers imitate Burney's use of maternal resemblance to make a similar point.

In Ann Radcliffe's *The Italian* the maternal impression is sexual. When the heroine unknowingly meets her missing mother she is attracted to her in terms that anticipate feminist psychoanalytic discussions of homoerotic incestuous love. Whereas Roxana experiences a fleeting passion for her daughter, in Radcliffe's novel the sexual bond between female parent and child is more enduring. Chapter 2 argues that though modern readers might think homoerotic incest would seem subversive in the eighteenth century, *The Italian* points to a historically different set of social tenets. Not only does Radcliffe depict homoerotic incestuous feeling as normal, she stresses its conservative value by referring to other gothic works—Horace Walpole's *The Mysterious Mother* (1768) and Matthew Lewis's *The Monk* (1796)—in which heterosexual incest has a disastrous effect. In the end, Radcliffe suggests, homoerotic incest is less likely to interfere with marriage and maternity and is thus a fairly reliable source of familial security.

Of all maternal responsibilities there was none more highly touted than that of breastfeeding—and none thought to have a more lasting impact. Chapter 3 opens with an examination of the popularization of maternal breastfeeding and the variety of political uses to which the image of the mother's bosom was put. Mary Wollstonecraft capitalizes on some of the most progressive of these in her posthumously published novel *The Wrongs of Woman.* In her earlier *A Vindication of the Rights of Woman* (1792), Wollstonecraft claims that the bodily basis of sexual difference has been culturally exaggerated. But in *The Wrongs of Woman* she adopts the kind of emphasis on maternal materiality exemplified in *Tristram Shandy* and *Evelina* to argue that women are physically different from men, similar to each other, and better suited to nurture and raise children. *The Wrongs of Woman* pays special attention to Maria's thwarted longing to breastfeed her daughter, ultimately intimating that the biological interdependence of mother and child proves that women deserve child custody rights. Four decades later a similar argument would be used in Parliament to help pass the Infant Custody Bill, the first legislation to grant English women the power to visit with and in some cases even retain their children in the event of separation or divorce.

Chapter 4 shows how Maria Edgeworth also locates sexual distinction around the mother's breast, but with different political effect. In *The Wrongs of Woman*, maternity is proof of woman's entitlement to legal rights. In *Belinda* it is deployed in the service of heterosexuality and empire, as Lady Delacour—the novel's emblematic mother—becomes the site upon which sexual, national, and racial distinctions are organized. In contrast to *The Italian*, in which mother and daughter share a socially sanctioned erotic attachment, in *Belinda* Lady Delacour needs to free herself of nonfamilial homoerotic alliances before she can perform as a parent. After doing so, she turns to colonial problems, playing the pivotal role in the extradition of Belinda's racially indeterminate Jamaican suitor. The mother's part in expelling first sexual and then racial ambiguity suggests that the need to demarcate the boundaries of gender difference on which heterosexuality and biological maternity depend was linked to a need to imagine national boundaries impervious to racial mixing.

In *Adeline Mowbray*, Amelia Alderson Opie's fictionalized account of Mary Wollstonecraft's life, the demarcation of racial difference is also central, but instead of serving heterosexuality it supports white female kinship. The novel follows a heroine who, after being rejected by her sexually rivalrous mother, becomes deeply attached to Savannah, her mulatto servant from Jamaica. It is not until the novel's end, when the dying Adeline meets Mrs. Mowbray again and literally gives her Savannah, that mother and daughter are reconciled. Chapter 5 maintains that the mother and daughter's utopian, if temporary, connection is made possible by the mulatto woman's commodification. Remarkably attuned to the political dynamics of psychological desire, *Adeline Mowbray* suggests that the sexual competition that characterizes Adeline's relationship with her mother is both produced and resolved by a colonial economy.

Jane Austen's *Emma* brings the mother-daughter story to psychological maturity in the context of an acutely nuanced examination of the rise of middle-class authority. The unprecedented combination of interior perspective and ironic detachment in *Emma* marks a turning point in representations of the mind, enabling Austen to fashion one of the most precise early models of the unconscious. More than any previous English novel, *Emma* invites a psychoanalytic interpretation by making it clear that there is a division between Emma's self-understanding and the actual cause of her behavior. Chapter 6 argues that Emma's several mistakes are driven by her unconscious and enduring sorrow about her mother's death and that this sorrow is exacerbated by her loss of upper-class privileges. If Austen rejects the mother-daughter formula in her earlier *Northanger Abbey, Emma* marks her much more confident effort to revise it.

By yoking the narrative inevitability of the mother's absence with growing assumptions about the child's need to be mothered, *Emma* brings the mother-daughter story to what, in hindsight, is its logical psychological conclusion: the mother, from whom every child is fated to separate, is at the root of the unconscious, an origin at once so remote that the feelings associated with her can never be directly understood and yet so influential that her imprint is indelible. It is a testament both to Austen's insight and to the entrenchment of the paradigms on which she drew that many still believe this is true.

Chapter 1

"The Lovely Resemblance of Her Lovely Mother"

Evelina *and Later Novels*

HENRY FIELDING'S *Joseph Andrews* (1742) concludes with an arresting revelation: only the mother can mark and recognize her children; leaving no signature and lacking discernment, the father is an unreliable parent. Thus, upon being informed that Fanny Goodwill is "his daughter who had been stolen away by gypsies in her infancy," Mr. Andrews declares that "he had never lost a daughter." But he learns otherwise after Mrs. Andrews "run[s] to Fanny, [and] embrace[s] her, crying out, 'She is, she is my child!'" (290). Similarly, Mr. Wilson—who claims that his missing son was "the exact picture of his mother" (189) and that he would know him "amongst ten thousand" (190)—ironically fails to recognize that son in Joseph, who is present even as Wilson recounts the story of the boy's loss and boasts about his own powers of recognition. It is only later, when Joseph's strawberry birthmark, "which his [pregnant] mother had given him by longing for that fruit," (190) is revealed, that Joseph is properly identified as the gentleman's son (293).

Jill Campbell argues that the imprint "links [Joseph] specifically to his mother rather than his father" (654), compounding other
textual suggestions that Joseph's gender identity is an ambiguous one.
I would add that both Fanny and Joseph are rescued from the stigma
of bastardy by their bodily connections with their female parents, who
deflect the danger of incest by proving that the foundlings are not
siblings.[1] The mother becomes the foundation of an orderly society,
which, if left to the father, would be based in error and misperception.

In Frances Burney's *Evelina* (1778), the mother's power of
identification plays an even more important role in guaranteeing paternal recognition than in *Joseph Andrews*.[2] Whereas questions about
Joseph's identity become a problem toward the end of Fielding's novel,
Evelina opens by focusing on the uncertainty of kinship. The heroine's
need to find her father provides the organizing structure for the narrative, making the mother's role in securing paternal acknowledgment
all the more central.

Like Mr. Andrews and Mr. Wilson, Evelina's father, Sir John
Belmont, cannot identify his descendants. He raises one infant as his
heir who bears no relation to him and is actually the child of Evelina's
former wet nurse (378); because he does not recognize him, Belmont
also engages in a duel with his illegitimate son, Mr. Macartney. Upon
being informed that Evelina is his real heir, he comically responds:
"how many more sons and daughters may be brought to me, I am yet
to learn, but I am, already, perfectly satisfied with the size of my family"
(371). Thanks to the social sanction of male promiscuity, Belmont has
no idea how many children he has propagated.

In the end, it is only the mothers who can identify Belmont's
kin and separate illegitimate children from legitimate ones. The wet
nurse reveals the history of the false daughter, Mr. Macartney's mother
names her son as Belmont's bastard, and Evelina's dead mother proves
that her child is the legitimate heir both in a posthumous letter and
in Evelina's astonishing resemblance to herself. When Evelina finally
meets the father who abandoned her and precipitated her mother's
death, he reads the mother's letter, looks at the daughter, and acknowledges her legitimacy based on her "dear resemblance" to "my departed
wife" (385–86). Though counterintuitive, it is because Evelina is the
mirror image of her mother that Belmont finally acknowledges his own
biological kinship with her.

This chapter focuses on the psychoanalytic, linguistic, legal,
and reproductive significance of the maternal mark in *Evelina* and

closes by suggesting that mother-daughter resemblance became a popular motif among late eighteenth-century women novelists. The plot
features examined here have a long history. The stories of the faithful
wife cleared of adultery, of feared incest among siblings, and of the
mother's textual certification of kinship all have classical roots.[3] The
recognition scenes that so often resolve the novels discussed are also
historic. Aristotle speaks of the dramatic value of recognition scenes
among unsuspecting family members (41–42), like the one that occurs
in *Oedipus the King,* and there are countless familial reunions portrayed
in a wide range of literature from ancient times to the eighteenth
century and beyond. Beginning with the classical novel, children are
typically recognized by some physical sign, including clothing, tokens,
documents, birthmarks, resemblance to one or both parents, or, in
Oedipus's case, bound feet.[4] Often these signs specifically link them
with their mothers.[5]

What distinguishes *Evelina* and subsequent women's novels
is not the originality of their preoccupation with mother-daughter resemblance but the insistence with which they evoke it when they might
have relied on other forms of recognition. In repeatedly employing the
motif, women writers signal an affiliation with one another as well as an
interest in the symbolic possibilities of mother-daughter connection.
In many novels, for instance, maternal resemblance becomes a form
of legal documentation. The father has the lawful right to name the
daughter, but the mother's imprint proves a more reliable record of
marriage, kinship, and legitimacy.[6]

In stressing the father's limitations, *Evelina* and the novels
that follow expose what Brian McCrea identifies as the instability and
"weakness" of paternal authority (150).[7] The father may be designated
the child's author by virtue of his right to name her, but he cannot be the
ultimate author because he does not know—or in some cases does not
publish—the true story of her origin. His inability to act as author in a
world in which only *he* has the legal sanction to do so proves the fallacy
of paternal definitions of kinship. The problems can be corrected only
when the maternal body exerts a new law.

The-Name-of-the-Father

Psychoanalytic theory offers a useful model of the confluence of language and law in the construction of familial positions. Freud's sug-

gestion that the prohibition against incest is the basis for both paternal authority and the development of social identity is central to this model. His classic account of the oedipus complex, rehearsed in his discussion of Little Hans, concerns the moment when the son comes "up against the incest-barrier" prohibiting his sexual access to his mother ("Analysis of a Phobia" 81); the son develops rivalrous feelings toward his father but is also afraid that he will be punished for these by being castrated. The problem is resolved when "the authority of the father or the parents is introjected into the ego and there forms the kernel of the superego, which takes its severity from the father [and] perpetuates his prohibition against incest." His social identity is shaped when the son internalizes paternal authority, giving up his mother in favor of an "identification" with the father's law ("Passing of the Oedipus-Complex" 169).

According to Freud, the daughter is in a different situation, although the mother remains her "original [love] object," who must be relinquished ("Some Psychological Consequences" 176). Since, in Freud's view, the girl is already castrated, the threat of castration is not operative for her, and her bond with her mother must be "loosen[ed]" (179) by another means. The solution for Freud is penis envy. Blaming her mother for her lack of a penis, the girl "takes her father as a love-object" and replaces her wish for a penis with a wish to bear her father's child ("Some Psychological Consequences" 181), which she must then sublimate. Many critics have denounced Freud's treatment of anatomical difference and his theory of penis envy. I want simply to note that while their experiences work out differently, Freud's oedipal boy and girl both substitute their attachment to their mother with an affiliation with the father that situates them in the larger social order represented by and based in the incest taboo.

Drawing on Ferdinand de Saussure, Jacques Lacan introduces the acquisition of language into the family romance and suggests that the loss of the mother creates the need for speech. The word is "a presence made of absence" (Lacan, "Function and Field" 65), and the first symbolization is "of the absence of the mother" (Lacan, "On a Question" 200).[8] "Words stand for objects, because they only have to be spoken at the moment when the first object is lost" (Rose, introduction-II 31). Julia Kristeva adapts Lacanian theory to "submit that the *entry into syntax constitutes a first victory over the mother,* a still uncertain distancing of the mother, by the simple fact of naming" (*Desire* 289).[9]

Language figures in another aspect of Lacan's model as well, for the law against incest, which constitutes the oedipal subject's separation from the mother, is itself based in the language of "kinship nominations . . . [that institute] the order of preferences and taboos." The law is thus "identical with an order of language" (Lacan, "Function and Field" 66). Whereas in Freud's schema the son is inducted into the social order by virtue of his identification with the father, for Lacan the father represents both this induction and an induction into the linguistic system on which social order is dependent. Of the various kinship nominations, "the Name-of-the-Father" becomes the predominate sign of the oedipal transition; substituted "in the place first symbolized by the operation of the absence of the mother" ("On a Question" 200), the Name-of-the-Father marks the interplay between language and the law: "It is in the *name of the father* that we must recognize the support of the symbolic function which, from the dawn of history, has identified his person with the figure of the law" ("Function and Field" 67).

Lacan can thus be read as suggesting that the father authors the subject by marking his separation from the mother and his entrance into identity and language;[10] the Name-of-the-Father regulates the "kinship nomination" that defines the subject's place in the law.[11] Madelon Sprengnether aptly summarizes the logic of this interpretation: "Language and society, for Lacan, can only have meaning within patriarchy. The father's prohibition of incest, his *non*, thus becomes synonymous with his *nom*, the order of naming by which the child takes its place in society" (196).

It must be stressed that Lacan emphasizes not an actual father but rather the Name-of-the-Father, distinguishing between the material person of a father and the linguistic position that marks his authority. "Even when in fact it is represented by a single person, the paternal function concentrates in itself both imaginary and real relations, always more or less inadequate to the symbolic relation that essentially constitutes it" ("Function and Field" 67). Because language itself is a fiction, because it appears as a presence when what is actually represented is absent, both the authority invested in the Name-of-the-Father and the subjective identity assumed with reference to this authority are precarious (Rose, introduction-II 40). The idealized paternal position provides the real father "with all too many opportunities of being in a posture of undeserving, inadequacy, even of fraud" ("On a Question" 219).

Evelina and The-Name-of-the-Mother

In his pontifications about birth and his thwarted attempt to name his son, Walter Shandy is a fitting exemplar of Lacanian theory—a father who turns to language in the hope that it will mask his abundant insufficiencies. But like Mr. Goodwill and Mr. Wilson in *Joseph Andrews*, who fail to recognize their children, Walter proves the futility of fatherhood even as he tries to shore up its power. The same can be said of Evelina's father, who offers ample evidence of paternal fraudulence.

Yet *Evelina*'s conclusions about the father differ from those of conventional psychoanalysis. Whereas the Name-of-the-Father secures a social identity (however illusory) that depends on the subject's prior separation from the mother, Evelina must first separate from her father and connect with her dead mother to find her place in the world. In the process, it becomes clear that the mother and not the father defines kinship nominations and that authorship itself is a transcendentally significant matrilineal act. So too, though the Name-of-the-Father marks the first law against incest, in *Evelina* the father's inability to distinguish familial relations creates incestuous dangers that the mother must rectify. As the only figure who marks the child and can define incest, the mother is the keeper, if not the maker, of the taboo.

The distinction between the family romance models in *Evelina* and psychoanalysis draws attention to their most trenchant similarity. Both narratives assume that there is an original period of mother-child physical connection that the father cannot directly rival. As the sign of the unique attachment between mother and child, the maternal mark in *Evelina* might be seen as a prototype of the preoedipal bond. In the psychoanalytic schema, paternal socialization is the consequence of the child's loss of the mother and movement out of the preoedipal period. In *Evelina*, the lost mother's material imprint shapes society. With relatively little tweaking, the same preoedipal logic underwriting the Name-of-the-Father propels another story.

The problem of naming and socialization is central from the outset of *Evelina*, where much is made of the heroine's status as a nameless nobody. Abandoned at birth by her father—who burned the certificate recording his marriage to her mother, Caroline Evelyn—Evelina has no legal surname; her first name is adapted from her dead mother's maiden name.[12] In many ways, Evelina's "nobodiness" is a liability, especially because her lack of paternal ownership makes her vulnerable to sexual attack. Most glaringly, Sir Clement Willoughby wants to seduce but not marry her, because no one "would recommend to me a connection of that sort, with a girl of obscure birth, whose only dowry is her beauty" (347). A baronet and rake like her father, Willoughby signals the potential for Evelina to be lured into repeating the history of her mother, whom Belmont seduced, impregnated, and deserted. Evelina needs to locate Belmont and compel him to legitimate her precisely because this is the only clear way to gain social protection.

Yet, in an epistolary novel composed primarily of the heroine's letters, fatherlessness also brings its own rewards. Since the plot is based on the trials Evelina experiences in her nameless state, its design dictates that when she meets her father, becomes somebody, and is married, her authorship will end. As the producer of the account of her orphan wanderings, Evelina benefits from having nobodiness as her literary subject. Were she named, Evelina would be spoken for; because she is nameless, she has both the occasion and the need to speak for herself.[13]

Such need is magnified by her father's perverse proclivity to distort female history. If in Lacanian theory the paternal signification of identity is precarious because of the inherent unreliability of language and the fraudulence of fatherhood, in *Evelina* the father's designation of kinship nominations is flat-out erroneous. When Belmont effectively murders Caroline Evelyn by burning their marriage certificate, he creates the false impression that Caroline was fallen and Evelina is illegitimate.[14]

Similarly, Mr. Villars, Evelina's apparently trustworthy surrogate father, aggressively suppresses the details of her familial past, telling Evelina the truth about her parental history but withholding the information from the public. "I am," he says, "very desirous of guarding her from curiosity and impertinence, by concealing her name, family, and story" (19). When we learn at the end of the novel that Belmont has mistakenly raised the wet nurse's child in an attempt to make amends to Caroline, it becomes clear that Villars's censorship supported the misrepresentation and actually interfered with Evelina's claims to a respectable heritage. As Evelina explains, "the name by which I was known, the secrecy observed in regard to my family, and the retirement in which I lived, all conspired to render this [the nurse's] scheme . . . by no means impracticable" (373–74).

Though Caroline had asked Villars to hide her daughter from Belmont until the latter reformed, Villars has his own reasons for concealing the heroine to whom he is deeply attached. Lacking other familial relationships, he is reluctant to act in a manner that might sever "the only tie I have upon earth" (16). That Villars is eager to die "with transport" (20) "in the arms of one so dear—so deservedly beloved!" (25) suggests he may harbor sexual feelings for his ward; she is, he says, as dear to him as her mother, who was herself as dear as his wife (14, 125).[15]

The depiction of Evelina's relationship with her dead mother, Caroline Evelyn, is remarkably different. Both fathers self-servingly circulate false stories, but Caroline is the source of linguistic certainty and legitimacy. By the novel's end, the mother has shaped the daughter's identity from the grave, achieving a privileged relationship to family and words that enables her to designate kinship positions.

This resolution pivots on the way the mother and daughter's mutual need for legitimation is reflected in their physical resemblance. Born shortly before Caroline's death, Evelina has grown into a perfect replication of the mother. She is "the lovely resemblance of her lovely mother" (132) and "the living image of an injured saint" (130); indeed, when Belmont sees Evelina for the first time he cries: "My God! does Caroline Evelyn still live!" (372).

It is, in part, through her uncanny resemblance to her mother that Evelina is able to correct the injustices perpetrated against both of them. After finally agreeing to allow Evelina to meet her father because the false daughter has made a public appearance, Mr. Villars assures Evelina that she will be legitimated on the basis of her looks alone: "without any other *certificate* of your birth, that which you carry in your countenance . . . cannot admit of a doubt" (337, my emphasis). In the eighteenth century, the "face's singularity" had what Deidre Lynch describes as "a special cachet" and legibility analogous to "imprinted texts" (33–35).[16] The novel capitalizes on this convention, harkening back to the "burnt . . . *certificate* of . . . marriage" (15, my emphasis) in suggesting that Evelina's maternal resemblance constitutes textual evidence of kinship. Indeed, when he first meets Evelina, Belmont senses that she is his real daughter and suspects that the child he has been raising for seventeen years is a fraud. As Evelina explains in words echoing Villars's above: "the certainty I carried in my countenance, of my real birth, made him . . . suspect . . . the imposition" (374).

In this first encounter, however, Belmont still resists legitimating Evelina and acknowledging his paternity. As Irene Fizer points out, "as long as Belmont himself refuses to . . . own her, the incest taboo, which should mediate their relationship, is inoperative" (79).[17] When Belmont calls Evelina the "image of my long-lost Caroline," for instance, he suggests the ease with which the daughter might literally repeat her mother's history with him.

Afterward, the wet nurse admits to having tricked Belmont into raising her child, an important step in deflecting incest by preparing Belmont to legitimate Evelina. But of equal importance is that when Evelina meets her father for a second time, she bears the letter Caroline wrote to Belmont before her death. The letter has the same effect as Evelina's countenance, functioning as a certificate of birth and a replacement for the burnt marriage certificate. "Thou know'st I am thy wife!" Caroline declares in legalistic language; "clear, then, to the world the reputation thou hast sullied, and receive as thy lawful successor the child who will present thee this my dying request" (339).

By virtue of the interactive force of the letter and Evelina's face, Belmont finally articulates kinship positions while simultaneously stressing the limitations of his own powers to name: "Oh my child, my child! . . . Oh dear resemblance of thy murdered mother! . . . — Oh then, thou representative of my departed wife, speak to me in her name" (385–86). When the father heeds the "Name-of-the-Mother," identifications are finally secured.

Such a resolution of the family romance has a significant effect both on the incest taboo and on language. In the traditional psycho-analytic model, the law of the father commences with the prohibition against incest with the mother, but in *Evelina* it is the mother who oversees the taboo. In establishing Belmont's paternity, Caroline arranges for Evelina to be "torn from the arms of [her] *more than father*," Mr. Villars (130), while ensuring that Evelina will heed Belmont's request to think "of me as thy father" (386) and nothing else. After Evelina is identified as his "lawful heiress" (372), Belmont also realizes that his illegitimate son's love for the false daughter was never taboo.

At the same time, the mother's linguistic certainty has a referential force the father lacks. Producing a daughter and an account of the birth at nearly the same moment, Caroline documents their seamless connection and the letter's material truth. Although Belmont needs to claim Evelina as "my daughter" and Caroline as "my wife" for the plot to be resolved, he exerts no authorial power but merely reads and publishes Caroline's bodily and textual inscriptions.[18]

The dedicatory poem to her father with which Frances Burney opens *Evelina* becomes retrospectively ironic in light of the mother's impact. In the poem, Burney calls Dr. Charles Burney the "author of my being," but, in the spirit of anonymity, refuses to name him and to name herself as author. The novel confirms and extends the erasure, suggesting that although the daughter must dutifully appeal to the father, her mother is her real creator. The frontispiece of the 1779 edition of *Evelina*, which depicts a classically dressed woman staring at a tombstone engraved with "Belmont," corroborates the plot. Beneath the illustration are the first two lines of the dedicatory poem, beginning with "Oh author of my being." As Caroline Belmont is the only dead Belmont in the story, the lines must refer to her and not to any father.[19]

Such maternal power is otherwise contained in the novel, not least by Caroline's sexual victimization and death.[20] Moreover, if namelessness affords Evelina the freedom to wander and write, Caroline's success in reuniting her with her father is repressive. As Evelina explains to Orville before traveling to see her father: "this journey will deprive me of all right to act for myself" (354). Named by her father, Evelina becomes a commodity to be exchanged and renamed by Orville, and her own authorship ends.[21]

But though it challenges neither the foundations of hetero-sexuality nor social constraints on female power, Caroline's imprint still demystifies paternal authority. *Evelina* moves inevitably to the reproduction of kinship based on women's exchange among men. In the process, however, the novel suggests that men neither understand nor can describe the very system over which they preside. For all the physical and authorial freedom Evelina's apparent illegitimacy offers, the suspicion that her mother was a whore makes her uniquely prone to be treated as one. Belmont has no motive to protect her, but her mother does and can.

The Mother's Law

In designating kinship, Caroline significantly adjusts the law, exposing the problems of normative legal standards for marriage, legitimacy, and child custody. While an eighteenth-century father had certain absolute rights—most notably that of child custody—legitimacy depended not on his word but on whether a child was born in wedlock.[22] Because Belmont has destroyed the marriage certificate, however, he appears to

EVELINA.

Oh author of my being! —far more dear
To me than light, than nourishment, or rest.

Frontispiece from *Evelina*, vol. 1 (London: W. Lowndes, 1794). Engraved by
J. Hall after J. H. Mortimer. Reproduced by permission of the William Ready
Division of Archives and Research Collections, McMaster University.

have the sole authority to determine legitimacy until the "certificate" of Evelina's maternal resemblance finally supersedes him.

Before this resolution, the same nobodiness that affords Evelina authorial freedom also points to the precariousness of her potential bastardy. As Justice Blackstone's *Commentaries on the Laws of England* (1765–69) explains, the bastard "can inherit nothing, being looked upon as *nullus filius,* no man's son. He may gain a surname by reputation, though he has none by inheritance. . . . He cannot be heir to any one. . . . He has no ancestor, from whom any inheritable blood can be derived, for he is kin to nobody" (199).[23] The language is so close to some of the novel's descriptions of Evelina that it almost seems to have influenced them. Indeed, the time was ripe for Burney's concern about illegitimacy since, as John Gillis explains, its incidence "rose rapidly from the 1750s onward . . . [and] accelerated at a rate unprecedented in the known history of the British population" (*For Better* 110; also see 112, 115, 127–28).

Even as she is prey to charges of illegitimacy, Evelina is not free to act on her own behalf. Whatever the world may think, she knows that she *is* kin to a father who has the legal right to direct her behavior. Thus, when Evelina refuses to marry Orville before she meets Belmont, explaining that "it would be highly improper I should dispose of myself" (370), she is quite right; as a "child under age" Evelina must acquire "the consent of the parent to the marriage . . . in order to make the contract valid" (Blackstone 196).

But to demonstrate that she is legitimate and—in addition to requiring her father's consent to marry—is entitled to be his heir, Evelina must prove that her own parents were validly married, not an easy task.[24] In the eighteenth century there was generally "no certainty concerning what did or did not constitute a marriage" (Stone, *Road to Divorce* 136). The problem is compounded for Evelina by the absence of a marriage certificate, since "a hard-to-prove ceremony could create havoc in the courts" (Stone, *Road to Divorce* 108). Because Caroline married without parental consent, not in England but in France, and because the arrangement generally appears to have been the kind of clandestine affair that was increasingly subject to attack in the wake of the Hardwicke Marriage Act, appealing to a court to prove the marriage's validity could actually have the reverse effect.[25]

Even if Evelina could overcome these problems and establish that her parents were legally married, there was no formal procedure for settling questions about the legitimacy of children until the passage of the Legitimacy Declaration Act in 1858 (Teichman 31). Moreover, since so many eighteenth-century familial laws were, as Susan Staves points out, designed to protect male property rights (4), there was little a lawsuit could do to guarantee a legitimate daughter's inheritance claims. Villars vehemently opposes legal action, explaining that "should the law-suit be commenced, and even should the cause be gained, Sir John Belmont would still have it in his power . . . to cut off . . . [Evelina] with a shilling" (128).[26]

Nevertheless, Villars admits that years ago he had favored a lawsuit, only abandoning the idea because Evelina's grandmother, Madame Duval, denied "all assistance and encouragement" (128). Now, however, Madame Duval promotes the suit, repeatedly insisting that she will, as Evelina explains, "go openly and instantly to law, in order to prove my birth, real name, and title to the estate of my ancestors" (122; see also 121 and 159). Even Lady Howard approves, telling Mr. Villars: "Can it be right, my dear Sir, that this promising young creature should be deprived of the fortune, and rank of life, to which she is lawfully entitled?" (124).

The confusion and debate about the value of a lawsuit against Belmont obscure a more sobering reality: the suit is unlikely to succeed not simply because of the problems surrounding Caroline's marriage but because the law is unresponsive to women's victimization, whatever form that may take. Madame Duval constantly threatens to "take the law" against the physically abusive Captain Mirvan and Willoughby, who, among other things, tie her up and throw her in a ditch (211; see also 52, 167). But the novel makes it clear that to expect such recourse is delusional, since male abuse of women is—for all practical purposes—legal.[27]

Caroline flouted such legal limitations when, shortly before dying, she "frequently and earnestly" urged Villars "that if her infant was a female, [he] would not abandon her to" Belmont (126). If Evelina is legitimate, as Caroline insists, then only Belmont has the authority to determine her guardianship. In the eighteenth century the father's powers of custody were so absolute that even an "action whereby a father attempted to divest himself of the custody of his legitimate children in order to give custody to the mother was void as contrary to public policy" (Teichman 41).[28]

The illegality of his long-term guardianship helps explain why Villars so "wholly and absolutely disapprove[s]" of the paternal lawsuit that could expose his own misbehavior (127). Caroline had intended to contain Villars's custodial rights, designating him the father *only* "till some apparent change in [Belmont's] sentiments and conduct should announce him less improper for such a trust" (126). But Villars cannot be relied on to secure the legitimation that is Caroline's greatest wish.

The maternal mark finally becomes the means by which both Villars and Belmont are controlled. Caroline bends the law to secure Villars's guardianship of Evelina, but, by proving Belmont's paternity in Evelina's looks and her letter, she also limits his authority. At the same time, she provokes Belmont to grant her and her daughter the legal acknowledgment only he can now supply.

The Power of Pregnancy

Caroline's signature also intriguingly rearranges eighteenth-century embryological theories. It had long been believed that certain marks on a child's body bore witness to its legitimacy or illegitimacy and that these marks were the consequence of maternal imprinting during conception and pregnancy. From ancient times until the end of the eighteenth century, a wide range of medical theories—broadly categorized as "imaginationist"—suggested that a mother's imagination and desire affected her child in utero, primarily in negative ways.

Least seriously, a maternal longing might produce a birthmark or blemish, such as the one Joseph Andrews sports from his mother's craving for strawberries.[29] Most seriously, a mother's desire could create a child with such severe birth defects it was designated a "monster," a being "seen as a visible image of the mother's hidden passions" (Huet 6). Because a monster reputedly reflected its mother's illicit sexual desires, and because he did not appear to resemble the father, he became the "most illegitimate of offspring" (Huet 33). There was, in fact, no legal difference between the monster and the bastard. Immediately after describing how the monster "has no inheritable blood, and cannot be heir to any land, albeit, brought forth in marriage," Blackstone writes: "Bastards are incapable of being heirs. . . . [T]hey have no inheritable blood" (368).

The very idea that a woman's mind could determine embryological development was part of a larger scientific debate. Until the mid-seventeenth century, most embryologists favored the Aristotelian notion that the female contributed the passive principle in conception and the male the active one that created the movement necessary for embryonic growth.[30] In his pathbreaking *De Generatione animalium* (1651), William Harvey challenged Aristotle, arguing that the material carried by the mother contained its own "power to develop" (Gasking 28) and was simply ignited by the semen.[31]

Other scientists favored preformation theory, believing that the offspring existed preformed at conception in either the mother's or the father's gonads (Gasking 55). By the end of the seventeenth century and especially during the eighteenth century, there were two competing groups in this category of thinkers: the ovists, who argued that the whole embryo existed preformed in the ovary, and the animalculists, who claimed the same for the sperm (and would therefore be appealing to a character like Walter Shandy).[32] Because it suggested that the embryo was shaped by the mother's mind and desire during gestation (Huet 42), imaginationism was not as predeterminative as ovism; but both imaginationism and ovism assumed that the mother exerted greater procreative power than the father.

Evelina confirms such a belief, especially because, as with the imaginationist mother, Caroline's mark records her most pressing desire during pregnancy: "to clear her own honour" and prove Evelina's legitimacy (128).[33] The pivotal difference is that instead of leaving a sexually suspicious birthmark or birth defect, Caroline "secure[s] from blemish the birth of her child" (128) by creating a beautiful twin image. The monsters of imaginationism raised the specter of illegitimacy by their lack of resemblance to their fathers. But when Caroline's beauty is identified in her daughter, paternity is guaranteed. Far from being a source of her problem, Evelina's dissimilarity from Belmont enables him to recognize her as Caroline's child and then necessarily his own. Whereas in imaginationism the desirous mother creates the illegitimate monster, in *Evelina* Caroline's desire erases the monster of illegitimacy.

Mother-Child Bonding and Social Reorganization

Although it is not the emotional link Freud would later describe, the record of material attachment between Evelina and Caroline anticipates the preoedipal bond in its tenacity and impact. Registered in the daughter's earliest infancy, the mother's presence has a lifelong effect. In assuming that the mother's imprint outlasts their separation, *Evelina* assembles some of the pieces of the model on which psychoanalysis comes to depend.

But unlike conventional psychoanalysis, *Evelina* imagines that mother-child affinity can afford the female parent a central role in the organization of kinship. Whereas in the psychoanalytic drama the child's social integration depends on his movement into the oedipal realm of the father, in *Evelina* the bonds between children and fathers are disposable or interchangeable. Evelina needs Belmont to name her, but Villars can, in the interim, be her "*more* than father" (130), and Orville appeals because he so resembles Villars (72), whose name is almost an anagram of his own.

In contrast, all the mothers in the novel who certify Belmont's paternity are indispensable to social order. In addition to Caroline, this includes Macartney's mother and Dame Green (Evelina's former wet nurse and the mother of the false heir, Polly), all of whom generate familial narratives more powerful than the father's botched designations. As if conscious of his own incapacity to know better, Belmont does "not hesitate to acknowledge" Macartney as his son immediately "upon reading [his] unhappy mother's letter" (362).

Dame Green—who secures Evelina's restitution by admitting she deceived Belmont into raising her own child—is especially interesting. Her conventional villainy notwithstanding (the story of the conniving wet nurse was formulaic), Dame Green resembles Caroline in that they both want their children to have the better future Belmont can provide. Before her baby is born Caroline experiences "all the tenderness of maternal pity" (339), and Dame Green "had little regard for any body but her child" (375). Caroline's imaginationist desire for Evelina's proper identification is matched by the wet nurse's wish "to give *her* [daughter] [Belmont's] fortune. . . . This wish once raised, was not easily suppressed . . . a mere idle desire, in a short time seemed a feasible scheme" (375).

Defying the rules of trade demanding she sacrifice her own child for a wealthier one (wet nurses were generally expected to wean their infants when serving other children), Dame Green puts her daughter before Evelina and satisfies her desires as surely as Caroline does hers. Polly Green ultimately acquires a substantial portion of Belmont's fortune, and, even after her real identity is exposed, she continues to be called Miss Belmont and treated as Belmont's daughter. Unwilling to have Polly "eternally stigmatized, as the bantling of Dame Green" (378), Belmont happily consents to the double marriage that will conceal her true identity and his own abundant mistakes. Orville does more, insisting, as Evelina explains, that "the so-long-supposed

Miss Belmont should be considered *indeed* as my sister, and as the co-heiress of my father! though not in *law*, in *justice*, he says, she ought ever to be treated as the daughter of Sir John Belmont" (387). Dame Green's crime is superseded by a "justice" designed not to serve the father's authority but to circumvent it. Even though the mother was lying, her familial narrative proves more valuable than Belmont's actual kinship.

Thanks to their mothers, all three children improve their social positions. Legitimated and made Belmont's heir, Evelina is identified by her highborn roots, and her connection to her vulgar (if rich) grandmother fades in significance. Polly Green, the "bantling" of a wet nurse and washerwoman, rises in fortune and status, making "a match . . . far superior" to the one she could have expected by birth (375). In marrying this "co-heiress," the bastard Macartney, who has "no inheritable blood," is positioned to inherit a good part of his father's fortune.

Although the mothers themselves do not fare well (Caroline and Macartney's mother die, and Dame Green is exposed), all three create a privileged legacy for their offspring of which they would otherwise be deprived. Inspired by maternal love and dedication, they reflect that increasingly idealized image of a female parent expected to commit herself to her child despite all obstacles.

The Resemblance Motif

By the end of the eighteenth century, it was quite common for popular novels to feature children who were the exact image of their mothers. Always a good parodic register of such conventions, Austen's *Northanger Abbey* explains that Catherine Morland is surprised that Eleanor and Henry Tilney look nothing like the picture of their dead mother. "The only portraits of which she had been in the habit of thinking, [bore] always an equal resemblance of mother and child" (191).

Indeed, the kind of novels Catherine habitually reads were likely to emphasize such a resemblance. Consider, for instance, the frontispiece and sole illustration in the early editions of Regina Maria Roche's gothic novel *Children of the Abbey* (1796). (Catherine is especially fond of gothic novels, as is Harriet Smith of *Emma*, who describes *Children of the Abbey* as one of her favorite books [29]). The illustration depicts the novel's heroine, Amanda, staring at what initially looks like a mirror but is in fact a portrait of her long-dead mother. As with

Evelina, Amanda's mirrorlike resemblance to her parent becomes the basis upon which her legal identity is secured.

Like Evelina, Amanda is an orphan who must uncover her true familial history to establish her superior social position. Her mother, Malvina, died at her birth, leaving Amanda the lawful heir of Malvina's wealthy and aristocratic father, Lord Dunreath. But Amanda's claims to inheritance have been obscured by Malvina's stepmother, who precipitated Malvina's death by turning Lord Dunreath against his daughter. After her husband died, Lady Dunreath suppressed his original will and produced a forged document that disowned Malvina's children.

Amanda's problems are resolved when she finds her mother's portrait in the gloomy Dunreath Abbey, where she is discovered by the now repentant Lady Dunreath. Recognizing Amanda by her likeness to her mother, Lady Dunreath exclaims: "Behold the hour of restitution is arrived! . . . I beheld the very form and face of Lady Malvina. . . . Ye sweet and precious descendants of this illustrious house; . . . May your virtues add to the renown of your ancestors. . . . May their line by you be continued. . . . May your names be consecrated to posterity" (III, 283–85).

Lady Dunreath writes a full history of Malvina's story and gives it to Amanda, along with Lord Dunreath's official will. The two documents vindicate Malvina's past, validate Amanda's entitlement to the Dunreath name, status, and property, and eventually make it possible for her to marry the nobleman who has been pursuing her. Having marked the heroine with her own features, the dead mother improves her daughter's social status and helps recuperate a textual account of kinship.

Several other contemporary women's novels similarly depend on maternal resemblance to orchestrate their conclusions, including Elizabeth Helme's *Louisa; or The Cottage on the Moor* (1787); Charlotte Turner Smith's *Celestina* (1791); Agnes Maria Bennett's *The Beggar Girl and Her Benefactors* (1797); and the anonymously published *Fatherless Fanny* (1811), parts of which have (perhaps inaccurately) been attributed to Clara Reeve.[34] All five novels were very popular. *Louisa* was reprinted three times in its first month of publication (Foster 270). *Celestina* was reprinted three times in two years, translated into French, and praised by the *Analytical Review* and *Critical Review* (Hilbish 138– 39). In 1798, *The Beggar Girl* and *Children of the Abbey* appeared on the Minerva Press's "Favorite Authors" list, ranked respectively in first and second place.[35] Reprinted numerous times and published well into

Children of the Abbey.

Vide. Vol. 3. Page. 239.

Frontispiece from *The Children of the Abbey* (Minerva, 1797). Courtesy of Annenberg Rare Book and Manuscript Library, University of Pennsylvania.

the second half of the nineteenth century, *Fatherless Fanny* even has a cameo role in *Vanity Fair* (1847–48) (742).

The popular repetition of the motif of maternal resemblance suggests it achieved something of a mythic status. It was, for instance, because she knew her readers were accustomed to such a resolution that Bennett could satirically title the key chapter of her final volume: "The Beggar proved to be like somebody; becomes useful; and, like the Heroines of all other famous Novels, carries a nostrum in her looks, to put M.Ds. out of practice" (VII, 3).

Louisa, Celestina, The Beggar Girl, Children of the Abbey, and *Fatherless Fanny* all feature a homeless heroine who, like Evelina, is mistaken for an orphan and a bastard.[36] The fact that the heroine's identity is in question necessarily raises questions about patriarchal authority. Like Evelina, these heroines have a narrative precisely because the father or grandfather is unreliable at best and dangerous at worst. Thus, in *Celestina* the grandfather punishes Celestina's mother (Genevieve) for marrying against his wishes by imprisoning her in a convent and removing the child she bears. Genevieve dies "in consequence of the anguish of mind she suffered at having her child taken from her" (IV, 276). Invariably, the patriarch is in some way responsible for having divided the mother and her legitimate daughter at the child's birth.[37]

In some of these books the mother is dead, in others she is presumed dead, but in either case her absence, which appears to have sprung from sexual suffering or patriarchal violence or both, is an exaggerated version of the daughter's plight. As in *Evelina,* the mother's marital history has usually been suppressed, and the heroine is stigmatized because of it. Thus, Celestina is informed that her birth "was disgraceful to her parents" (I, 126), and Rosa of *The Beggar Girl* mistakenly believes her mother is an alcoholic beggar. The heroine's mission is to resolve the problem of the mother's victimization and reputation so that she herself can be socially sanctioned for marriage. Since the mother's absence directly links marriage, sexuality, and the very real dangers of childbirth with death, the heroine must also change the meaning of her mother's finale to embark on her own happy ending.[38]

These conflicts are settled at the novels' end when the heroine either discovers her absent mother or discovers new proof of the mother's marriage that alters its ominous associations. When the second Lady Dunreath assumes full responsibility for Amanda's mother's death in *Children of the Abbey,* for instance, Amanda, who had imagined Malvina expiring in childbirth "under the greatest torture" (I, 73), learns that parturition was not at fault. Even more wonderfully, Louisa, Rosa (of *The Beggar Girl*), and fatherless Fanny find their missing mothers and reunite them with their fathers. The parents' joyful reunion rectifies the threat of marital violence, and the mother's very survival proves that sexuality is not fatal.

As in *Evelina,* this solution is made possible either by the heroine's mirrorlike resemblance to her mother or by her mother's bodily imprint. Lady Dunreath recognizes Amanda because she looks like Malvina; the heroine's father in *Louisa* identifies his daughter by her "extreme likeness to an angel, who for a short time blessed the earth" (II, 12); and Fanny's father tells her "every feature in that lovely face recalls thy sainted mother" (242). [39]

Most of the novels also make an explicit association between body and text, investing the mother with joint reproductive and literary authority. In *Children of the Abbey* and *Louisa,* the heroine's resemblance prompts the discovery of a legitimate will. In *The Beggar Girl,* Rosa's family history appears to be "written on [her countenance] in legible characters" (IV, 6; see also I, 25). Most remarkably, the wet nurse imprints Rosa's parents' initials in gunpowder on the left side of Rosa's chest (VI, 317). Like the wet nurse's "fictitious daughter" in *Evelina,* the artificial mark proves that a woman need not be highborn or even the heroine's biological kin to exert textual power.

The conservative implications of these finales are obvious. After lamenting women's lack of legal rights and rehearsing the dangers to which marriage and sexuality expose them, the novels cheerfully orchestrate the heroine's entrance into heterosexuality. Once she recovers her mother's true history, the heroine's upper-class identity is determined and valorized in a way that secures her commodity status. Given by her father (or a surrogate) to a husband—together with whatever property she has inherited—the heroine is no longer free to wander the world on her own. Not only does the story of the mother's domestic abuse do nothing to change the domestic system, the maternal mark guarantees that a new generation of women will be bound by it.

The mother has, however, made one crucial difference. By documenting her daughter's legitimacy and lineage in her looks, she offers her child protection from further social stigma. Though childbirth may kill her, gestation gives the mother the final word on kinship. If such a narrative was a compensatory fantasy for female writers and readers, within its parameters, at least, the father is lacking. He has the legal right to design wills and the custodial authority to separate mothers and daughters, but only the pregnant parent can rectify the chaos he creates. The mother's imprint tells the daughter's story, and the daughter's story revises the mother's apparent past. Like *Evelina* before them, these novels link textual production with pregnancy and, for perhaps the first time in Western literary history, repeatedly represent authorship as a maternal preserve.

Ultimately, the mother positions the daughter in a family designed to replicate upper-class paternal rule. Yet in the process, her inscription highlights the fallacy of the father's law, exposing the inequity, illogic, and downright danger of his right to name the kin.

Chapter 2

Gothic Mothers and Homoerotic Desire

Incestuous Longing in The Italian

THE RESEMBLANCE motif in *Evelina* and later novels signals the mother's lasting impact on her daughter. It literalizes the growing assumption that the mother's centrality to her child begins in pregnancy and suggests that even when she does not survive childbirth her impression is indelible. Registering the material closeness between mother and child without insisting on its emotional intensity, the mark might be seen as an early version of the preoedipal bond.

In this chapter I suggest that Ann Radcliffe's *The Italian* (1797) more closely evokes the modern understanding of the preoedipal period. Lingering on the daughter's physical desire for her parent, the novel assumes that the mother's early imprint is sexually and psychologically charged. If psychoanalysis cannot finally accommodate the kind of maternal authority evident in *Evelina,* its account of the daughter's sexual attachment to her mother—especially as elaborated upon by feminist theorists—bears striking resemblance to the description of female kinship in *The Italian.*[1] The congruence between Radcliffe's novel and feminist psychoanalytic theory suggests something of the role popular fiction may have played in constructing the idea of the daughter's homoerotic love. At the same time, the political meaning of this love appears to have changed. In *The Italian,* the daughter's passion for her mother initially poses a social challenge but ultimately emerges as a moral and even conservative good. In our own day, such a feeling seems more subversive, falling among the "prohibited desires" that, at least in part, constitute the basis of psychoanalytic expertise.

Psychoanalysis and the Daughter's Desire

Feminist psychoanalytic theorists generally stress that the identity a child acquires during the oedipal phase is a gendered one that prepares the subject for heterosexual obligations. As Judith Butler puts it, the "*regulatory practic[e]* of gender formation and division constitute identity" as part of "a system of compulsory heterosexuality" (*Gender Trouble* 16, 18). Read from this perspective, a novel like *Evelina* is notable for its linkage of identity, feminine propriety, and marriage. Since Evelina's declaration of self depends upon her vindication of her mother's—and by extension her own—chastity, her acquisition of identity and feminine virtue is simultaneous and promptly followed by her readiness to marry.

　　The idea of mother-daughter love has appealed to feminist theorists because it offers a structural alternative to compulsory heterosexuality—a means of using psychoanalysis to challenge its own heterosexual teleology. If the oedipal story of patricide, incest, and the value of exogamous marriage is as old as the origins of patriarchy and "paradigmatic of all narratives" (de Lauretis, *Alice Doesn't* 112), Freud's contribution inheres in his designation of a more innocent preoedipal moment of mother-child connection. Recognizing the mother as love-object for the girl as well as the boy child, Freud makes possible the formulation of an alternative story that appears to precede and potentially challenge the oedipal one advocating marriage. Though some feminists have objected to Freud's chronology and the "hierarchical ordering of the preoedipal and Oedipal periods . . . [that] subordinates the role of mother to that of the father" (Sprengnether 7),[2] many have nevertheless capitalized on his suggestion that the daughter experiences a homoerotically charged affection for her parent. The "homosexual-maternal fantasy" has become so central among feminist theorists that

Teresa de Lauretis describes it as the "necessary imaginary of feminism" (*Practice of Love* 182–83).[3]

Such a fantasy is, by definition, also a fantasy of incest. As discussed in chapter 1, the incest taboo plays a central role in the psychoanalytic model of identity development and language acquisition. It is, of course, equally central in the psychoanalytic account of sexuality, which, as Foucault explains, "has its privileged point of development in the family" and is thus "'incestuous' from the start" (108). Freud's little boy is fated to love his mother, but when he develops castration anxiety and accepts his father's prior claim to her, he is rewarded with the promise that he will eventually have his own wife. From a psychoanalytic perspective, the heterosexual incestuous feeling the family both generates and forbids in the boy helps guarantee the replication of familial life.

The incest taboo plays a different though related role in Claude Lévi-Strauss's *The Elementary Structures of Kinship*, where it also serves as structural reinforcement for marriage. Lévi-Strauss famously argues that "the relationship of reciprocity which is the basis of marriage is not established between men and women but between men by means of women" (116); "the prohibition of incest is less a rule prohibiting marriage with the mother, sister or daughter, than a rule obliging the mother, sister or daughter to be given to" other men. The law is primarily designed, in other words, not to attach men to exogamous women but rather to enable men of different families to bind together by exchanging women (481, 480). Thus, Luce Irigaray argues that "the very *possibility of sociocultural order requires homosexuality* as its organizing principle" (*This Sex* 192), and Eve Kosofsky Sedgwick suggests that the triangular exchange of women among men supports a continuum of male "homosocial" bonds.[4]

Despite their different implications for heterosexuality, the outcomes of the psychoanalytic and anthropological models are essentially the same, for both assume the inevitability of exogamous marriage. The different processes the models reflect may also be linked in social effect. As Gayle Rubin explains, "kinship systems include sets of rules [about incest] governing sexuality. The Oedipal crisis is the assimilation of these rules and taboos" (198).

The models are also linked in their attention to the male subject and their inability to account fully for woman's experience of and acquiescence to the incest taboo. For Lévi-Strauss, the female relative—as the prohibited *object* of desire—has only a passive part to play in the transaction. Her own desire—whether incestuous or not—cannot interfere with the system. Even in cases where a woman wants to marry the man to whom she is given, she is simply not "one of the partners between whom the exchange takes place" (Lévi-Strauss 115).

Freud is more interested in woman's subjective experience when he describes the girl's resolution of the oedipus complex. But as he himself notes, if the mother is the original love object for both preoedipal boys and girls, the girl must transfer this love to her father before she can be influenced by the heterosexual incest taboo. How "does a little girl find her way to her father? How, when and why does she detach herself from her mother?" ("Female Sexuality" 184). Though Freud tried to resolve these questions with his theory of penis envy (which concludes with the daughter's blaming and hating her mother for her own lack of a penis), he remained skeptical about his assumptions: "one [has] to give due weight to the possibility that many a woman may remain arrested at the original mother-attachment and never properly achieve the change-over to men" ("Female Sexuality" 185).[5] More than once he intimated that the daughter's enduring love for her mother created a "homosexual factor in all feminine sexuality" (Rose, *Sexuality* 35).[6]

Their discussions differ in ideological nuance and detail, but feminists have seized on Freud's account of the daughter's mother-love and been nearly uniform in emphasizing the complications it poses to compulsory heterosexuality. In her highly influential *The Reproduction of Mothering*, Nancy Chodorow argues that the daughter's preoedipal attachment to her mother prevents her from making a final commitment to heterosexual love (125–29, 166–68) and that the appeal of "mother-*daughter* incest" is the major threat to the "formation of new families" (132). Though Chodorow has been criticized for her studious avoidance of a discussion of lesbianism,[7] Adrienne Rich insists that Chodorow's findings lead "us implicitly to conclude that heterosexuality is *not* a 'preference' for daughters" raised by mothers (636). Similarly, Kaja Silverman suggests that the daughter's maintenance of an "erotic investment in the mother" creates a "homosexual axis" of female desire (*Acoustic Mirror* 123). "The body of her mother," says Julia Kristeva, is the "one toward which women aspire all the more passionately simply because it lacks a penis: that body cannot penetrate her as can a man when possessing his wife" (*Desire* 239).[8]

The idea of mother-daughter love and the possibility of homoerotic desire complicate the conventional understanding of the law against incest by making clear, as Rubin puts it, that the incest "taboo presupposes a prior, less articulate taboo on homosexuality. A prohibition against *some* heterosexual unions assumes a taboo against *non-heterosexual unions*" (180). More specific in her familial and sexual designations, Judith Butler suggests that a taboo against "homosexual incest" "must *precede* the heterosexual incest taboo" (*Gender Trouble* 69, 64). If Irigaray is correct in arguing that the exchange of women between men "*requires homosexuality* as its organizing principle" (*This Sex* 192), then the male homosexuality or homosociality of this exchange is predicated on the prohibition of women's relations with other women and especially with female kin.

Homoeroticism and History

Having mapped the trends in feminist discussions of female kinship and homoerotic love, I would like to note, and possibly preempt, two objections that can be raised to my drawing on them to interpret Radcliffe's novel.

First, there are theoretical problems with linking sexual orientation to familial attachments, for such a perspective narrows the erotic and political implications of desire.[9] Queer theorists have been particularly critical of the extent to which lesbian love has been explained as an outgrowth of the mother-daughter bond.[10] In my discussion of Radcliffe's novel, however, I aim not to limit lesbianism to familial origins but rather to consider how the possibility of female homoeroticism adjusts the conventional understanding of the family. One need neither taper lesbianism to a family mold nor insist on the historical universality of mother-daughter love to acknowledge that homosexual incestuous desire can have social implications.

The second objection concerns the problem of history and whether it is anachronistic to apply the modern notion of "homosexual incest" to an eighteenth-century novel like *The Italian*, which arguably predates the conceptualization of such a term. I will argue, however, that the novel itself indicates the contemporary relevance of such an idea, reflecting a cultural investment in the possibility of mother-daughter sexual love—though recognizable linguistic codes might not yet have existed to define it.

Feminists have long discussed the historical difficulties raised in interpreting early modern women's relationships with each other—

particularly when these appear to have involved a romantic or sexual component. In her pathbreaking article on the subject, Caroll Smith Rosenberg cautioned against defining women's romantic friendships as sexual or subversive in the modern sense affixed to lesbianism. A few years later, however, Lillian Faderman used "lesbian" to connote any early modern "relationship in which two women's strongest emotions and affections are directed toward each other," whether or not it involved sexual contact (17–18). Adrienne Rich was even more global, coining the term *lesbian continuum* to describe "a range—through each woman's life and throughout history—of woman-identified experience; not simply the fact that a woman has had or consciously desired genital sexual experience with another woman" (648).

As numerous critics have since noted, such expansive definitions of lesbianism erase the historical, cultural, and sexual specificities of women's lives. Others have argued that because there was no universally identifiable English term to define sexual love between women until the early twentieth century, earlier English or American same-sex relations would not have been understood in the sense we now attach to "lesbian"; without linguistic designation, lesbians and lesbianism did not exist.[11]

Recent scholarship on the subject tends to argue differently. Opposing both those who define lesbianism broadly and those who insist that the premodern lesbian is a historical impossibility, a variety of scholars have documented an early modern cultural awareness of female homoerotic desire and behavior. Thus, Randolph Trumbach suggests that by the end of the eighteenth century, the terms "tommy" and "sapphist" may have been used to describe female same-sex love ("London's Sapphists" 112–13), and Emma Donoghue notes that "early texts are full of . . . specific labels for women who would [now] be called lesbian" (3). Drawing on a wide range of evidence, including Anne Lister's famous diaries, Terry Castle demonstrates that "one can find striking evidence of a certain incipient lesbian self-awareness well before the so-called invention of the lesbian around 1900" (*Apparitional Lesbian* 10). A number of other scholars, including George Haggerty, Claudia L. Johnson, Lisa Moore, and Felicity Nussbaum, have used eighteenth- and nineteenth-century women's novels to suggest how powerful the category of female-female desire was "in the cultural imaginary of the [early modern] period" (Moore, *Dangerous Intimacies* 11).[12]

My reading of *The Italian* not only supports the possibility that there was a recognizable category of female homoerotic desire in the eighteenth century, it also suggests that a daughter's love for her mother could be portrayed in sexual terms. Even if the modern word "lesbian" does not precisely define it, the daughter's reaction to her mother is unmistakably erotic. In what follows, I seek both to document the role of same-sex love in the novel's familial narrative and to consider the part familial relations may have played in defining the range and appropriateness of female homoerotic expression. I use the word "homoerotic" because, unlike "lesbian" and "homosexual" (which are nouns as well as adjectives) it is purely descriptive and does not necessarily connote a form of modern sexual identity.

Homoerotic Incestuous Desire in *The Italian*

Anyone well versed in eighteenth-century fiction knows that heroines are typically figured as objects of male desire and prohibited from overt expression of heterosexual interest. Often this is rendered by means of a scopic economy that accords well with film theory's description of woman as "icon . . . of the gaze: an image made to be looked at by the spectator, whose look is related by the look of the male character(s)" (de Lauretis, *Alice Doesn't* 139). As E. Ann Kaplan famously put it decades ago, the male "gaze carries with it the power of action and possession. . . . Women receive and return a gaze, but cannot act on it" ("Is the Gaze Male?" 311).[13] When Lord Orville takes pleasure in looking at Evelina and says "whoever has once seen Miss Anville, must receive an impression never to be forgotten," Evelina responds with predictable modesty: "I . . . felt myself change colour, and stood, for some moments, silent and looking down" (71). Evelina's visual inaction is intensified by her inability to control who views her (hence she cannot "*forbid* [Willoughby] my *sight*" [218]), and by the many times she is misinterpreted—as when Orville sees her in the company of prostitutes. The distinction between a woman's being seen as beautiful and her being seen as a whore is easily confused.

Such dynamics can change, however, if the woman is the spectator of another woman, as occurs in the climactic scene in *Children of the Abbey*.[14] When Amanda discovers her dead mother's mirror-like portrait, the narrative lingers on Amanda's visual and emotional reaction to the picture. "Though [the maternal image was] faded by the damp," she sees that it "retained that loveliness for which its original was to be admired." Amanda thinks of her father, who first fell in love with her mother upon viewing the portrait, and remembers him describing "his emotions as he gazed upon it." Shortly after, her own "heart swelled with the emotions [the picture] excited" (III, 241–42).

One might argue that Amanda is simply identifying with the male gaze or alternating between this and an identification with the objectified image (since she looks just like her mother, she is objectifying herself).[15] But as film theorists like de Lauretis remark, such a formulation of female spectatorship is not nuanced enough (*Alice Doesn't* 142). Even if Amanda's scopic interest replicates male desire, her own sexual identity is thereby complicated. In her excitement, for instance, Amanda becomes "determined . . . [to] visit the apartments that were her mother's" (III, 242)—a desire she satisfies with uncharacteristic bravado.

Fatherless Fanny is equally desirous and courageous when given the opportunity to view her mother's ghost. "The possibility of beholding [the ghost] . . . seemed to change her timid nature. . . . So entirely was her mind engrossed by her desire of seeing her mother, that fear was entirely forgotten" (325–26). When the apparition arrives, Fanny gazes with intensity, her feelings "worked up to such a pitch of enthusiastic awe . . . that she could not have uttered a syllable, or moved from the spot." With obvious interest in her mother's naked body, she strains to see beyond the robes "calculated rather to hide than display [her mother's] symmetry" (324–26). Ultimately, the ghost proves to be her actual parent; mother and daughter are reunited, and the mother superior of a nearby convent invites them to pass the night in her bed: "[it] is big enough to hold you both, and then I trust that when the first ebullitions of joy have subsided, nature will assert her rights, and sleep restore your exhausted faculties" (338).

It is hard to know how much license to take in analyzing such scenes. To read Amanda's mother's apartment as a genital symbol or to claim that the "ebullitions of joy" Fanny and her parent experience in bed are orgasmic is perhaps anachronistic. What is clear, though, is that in each scene the heroine shifts from being an object of male desire to being a desiring subject and that her passion for her mother is analogous to the sexual feelings generally reserved for male characters.

As its title suggests, *Children of the Abbey* is a gothic novel, and (though the book is more of a hybrid) the portion of *Fatherless Fanny* involving a ghost is gothic as well. Notorious for its preoccupation with incest and familial death, the gothic has consistently lent itself to psychoanalytic interpretation, though this has only recently included some attention to the gothic's investment in mother-daughter love.[16]

Radcliffe's *The Italian* offers a particularly rich and explicit example of the relevance of such attention. It follows Ellena Rosalba, who, after repelling the hero's overtures, becomes passionately and arguably erotically attached to her unrecognized mother. The attachment is central to the narrative's double movement, first away from the marriage plot, and then toward it.

An overview is helpful: in the first half of *The Italian*, Ellena's love for her mother interferes with her exchange among men, corroborating Judith Butler's suggestion that the heterosexual incest taboo on which women's traffic is based presupposes the prohibition of homoerotic incest. Initially Ellena inhabits a kind of preoedipal world where the prohibition against homoerotic incest is not yet operative. Because she yields neither to it nor to the law against heterosexual incest that follows, Ellena is free to experience homoerotic feelings for her mother and to stand outside the system of exchange.[17] As Claudia Johnson argues, "Radcliffe's fiction . . . turns to the alternative of homoerotic relations" to provide the heroine with "a respite of free space, where [her] own affectivity can for once be indulged and enjoyed" (*Equivocal Beings* 136).

In the second half of the narrative, the incest taboo is institutionalized. Ellena separates from her mother, meets her reputed father, barely escapes his sexually charged attack, discovers her real father, and, predictably enough, weds the hero she has avoided. Though it initially appears capable of challenging heterosexuality, homoerotic incest instead becomes the first of many stages in Ellena's inevitable exchange. The novel lingers on the daughter's love for her mother, yet finally positions it as only a temporary alternative to her appropriation by men.[18]

Like *Children of the Abbey* and *Fatherless Fanny*, *The Italian* renders Ellena's desire by means of a scopic economy generally reserved for men—in this case, the hero Vincentio di Vivaldi. The book opens with an account of his instantaneous attraction to Ellena, whom he first sees in church. Fixating on the veil that obscures her face, Vivaldi experiences "a most painful curiosity . . . as to her countenance" (5). He is " 'fascinated,' 'excited,' 'rapt,' and 'embarrassed,' " when watching the fetishized veil (Sedgwick, *Coherence* 144), but he is also "entranced" (11) and "agitated" (12) when later observing Ellena without it.[19] In both cases, his perspective of the heroine frames the reader's view of her.

In contrast, the opening chapters rarely feature Ellena's perspective of Vivaldi, instead recounting her persistent efforts to avoid him.[20] When the wind lifts her veil, Ellena draws the material back over her face (6); when Vivaldi reveals himself before her window, she closes it with "haste" (12); while he fantasizes about her, she seeks "to dismiss his image from her mind" (9). Though obvious staples of female modesty, such gestures function as part of a larger pattern of resistance. Ellena, for instance, refuses Vivaldi's marriage proposal on the basis of his family's—and particularly his mother's—disapproval of her. Her resistance is so extreme that her aunt and surrogate mother, Signora Bianchi, must urge Vivaldi's suit along with him (38). It is only after Signora Bianchi's death that Ellena agrees to marry Vivaldi: "the sanction given by her aunt to this choice . . . endeared him to her heart. . . . The more tenderly she lamented her deceased relative, the more tenderly she thought of Vivaldi" (57).

Vivaldi's mother exerts a similar—if negative—influence, as her disapproval of the heroine's dubious birth underscores Ellena's hesitancy about the marriage. Reversing conventional gender expectations, the Marchesa seeks to control her son's exchange and loves him "rather as being the last of two illustrious houses, who was to re-unite and support the honor of both, than with the fondness of a mother" (7–8). Though framed as the enemy, she actually serves as figural support for Ellena's resistance.[21] Thus, while Ellena veils her face and closes the window, the Marchesa has Ellena kidnapped so as permanently to remove her from Vivaldi's view. Such abuse notwithstanding, Ellena continues to respect the Marchesa's opposition to the marriage, asking Vivaldi upon her rescue: " 'Tell me yourself . . . whether I ought to give my hand, while your family—your mother'—She paused, and blushed, and burst into tears" (150). Accurately capturing the strength of his mother's influence, the heartbroken Vivaldi responds: "It is too certain that you do not love me!—My mother's cruelty has estranged your heart from me!" (152).

Signora Bianchi and the Marchesa di Vivaldi may have different attitudes about Ellena's prospective marriage, but both women inform the heroine's romantic response to the hero more than he does himself. The primacy of Ellena's involvement with these maternal figures foreshadows her passionate response to her actual (though unrecognized) mother, whom she meets after the Marchesa has Ellena kidnapped and imprisoned in a convent, that place frequently evoked in sentimental literature for its "independence from the structures of heterosexual affectivity" (C. L. Johnson, *Equivocal Beings* 131). Unlike the opening chapters of the novel, which focus on Vivaldi's desire for Ellena but rarely offer her perspective of him, the scenes in the San Stefano convent are rendered through Ellena's eyes, marking her shift from an object of attraction to a subject with a gaze.

When readers finally witness events from Ellena's view, she is listening to a choir in church and is immediately struck by the voice of a nun, whose face is hidden by a veil. She stares at the woman with rapt attention, overwhelmed by an inexplicable feeling. Ultimately the heroine will learn what many eighteenth-century readers would have guessed at once—that the nun, named Olivia, is her missing parent, believed to be long dead.

Remarkably, this first sustained rendition of Ellena's view repeats, almost word for word, the novel's original description of Vivaldi's desire for Ellena. Vivaldi sits in church and "the sweetness and fine expression of [Ellena's] voice attract[s] his attention to her figure" (5). In the San Stefano church, Ellena is attracted by Olivia's voice "whose expression immediately fix[es] her attention" (86). Vivaldi is so "fascinated by the voice, that a most painful curiosity [is] excited as to her countenance" (5). Ellena looks "to discover a countenance, that might seem to accord with the sensibility expressed in the voice" (86). Vivaldi listens "with a rapt attention, and hardly with[draws] his eyes from her person till the matin service ha[s] concluded" (5). Ellena regards "the nun with a degree of interest which render[s] her insensible to every other object in the chapel" (86).

In a gender transposition considerably more involved than that in *Children of the Abbey*, the narrative reiterates each detail of Vivaldi's desire for Ellena in recounting Ellena's reaction to Olivia. Like him, she is obsessed with a woman's voice, face, and veil; like his, her gaze is transfixed. Even if the repetition is cited as proof of the book's hyperbole, it indicates the acceptability of describing the daughter's love for her mother in narratively established sexual terms.

The psychoanalytic suitability of Ellena's response is considerable. Eventually we learn that she last saw her mother when she was "not [yet] two years old" (382)—an age that marks the end of the preoedipal period, when the child is still intimately involved with its mother but on the borderline of separation and the entrance into language and culture. Like the preoedipal infant, who hears better than it sees and is especially drawn to the mother's voice (familiar from the experience in utero), Ellena is first riveted by Olivia's singing. The acquisition of sight follows upon that of sound, as she next tries to focus on the hazy countenance behind the veil.[22] It is a testament to the enduring power of their original attachment that Ellena and Olivia are magnetically drawn to each other despite the passage of time.

Moreover, unlike in the opening of the book where Ellena conceals herself from Vivaldi, at San Stefano she throws back her veil and displays her face to Olivia. She gazes at Olivia, who gazes back, blushes, and is unable to withdraw her eyes (87). On several occasions the two women lift their veils with suggestive results. Watching the un-veiled Olivia, Ellena enters a kind of trance and, forgetting "the decorums of the place," begins to approach Olivia (88), much as Vivaldi had earlier followed her. When examining Ellena, Olivia blushes, grows pale, and portrays "an air of such universal languor as precedes a fainting fit" (91). Like the similarly named heroine of *Twelfth Night* (qtd. in one of the chapter epigraphs [23]), Olivia apparently falls in love with a woman.[23]

When Vivaldi finally comes to rescue the heroine from the convent, the veil's sexual resonance intensifies. Olivia gives Ellena her garment so that the girl can disguise herself as a nun during the escape. "Wrapt" (129) in the cloth, Ellena travels through the narrow avenues of the convent into the open air of the garden. Corroborating the reproductive imagery, the mother guides her daughter to the outside world and informs her that "my veil . . . has . . . protected you" (133). When Ellena reaches the garden, she is so reluctant to be delivered by Vivaldi that he must employ "gentle violence" to "disengag[e] her from the nun" (135). As when he worries about his own mother's effect on her, Vivaldi asks Ellena: "Do I then hold only the second place in your heart?" (135). Although Ellena attempts to reassure him, Vivaldi is not convinced: "I envy your friend those tears . . . and feel jealous of the tenderness that excites them" (136).

Vivaldi has ample reason to feel anxious about Ellena's love for her mother. Throughout their escape and seclusion in the Ursaline convent, she continues to resist him and to wear Olivia's veil, though she no longer needs it for disguise. Vivaldi tries to get Ellena to marry him, but she "assert[s] her own rights" (181) and refuses. When Ellena finally agrees to a secret wedding, she fixes her eyes "on the ground" during the ceremony, Olivia's "veil but ill conceal[ing]" her "dejected countenance" (185). Then, as if by an extraordinary projection of Ellena's wishes not to marry, the wedding ceremony is interrupted by Schedoni's men, disguised as members of the Inquisition. Pointing to Olivia's veil, they abduct Ellena, accusing Vivaldi of having kidnapped a nun.

The veil's role in interrupting the wedding thus marks the complication mother-daughter attachment poses to heterosexuality and women's exchange. Never having noticed "that the veil she wore was other than her usual one" (188), Ellena appears influenced by a maternal love so powerful that it determines her behavior, yet also so unconscious that it goes undetected. If, as Gayle Rubin suggests, the "woman [who] not only refuse[s] the man to whom she was promised, but ask[s] for a woman" stages a "double refusal" to the economy of marriage (183), then Ellena's unwillingness to abide by the taboo on homoerotic incest constitutes a triple refusal. It is also her last one.

Compulsory Heterosexuality

In the second half of *The Italian*, Ellena moves through one and then the other stage of the incest taboo. She gives up her attachment to her mother, is introduced to her reputed father, engages in a sexually charged relationship with him, and then moves back to Vivaldi. As in the conventional psychoanalytic narrative, the father's entrance reorganizes the family drama, shaping the heroine as a heterosexual subject whose internalization of the incest taboo finally makes her suitable for marriage.

The shift begins with Father Schedoni's replacing Olivia as the central focus of Ellena's attention. Having overseen Ellena's abduction, he begins the process of forcing her to comply with male desire by assuming an obviously sexual posture when trying to murder her: "He searched for the dagger, and it was some time before his trembling hand could disengage it from the folds of his garment. . . . Drawing aside the lawn from her bosom, he . . . raised it to strike; when, after gazing for an instant, some new cause of horror seemed to seize all his frame" (234). All the fumbling with undressing forestalls the need for violence but evokes the threat of incest. Schedoni sees that Ellena is wearing a locket with his picture; he wakes the sleeping heroine with the news that he is her father and begins to caress her (237). Though the embrace goes no further, and the familial revelation is misleading (he is her uncle, not her parent), Schedoni is the first man to unveil and expose the heroine, succeeding where Vivaldi has failed.

So too, whereas Ellena continues to wear Olivia's garment in

Vivaldi's presence, when Schedoni disguises her in "a lay-habit," Ellena puts "aside the nun's veil, for one of a more general fashion" (257). Once Ellena "dismiss[es]" (257) Olivia's veil, the image disappears from the text. Olivia herself re-emerges at the novel's end, but when she does, Ellena learns that she is her natural mother. Stunned, the heroine "no longer return[s] [Olivia's] caresses; surprize and doubt suspen[d] every tender emotion" (378). The novel suggests that the daughter can and will desire her mother so long as such feelings are preverbal and unconscious. But once Ellena becomes aware of familial terms, the homoerotic incest taboo is operative and her passion for Olivia must cease. Perhaps because her own behavior can be categorized as motherly affection, Olivia is delighted by the identification. But "joy was evidently a more predominant feeling with the parent than with the child" (378).

The incidents are rendered as discrete events, but the cessation of Ellena's "tender emotion[s]" for Olivia—her apparent rejection of her mother—is directly dependent on Schedoni's intrusion. Paternal interruption is marked in another respect as well, for no sooner is Olivia and Ellena's attachment desexualized than we learn that the Marchesa di Vivaldi is dead. In attempting to orchestrate her son's marital exchange, the Marchesa had usurped the father's privilege, but after her death Vivaldi's father assumes his marital role. When Vivaldi asks Olivia for permission to wed Ellena, Olivia refuses to claim authority, telling the hero he can only "hope for her acquiescence" to the engagement if the Marchese is the "suitor" (410).

Luckily for Vivaldi, a final father emerges to guarantee him satisfaction. This is Ellena's real father, the late Count di Bruno, whom Olivia names when she reveals the family's authentic history. When the Marchese learns that the Count di Bruno—not the now dead Schedoni—was Ellena's actual parent, he sanctions the couple's union. Anxious to mark his association with her father, the Marchese accepts Ellena into his family as the daughter of a man of "character" and "rank" (410). In keeping with the role the exchange of women plays in cementing male bonds, Vivaldi requires the involvement of both fathers to overcome Ellena's resistance.

Thus, Ellena enters the symbolic order. Losing her romantic attachment to her mother, she must prepare to become a mother; she must take the place of the mother. Accordingly, we learn that her experiences with Schedoni mimic her mother's history: years earlier he had kidnapped, raped, and almost killed Olivia with a dagger

(339–40). The rape was implicitly incestuous since Schedoni was the Count di Bruno's younger brother. Though more a victim of her male relative than Freud's actively desirous little girl, Ellena (like many gothic heroines) is nevertheless drawn to the family man who would destroy her.

Schedoni proves that the daughter's love for her reputed father, like that for her mother, must be tempered. Ellena must give up her feelings for Olivia because they interfere with male desire and her own exchange. She must give up her feelings for Schedoni because he is violent enough to rape and kill her, which would also prevent her exchange. In the psychoanalytic scheme, the father initiates the taboo against incest and marks the child's gendered identity in a heterosexual order. In *The Italian,* the functions are divided: Schedoni serves as a warning against incest, and the respectable real father, Count di Bruno, certifies the heroine's marketability.

Olivia seals the arrangement by clarifying Ellena's heritage. She may not leave a physical mark on her daughter like the mothers in chapter 1 (which is why recognition is delayed), but she similarly holds the clue to biological identity. As the formula dictates, once the mother names the father, the heroine is fit to be married. Ellena's attachment to her mother poses the greatest challenge to the exchange of women in the first half of the novel, but Olivia's defense of paternal authority ultimately secures the system.

Heterosexual Incest in *The Mysterious Mother* and *The Monk*

Although they bode badly for her happiness, Ellena's ambivalence about Vivaldi and desire for her mother do not preclude her availability for marriage. Like *Children of the Abbey* and *Fatherless Fanny, The Italian* presents a daughter's experience of homoerotic incestuous love as a relatively safe stage of sexual development. Even if Ellena remains vaguely resistant during the final wedding scene (leaving her veil only "partly undrawn" [411]), her feelings have no permanent impact on the inevitability of marriage. What matters is that she be viewed by men as suitable for exchange, and homoerotic incestuous desire does not actually challenge this. Thus, Vivaldi continues to pursue Ellena despite his open jealousy of her affection for Olivia (135).

Heterosexual incest has a much more damaging potential. Had Schedoni actually raped Ellena, as he had done with her mother, she would have been unmarketable, narratively doomed to a convent should she even survive. There is no unambiguous sign that Ellena and Olivia have consummated their love (though the scene where Ellena wraps herself in Olivia's veil is highly suggestive); but the relationship's harmlessness inheres not in its chastity but in its incapacity to stain the daughter's virginity regardless of sexual contact.

The relative safety of homoerotic incest becomes especially clear when *The Italian* is read against the gothic texts to which it directly refers—Horace Walpole's play *The Mysterious Mother* (1768) and Matthew Lewis's novel *The Monk* (1796). Routinely and explicitly contrasting Ellena and Olivia's relationship with the disastrous hetero-sexual incest in these works, Radcliffe stresses the conservative value of female kinship ties. She also offers a more positive vision of maternity than her male predecessors, who tend to blame the mother for incest.

Horace Walpole inaugurated the gothic novel in England with his sensationally popular *The Castle of Otranto* (1764), and for this reason alone Radcliffe is indebted to him. More specifically, the affectionate mother-daughter relationships in Walpole's novel (which differ considerably from the maternal corruption in his play) may have served as a precedent for subsequent representations of the bond. In *Otranto*, Hippolita is Matilda's natural mother and Isabella's surrogate one; both adore her and long to defend her from her cruel husband, Manfred. Though the daughters are rivals for Theodore's love, this is overshadowed by their maternal devotion. When Manfred fatally stabs Matilda, for instance, Theodore still tries to marry her, but, "lost in tenderness for her mother," Matilda ignores him and arranges for Isabella to "supply my fondness for this dear, dear woman" (106, 107). Such affection contrasts sharply with the father's drive toward incest. It is because Manfred is desperate to marry and violate Isabella, whom he has raised as a daughter to wed his now deceased son, that he mistakenly stabs Matilda. Female familial love is obviously the more palatable—if less effective—alternative.

It is, however, not *Otranto* but *The Mysterious Mother* to which Radcliffe directly alludes in *The Italian*. Produced four years after his novel, Walpole's play features a female parent more abhorrent than Manfred. Radcliffe quotes *The Mysterious Mother* three times, beginning with the epigraph of her first chapter: "What is this secret sin, this untold tale, / That art cannot extract, nor penance cleanse?" (Radcliffe 5; Walpole, *Mysterious* 9). In the play, these lines refer to "the mysterious mother," the Countess of Narbonne, whose secret guilt results from her incestuous union with her son, Edmund. In *The Italian*, the mysterious mother is Olivia, whose difference from the Countess of Narbonne is telling. Olivia is not the instigator of incest but rather its victim, and it is the father whose sin cannot be cleansed.

Unlike Ellena, who escapes Schedoni's attack, and Olivia, who is ruined because he rapes her, the Countess of Narbonne is doomed by her own uncontrollable desire; she is "a sensual woman" who knows "pleasure's relish" (17). The innocent party is her son, Edmund, whom she (unbeknownst to him) tricked into intercourse sixteen years earlier after waiting for her dearly loved husband to return to "my bed":

> Love dressed his image to my longing thoughts
> In all its warmest colours—but the morn,
> In which impatience grew almost to sickness,
> Presented him a bloody corpse before me. (60)

Yoking maternal desire and paternal death, the passage highlights the destructive nature of female sexuality. This is corroborated when the countess explains how "the storm of disappointed passions" (60) drove her toward her son, who was "his father's very image" (8; also see 35, 60). Knowing that Edmund planned to sleep with the servant Beatrice that night, the countess made other arrangements.

> Yes, thou polluted son!
> Grief, disappointment, opportunity,
> Raised such a tumult in my madding blood,
> I took the damsel's place; and while thy arms
> Twined, to thy thinking, round another's waist,
> Hear, hell and tremble!—thou didst clasp thy mother!
> (60)

Unlike *Evelina*, in which her daughter's mirror image certifies the mother's chastity and defers incest, in *The Mysterious Mother* the resemblance between father and son ignites the mother's lasciviousness and provokes it.

As if such revelations were not damning enough, the Countess next reveals that Adeliza—the young woman Edmund has forcibly married and perhaps ravished (50, 52)—is "thy daughter [and sister], / Fruit of that monstrous night!" (60). In keeping with imaginationist theories about fetal impressions, the mother describes the child as the product of her mental perversities: "Thou canst not harbour a foreboding thought / More dire, than I conceived" (60). Instead of marking Adeliza in a way that protects her heritage, like the mothers in chapter 1, the Countess dooms her descendants. Polluted by her father and brother, the illegitimate daughter can never be exchanged and must become a nun.

Radcliffe seems especially irritated by the idea that a mother could be driven to such sexual extremes. Though in *The Italian* the Marchesa attempts to ruin her son, she is prompted by socioeconomic interests, not sexual ones, and Olivia's history reveals that the father—not the mother—is the perpetrator of familial sin. For Walpole, the daughter marks the epitome of incestuous chaos, but Radcliffe presents the mother-daughter bond as an alternative to the father's threat, and in so doing seems deliberately to revise the play's paradigms.

Thus, in scenes that parallel those in *The Mysterious Mother*, Radcliffe replaces heterosexual incest with mother-daughter attachment. In Walpole's play, Adeliza is forced to marry Edmund even though she faints during the ceremony, never consents to the vows, and cries and "shrieks" during the attempted consummation (whether the act actually occurs is unclear [50, 52]). But when Ellena is unwillingly involved in the first wedding, Olivia's veil interrupts it. Similarly, in the play, the servant named Beatrice facilitates incest since the mother takes her place in Edmund's bed. But in the novel, the servant named Beatrice mediates the mother-daughter reunion, becoming the means by which Olivia recognizes her daughter (377–78). In functioning as a substitute for heterosexual incest, Ellena and Olivia's bond emerges as a conservative force, a form of erotic connection distinguished for its comparatively limited capacity to disturb.

The same pattern emerges in relation to *The Monk*, the shocking and graphically sexual novel that had "an enormous impact on Radcliffe" (C. L. Johnson, *Equivocal Beings* 122) and to which *The Italian* seems her conservative response (Garber xi–xii). The opening of *The Italian* mimics that of *The Monk*, but mutes its heterosexual intensity. In both texts the heroine arrives with her aunt at church and is spotted by the voyeuristic hero, who wants to lift her veil. By contrast, Lewis's heroine is forced to remove it (11). Unlike the more modest Ellena, Antonia looks directly at her admirer. Then she "eagerly" gazes at another man, a "pleasure fluttering in her bosom" (18). He is the

Monk, Ambrosio, who will rape and murder her before learning that she is his sister.

While Ambrosio bears much of the blame for the crime, their mother, Elvira, is his unwitting accomplice. She left Ambrosio when he was "scarcely two years old" (13)—the age Ellena was when Olivia disappeared. When they meet decades later, Elvira does not recognize her son, and it is the combined effect of this failure and the earlier abandonment that provokes his violence. The unmistakable implication is that if Elvira had been a good mother, incest and death would have been avoided.

Indeed, *The Monk* is replete with failed and monstrous mothers. The novel's other major plot, for instance, concerns the pregnant novitiate, Agnes, whose mother superior, Mother St. Agatha, buries her alive. Agnes's baby is born in the "Vault" but dies because she does not know how to breastfeed it. Agnes's inadequacy can be traced not only to Mother St. Agatha, but also to her biological mother, who originally pledged Agnes to the convent when she was pregnant with her. The cavern where Agnes gives birth is a horrible maternal space, reached by entering the body of a female statue. Engulfed by "thick darkness" at the bottom of a winding passage, the "gloomy dungeon" is "buried in obscurity." Its "damp walls" echo with Agnes's "groans" (368).

If Agnes's story marks the horror of the womb, parturition, and failed breastfeeding, Ambrosio's story is the nightmarish sequel. After being abandoned by Elvira, Ambrosio is raised by the fathers of the Capuchin order. Though he seems to become an ideal monk, he is overwhelmed by lascivious desires, arguably born out of hunger for his missing mother—as if he fails to move from the preoedipal period to the incest taboo. As a grown man, for instance, Ambrosio worships a picture of the Madonna, who is both the only mother he has ever known and, according to popular rumors, his actual parent; many believe he was a "present . . . from the Virgin" (17). "His unsatisfied Desires placed before him the most lustful and provoking Images" (67) of her.

Ambrosio's attraction to Matilda, a woman disguised as a monk and living in the convent, is a product of this lust. After learning that Matilda was the model for the painting of the Madonna, Ambrosio sees her naked breast, foreshadowing the breastfeeding scene in the vault. The sight drives him to distraction: "The blood boil[s] in his veins, and a thousand wild wishes bewilder his imagination" (65). The repeating letters in Madonna and Matilda evoke the missing "Mama," and Ambrosio finally consents to sexual relations with Matilda because he is afraid she too will abandon him.

"The over-whelming torrent of [Ambrosio's] desires" (238) increases when he meets his unrecognized sister, Antonia, who petitions him to help her ailing mother. First attracted by her voice (240), Ambrosio becomes sexually frantic when a magic mirror shows a bird "nibbl[ing]" (271) at Antonia's breasts. Again provoked by anxiety about abandonment, he worries that Antonia will be "lost to me" (243) and grows determined to possess her at all costs. Perhaps in Antonia, Ambrosio sees the mother of his infancy, for Elvira "must have resembled her Daughter in her youth" (203).[24]

If the mother's absence is, in part, the source of Ambrosio's desire for his sister, then Elvira's ignorance of his identity compounds the problem. Though Elvira was fleeing her brutal father-in-law when she left her son, this does not excuse her failing to remember him later, especially since she has fond memories of other lost children.[25] Indeed, Elvira recognizes something familiar in Ambrosio's voice, telling Antonia: "Either I must have known the Abbot in former times, or his voice bears a wonderful resemblance to that of some other, to whom I have often listened" (250). But instead of reaching the conventional conclusion that she is hearing her husband's echo in their son, Elvira dismisses the coincidence.

In *The Italian* Olivia lacks such physical clues but is nevertheless drawn to the child last seen at two years old. Elvira has no sense of connection to the son she lost at the same age, in part because she is single-mindedly preoccupied with his sister. This may not be the least of the reasons why Ambrosio kills them both, beginning with Elvira. It is symptomatic of their attachment that even after she is murdered, a sepulchral Elvira promises Antonia they will soon be reunited—a promise fulfilled three days later when Ambrosio rapes and kills her. In fitting testament to the role maternal insufficiency plays in the crime, the violence occurs in the caverns housing Agnes and her dead baby.

Both murder scenes feature the problem of voice, as Ambrosio kills first his mother and then his sister to silence them (303, 391). Reminiscent of Elvira's confusion about Ambrosio's voice, the detail points to Ambrosio's early age at desertion, a time when he "had no voice at all" (252). As a man, Ambrosio develops a sexually magnetic voice, the source of both Matilda's and Antonia's attraction to him (20, 60, 262). Antonia explains that "his voice inspired me with such interest, such esteem, I might almost say such affection for him, that I am myself astonished at the acuteness of my feelings" (20). Lacan argues that speech emerges when the son gives up his mother and accepts the law against incest—language is his compensation for her absence. But having relinquished his mother before he could symbolize her loss, Ambrosio speaks with a vengeance, demonstrating not his acceptance of the taboo but rather his continued desire and ability to attract maternal figures.

In revising *The Monk*, Radcliffe changes the voice's sex. At the opening of *The Italian*, it is Ellena's voice that is arresting, and she attracts not her sibling but Vivaldi. Later, when Ellena, like Antonia, *is* entranced by a voice, she is listening to Olivia. Drawn to her missing mother and not her brother, she has a distinct advantage over Lewis's heroine. Whereas Ambrosio's voice "penetrate[s] into [Antonia's] very soul" (18), foreshadowing his rape, Olivia promises her daughter sentimental reciprocity. Listening to her unknown mother, "Ellena felt that she understood all the feelings of the breast from which it flowed" (86). By replacing Ambrosio with Olivia—changing the doomed sister's fascination with her brother into the daughter's interest in her mother—Radcliffe questions the inevitability of heterosexual incestuous desire and posits mother-daughter love as a healthier form of attraction. As when she substitutes scenes of heterosexual violence in *The Mysterious Mother* with moments of mother-daughter attachment, she again emphasizes the conservative value of female kinship bonds.[26]

Her replacements revise both Walpole's and Lewis's need to blame the mother for heterosexual incest. In *The Mysterious Mother*, the Countess seduces her son, who forcibly marries their daughter and his sister. In *The Monk*, Elvira ignores her son, who rapes her daughter and his sister. Olivia bears no such onus. Rather, by attracting her daughter, she secures her child's marital future. Because their homoerotic tie delays but never eradicates the daughter's exchange, it proves less subversive than the heterosexual relationships to which it is compared. In the gothic, heterosexual incest is violent, leaving a mark on a woman that prohibits exogamy. Thus, Adeliza joins a nunnery, and, after being raped by Ambrosio, Antonia is happy to die; as she tells her would-be husband, "deprived of honour and branded with shame . . . She could not have been his Wife" (392).

Radcliffe opposes the daughter's sexual attachment to her mother with the horror of incestuous violence, ironically suggesting that their homoerotic tie is the best bolster of heterosexuality.[27] Ellena's mother is safe because she does not rape her kin, because she does not generate a sexually dangerous son, and because her love for her female child is preservative, making it possible for the daughter, who has resisted heterosexuality, to become a mother despite herself.

Chapter 3

The Maternal Bosom

Sexual Difference and Custody in
The Wrongs of Woman; or, Maria

EVELINA AND *The Italian* capitalize on different aspects of the ideal-ization of maternity. Caroline's signature on Evelina marks the physical tenacity of a bond between mother and child that begins with preg-nancy and lasts beyond death, and Olivia and Ellena's instantaneous love proves that bond's instinctive basis and emotional weight. Both offer incipient versions of what psychoanalysis would later describe as the preoedipal attachment between mother and child. The novels acknowledge that not all mothers are "good" ones (witness Madame Duval and the Marchesa di Vivaldi) and that good mothers are more than likely to die or disappear. But despite its hazards and infrequency, good motherhood remains a female parent's noblest goal.

By the end of the eighteenth century, being a good mother meant that a woman had to suckle her own children. Celebrated for her physical and emotional attachment to her child, the breastfeeding mother was instrumental in solidifying the notion of the preoedipal bond and epitomized femininity in a wide range of writings—from medical texts to political tracts to conduct books to novels. Perhaps no other maternal activity garnered such cultural consensus. Conservative, moderate, and progressive authors generally agreed on the importance of maternal breastfeeding and tended to render it as the foundation of familial security.

They also tended to render it as the basis of national success, an association symptomatic of a variety of related historical changes, including the rise of nationalism, colonialism, and population studies. The attachment to a sovereign nation that was an increasingly important source of identity in the Western world was influenced as well as complicated by colonialism.[1] Though imperial expansion was a source of English pride and wealth, its attendant revolts—by West Indian slaves, the Irish, and American colonists—fueled its fears (see chapter 4). The new science of population contributed by suggesting that a variety of groups—the domestic poor, the Irish, West Indian slaves, and Africans—might gain a reproductive advantage that would undermine national and imperial safety.[2]

In the midst of such concerns, the mother—and particularly the breastfeeding mother—became a figure of special political interest. As the producer and nourisher of new citizens, she appeared to be the source of a population growth that could work either for or against national stability. If an excess of poor children at home,[3] or colonized children abroad, could threaten English security, middle- and upper-class female citizens needed to gain a competitive advantage by reproducing and maintaining their own population.

The linkage between maternal breastfeeding and population growth brought concerns about sexual, class, and racial differences into close proximity. As a powerful image of woman's incommensurability with man, the suckling mother often (though not always) signaled the logic of measuring human differences and of organizing power accordingly. Thus, many eighteenth-century authors suggest that the proper deployment of maternal breastfeeding will enforce female obedience in the family, lower-class subservience in the nation, and racial containment abroad. As I suggest below, however, what is perhaps most telling about the discourse on maternal breastfeeding is its ideological variability—its capacity to represent both conservative *and* progressive interests.

The following two chapters, on Mary Wollstonecraft's *The Wrongs of Woman; or, Maria* (1798) and Maria Edgeworth's *Belinda* (1801), explore this flexibility in detail, paying special attention to the role the maternal bosom played in articulating systems of difference.

Because I am primarily interested in political history here, I depend less on psychoanalytic theory than in earlier and later chapters. *The Wrongs of Woman* and *Belinda* are also arguably less suited to the psychoanalytic family romance because they focus on the mother's as opposed to the daughter's point of view; the psychoanalytic model is notoriously neglectful of the mother's perspective.

On the other hand, psychoanalysis has been an invaluable participant in discussions about the construction of difference. The oedipal crisis is a crisis of difference, marking the painful moment of maternal separation when the subject must assume a position of gender difference in a linguistic economy organized around the difference between word and thing. The history of systems of difference in chapters 3 and 4 provides a framework for a return to psychoanalysis—and particularly to its treatment of difference—in chapter 5.

The Politics of Maternal Breastfeeding

Although for centuries medical and religious writers had urged women to breastfeed their children, it was not until the end of the eighteenth century that maternal breastfeeding became a fashionable alternative to hiring a wet nurse (Fildes, *Breasts* 106).[4] At around the same time, Thomas Laqueur suggests, the female body began to be seen as categorically different from the male body. Lactation became crucial evidence of woman's fundamental difference from man and of her natural and unique capacity to serve as a full-time mother.

All three of the most important endorsements of maternal breastfeeding—Dr. William Cadogan's *Essay Upon Nursing* (1748), Jean-Jacques Rousseau's *Émile* (1762) (which was enormously popular in England), and Dr. William Buchan's *Advice to Mothers on the Subject of Their Own Health and on the Means of Promoting the Health, Strength, and Beauty of Their Offspring* (1803)—argue for the natural basis of nursing and stress the deviance of women who resist it. Rousseau calls women's refusal to nurse the "first sin" (13) and Dr. Buchan bemoans the "shocking" fact that "of all animated nature . . . woman [is] the only monster capable of withholding the nutritive fluid from her young" (76). Precisely because it is their natural duty, Dr. Cadogan suggests, mothers who fail to suckle risk illness and death (14).

In a variety of ways these authors link the sexual difference breastfeeding represents with the maintenance of male power. Nursing is women's biological duty, but they "cannot be supposed to have proper

Knowledge to fit them for such a Task," Dr. Cadogan explains, so they must turn for advice to men, who have "a Philosophic Knowledge of Nature" (3).[5] Similarly, though he notes that "if the author of nature had meant to assign [the education of young children] to men he would have given them milk to feed the child," Rousseau sees no contradiction in offering lengthy advice on the subject (5). Fathers are urged to assert comparable authority by supervising their nursing wives for "the Love of Posterity" (Cadogan 24) and for the maintenance of male sexual rights: "Neither conjugal love, fidelity, modesty, chastity, nor any other virtue, can take deep root in the breast of a female that is callous to the feelings of a mother" (Buchan 170).

The problem of sexual difference is closely aligned with concerns about class. "Most of our People of Condition are . . . a puny valetudinary Race," Cadogan laments, "chiefly owing to bad Nursing." But the poor mother, who has "little more than her own Breast to feed" her child, "sees it healthy and strong" (Cadogan 5, 7). Rousseau makes the same point: "The children of the poor . . . are generally less frail and weakly, more vigorous than those who are supposed to be better brought up" (33). The reality, of course, was much more harsh; poor children were at risk of death and desertion and were often sent out to disreputable nurses (George 55–59, 213–16). Ironically, Cadogan's treatise provided the basis for infant care at the London Foundling Hospital, itself a testament to the tragic fate of many children whose impoverished mothers were forced to abandon them.[6] The discrepancy between romanticized claims about poor children and the likelihood of their early demise or abandonment brings the political stakes into relief. The rhetoric plays on the fear that the poor will gain reproductive and physical superiority; the hope is that such disorder can be simply enough averted by middle- and upper-class mothers' choosing to nurse.

The anxiety about population includes concerns about racial and colonial supremacy. Like poor English women, "savage" mothers are described as having a competitive advantage. As Dr. Buchan explains, "the mother in civilized society, who . . . denies her infant the vital stream with which she is abundantly supplied for its sustenance" does not care about her child's life nearly as much as "the poor savage" (77). "The Caribs are better off than we are," Rousseau laments (10), footnoting George Buffon, who astonishingly insists that the well-suckled "little negroes" in Africa "begin to walk at two months, or rather to crawl" (27–28n). Because Western mothers have "ceased to suckle their children," all of Europe's fate is endangered. "Her arts and

sciences, her philosophy and morals, will shortly reduce her to a desert"
(Rousseau 12).

As in the earlier passages, the negative examples here emphasize the obverse potential of the genteel female body. If maternal
breastfeeding were only well deployed, the authors intimate, sexual,
class, and racial order could be preserved. Such associations confirm
Ruth Perry's provocative suggestion that maternal breastfeeding was "a
colonial form—the domestic, familial counterpart to land enclosure at
home and imperialism abroad" ("Colonizing" 206).

Yet discussions of maternal breastfeeding could also serve different political interests and have what were for the time progressive
implications. In part this stems from the role images of breastfeeding
played in critiquing aristocratic values. In the passages quoted above,
the difference between the middle and upper classes is elided as attention is focused on the danger posed by the poor. As Toni Bowers notes,
however, the idealization of maternal breastfeeding also signaled the
superiority of middle-class to aristocratic morality. In certain contexts,
the nursing mother distinguished "the selfless, virtuous, and affectionate [middle-class] domestic mother from the idle, selfish aristocrat"
("Point of Conscience" 142).

Indeed, maternal breastfeeding conflicted with the demands
of an aristocratic property system by threatening the generation of
paternal heirs. Though some, like Dr. Buchan, insisted that the failure
to nurse led to "barrenness" (78), the scientific reality that lactating
women are less likely to conceive was well known (Fildes, *Breasts* 108–
9). Anxious for sons, aristocratic families often discouraged mothers
from nursing and especially from nursing daughters. Thus, in 1783 the
Duchess of Devonshire "complained . . . that her husband's relatives
'abuse' the nursing of her daughter because of 'their impatience for a son
and their fancying I shan't [have one] so soon if I suckle'" (J. S. Lewis
61).[7] The popularization of maternal nursing implicitly challenged the
idea that an aristocratic mother's main function was to supply heirs for
the paternal estate.

Though writers like Buchan, Cadogan, and Rousseau suggest
otherwise, maternal nursing also had the capacity to weaken the father's
authority—both within and without the aristocracy. If Caroline's mark
on Evelina highlights the illogic of paternal kinship nominations, the
more credible role a mother might play in nourishing and raising her
child could be cited to similar effect. The growing belief in the mother's
centrality exposed the senselessness of an exclusive privileging of male

lineage. It is a testament to this skepticism that by the beginning of the nineteenth century, many aristocratic women began giving birth in the presence of their own relatives rather than under the direction of their husbands' mothers (J. S. Lewis 52).

Most important, in 1839 Parliament passed the Infant Custody Bill, which gave a legally separated woman the unprecedented power to visit with or in some cases even retain her young children. The Infant Custody Bill epitomized the cultural consensus that children and mothers belonged together, and it was the first act in English history to suggest that "married women had a legal existence independent of their husbands" (J. S. Lewis 59). As I discuss in more detail in the final section of this chapter, parliamentary supporters of the act repeatedly drew on images of breastfeeding to demonstrate the naturalness of maternal custody rights.

Ironically, even as breastfeeding proved the inextricable bond between mother and child, its value as birth control also made it possible to imagine an escape from maternal duties. When nursing delayed pregnancy, child care became a means (at least temporarily) of avoiding more child care. Mary Wollstonecraft, who was particularly impressed by this advantage, argued that nursing mothers had the freedom to move beyond the domestic sphere and attach "themselves to a science, with that steady eye which strengthens the mind, or practis[e] one of the fine arts that cultivate taste" (*A Vindication of the Rights of Women* [*VRW*] 191).

Thus, as much as the middle- and upper-class nursing mother could be seen as strengthening traditional hierarchies, she also had the potential to disrupt them. The campaign for maternal breastfeeding challenged the aristocratic property system and was instrumental in establishing women's first independent legal rights. Breastfeeding might shore up the father's familial authority, but it could also make him seem dispensable, just as it could theoretically enable women to move beyond the family and develop public interests.

Mary Wollstonecraft

Though many readers have noticed Wollstonecraft's preoccupation with motherhood, less specific attention has been paid to her representation of breastfeeding.[8] Wollstonecraft promotes maternal suckling in virtually all of her major works, often demonstrating its healthiness for both mother and child. Thus, the mother in *Mary* (1788), who sends her children out to nurse, develops lifelong bouts of consumption, and all but two of her children die (4). But when she suckled her own daughter, Fanny Imlay, Wollstonecraft maintained that the two-month-old was "not only uncommonly healthy, but already, as sagacious as a child of five or six months old, which I rather attribute to my good, that is natural, manner of nursing her" (Wardle 256). Like the well-suckled "little negroes" Buffon describes as walking at two months, Fanny has secured an extraordinary advantage.

Whereas Buffon is implicitly concerned about the maintenance of European supremacy, Wollstonecraft suggests that categorizations of difference must themselves be adjusted if maternal breastfeeding is to become widespread in England. Though she does not always reach equally progressive conclusions, she consistently suggests that sexual, class, and racial hierarchies inhibit good mothering and must be rearranged before proper parenting can begin. At some of her most radical moments, Wollstonecraft opposes motherhood and heterosexuality, suggesting that romantic conventions and marriage itself are incompatible with maternal suckling.

Many of Wollstonecraft's arguments about maternity are tied to an interrogation of property distribution, which had its own sexual, class, and racial valence. The inheritance of landed property separated the upper from the lower ranks; husbands had legal ownership over their wives, who generally could not maintain independent land or wealth;[9] and African slaves were seen as material property with no authority over their own bodies. Expanding the challenge maternal nursing actually posed to the aristocratic inheritance system, Wollstonecraft generally associates breastfeeding with a more equitable distribution of property rights in the broadest sense of the terms.

Thus when, in *A Vindication of the Rights of Men* (1790) (*VRM*), she hopes for a day when "the only security of property" will be "the right a man has to enjoy the acquisitions which his talents and industry have acquired," Wollstonecraft makes it clear that "man" includes "woman" and that such changes would improve motherhood. Were property distributed according to desert, she suggests, "women would probably . . . act like mothers, and the fine lady, become a rational woman, might think it necessary to superintend her family and suckle her children, in order to fulfill her part of the social compact" (*VRM* 51–52). According to such logic, the aristocratic inheritance system itself—based in birth and not in labor—

discourages women from performing maternal work. Like land and wealth, children have yet to be owned by those whose "talents and industry" produce them, and until such terms change, the aristocratic status of "lady" will be more appealing than the duties of motherhood.

In *Rights of Men* women are aligned with younger sons and West Indian slaves—other groups who lack property (albeit in different ways). After calling Edmund Burke "the champion of [aristocratically inherited] property" and primogeniture (*VRM* 20), Wollstonecraft blames him for condoning the slave trade: "The whole tenor of his plausible arguments settles slavery on an everlasting foundation" (*VRM* 23). Arguing against "hereditary property—hereditary honours" (*VRM* 12) and presenting the nursing mother as the symbol of the benefits that would accrue if this system were changed, Wollstonecraft affiliates maternal breastfeeding with the values of the French Revolution and the spirit of abolition.

In both *A Vindication of the Rights of Woman* and *The Wrongs of Woman; or, Maria,* the nursing mother continues to signal the need for a change in the understanding of property and material assets. But Wollstonecraft's depiction of sexual difference alters from one text to the other, as does her focus of political urgency. In the *Rights of Woman,* Wollstonecraft bases her arguments for improving female education on the claim that the most debilitating sexual differences are learned, not innate. Women tend to be bad mothers because they behave like aristocrats, valuing the inherited property of their appearance over a middle-class and male investment in work and character. The rare woman who breastfeeds her child demonstrates the kind of manly middle-class virtue that supports marital contentment. In the *Rights of Woman,* the breastfeeding mother breaks down sexual difference to shore up middle-class heterosexuality.

As signaled by its more pessimistic title, *The Wrongs of Woman; or, Maria* is less a cry for change than an exposition of inequity. Here Wollstonecraft focuses on the law, which discriminates against women of all classes and favors all men by treating the female body and its offspring as male property. Instead of urging the improvement of sexual relations, as she does in the *Rights of Woman,* here Wollstonecraft puts motherhood before men, anticipating the parliamentary argument for maternal custody and demonstrating the impossibility of heterosexual security when women are "the *outlaws* of the world" (*The Wrongs of Woman; or, Maria* [*WW*] 156).

A Vindication of the Rights of Woman

A Vindication of the Rights of Woman continues from the *Rights of Men* in suggesting that maternal breastfeeding will become widespread only when inequitable hierarchies are challenged. Women will not be affectionate, suckling mothers, Wollstonecraft warns, "till more equality be established in society, till ranks are confounded and women freed" (*VRW* 191). Wollstonecraft is not as aggressive about West Indian slavery as in the *Rights of Men*, where slavery is a problem in its own right; in the *Rights of Woman*, it is generally evoked as a metaphor for English women's oppression. But her objection to the aristocracy remains largely the same, as she "pay[s] particular attention to [women] in the middle class" (*VRW* 9) in hopes of freeing them from an investment in aristocratic values, which, she insists, men encourage. Like the aristocracy, which privileges "hereditary property," men value women for the inherited "sovereignty of beauty," not their domestic work (*VRW* 55). Because breastfeeding might alter their figures, women "neglect to discharge the indispensable duty of a mother [to suckle]. . . . Natural and artificial duties clash" (*VRW* 142). The mother who breastfeeds complies with nature by adopting a middle-class working position. But most women, taught to be ornaments for male pleasure, behave like leisured aristocrats and do not.

According to such logic, "natural" duty is not necessarily in-stinctive. The word "natural" was ambiguous in the eighteenth century and only beginning to be understood in the modern sense of "innate." This helps explain why Wollstonecraft can argue that "the care of children in their infancy is one of the grand duties annexed to the female character by nature" (*VRW* 151; also see 167), while maintain-ing that breastfeeding is important because it evokes maternal feelings that might otherwise not exist: since "natural affection . . . is . . . a very faint tie," the "duty" of suckling—"calculated to inspire maternal . . . affection"—is crucial (*VRW* 152). Maternal sentiment is not so much an essential condition of the female body but rather the product of "habit" (*Thoughts* 4).[10]

Wollstonecraft's perspective on the "natural" basis of sexual difference is equally complex. On the one hand, as Claudia Johnson points out, Wollstonecraft "cannot stop talking about the preeminence for which Nature has evidently designed men's bodies" (*Equivocal Beings* 40); thus she argues that "the female in point of strength is, in general inferior to the male. This is the law of nature" that "cannot . . .

be denied" (*VRW* 8; for other examples see C. L. Johnson, *Equivocal Beings* 40–41). But just as she is critical of the aristocratic overvaluation of inherited assets, Wollstonecraft is anxious to stress that the bodily source of sexual difference has been culturally exaggerated. Woman might acquire greater "strength, both of mind and body" (*VRW* 9) were she not taught "to labour to become still weaker than nature intended her to be" (*VRW* 41).

What links Wollstonecraft's representation of maternal breast-feeding and sexual difference is her suspicion of explanations based in nature and the body. If breastfeeding is valuable because maternal affection is not inborn, innate sexual differences need to be downplayed. Whatever the foundation of their bodily distinctions, the sexes would be more similar if women cultivated their characters and minds. "I see not the shadow of a reason to conclude that [the] virtues [of men and women] should differ in respect to their nature" (*VRW* 26). "I . . . deny the existence of sexual virtues" (*VRW* 51; also see 193).[11]

Claudia Johnson notes the disappointment with which some feminists receive Wollstonecraft's failure to produce a "positive culture of the feminine and of female solidarity" in the *Rights of Woman* (*Equivocal Beings* 23; see also 210n).[12] Wollstonecraft suggests not only that no value inheres in a separate feminine identity but also that woman's only hope for advancement is to "grow more and more masculine" (*VRW* 8). Such a perspective, G. J. Barker-Benfield argues, is the logical outgrowth of Wollstonecraft's commitment to "the Harrington ideal of masculine civic consciousness" ("Mary Wollstonecraft" 108). Johnson adds that Wollstonecraft is especially concerned with the problem of feminized men: "The strategy of the *Rights of Woman* is to rouse men to claim the liberties of their sex, and to convince them to invite women to share those liberties" (*Equivocal Beings* 31). I would stress the logic underlying Wollstonecraft's call for women to be more masculine and for men to be less feminine. In both cases, she insists that the sexes need to be more similar and that heterosexuality and motherhood depend upon gender parity.

Education plays a central role in the *Rights of Woman* precisely because it has the potential to draw out the similarities between men and women, although in its current form it exacerbates their differences. "Girls and boys would play harmlessly together, if the distinction of sex was not inculcated long before nature makes any difference" (*VRW* 43). The separation that begins in youth undermines the prospect of marital happiness: "The affection of husbands and wives cannot be pure when they have so few sentiments in common" (*VRW* 193). To cure such heterosexual ills the government needs to establish coeducational institutions that promote common interests (*VRW* 168–69). "If marriage be the cement of society, mankind should all be educated after the same model, or the intercourse of the sexes will never deserve the name of fellowship" (*VRW* 165).

Coeducation would also advance middle-class interests. Wollstonecraft envisions a school in which "boys and girls, the rich and poor, should meet together" until they reach the age of nine. At that point, "girls and boys, intended for domestic employments, or mechanical trades, ought to be removed to other schools" and trained for sex-segregated work. Children "of superior abilities, or fortune" would remain together and be educated in politics, science, history, and literature (*VRW* 167–68). Combining boys and girls of "fortune" and "superior abilities," Wollstonecraft's elite school levels distinctions of sex and birth (a smart child is just as deserving as a rich one) while reinforcing the separateness of the working class.

The danger of sex-segregated schools is that they operate in the reverse, maximizing differences of gender while encouraging a bodily familiarity among women that obscures working-class boundaries:

> In nurseries, and boarding-schools, I fear, girls are first spoiled; particularly in the latter. A number of girls sleep in the same room, and wash together. And, though I should be sorry to contaminate an innocent creature's mind by instilling false delicacy . . . I should be very anxious to prevent their acquiring nasty, or immodest habits; and as many girls have learned very nasty tricks, from ignorant servants, the mixing them thus indiscriminately together, is very improper. (*VRW* 127)

The denunciation of indiscriminate class "mixing" continues when Wollstonecraft asks: "Why in the name of decency are . . . ladies and their waiting-women, to be so grossly familiar" as to wash, dress, and evacuate before each other? (*VRW* 127).

If the attack on women's "bodily wit" (*VRW* 128) points to an underlying anxiety about female homoeroticism,[13] Wollstonecraft's more explicit concern is with the threat female cross-class intimacy poses to heterosexuality. The "marriage state" is "so frequently render[ed] . . . unhappy," she suggests, because "women are, in general, too familiar with each other" (*VRW* 127). "The decent personal reserve which is the foundation of dignity of character, must be kept up between woman and woman, or their minds will never gain [the] strength and modesty" (*VRW* 128) on which successful marriage depends. If man and woman need to learn that the significance of their bodily differences has been exaggerated, "woman and woman" need to learn that their shared bodily activities are not the grounds of legitimate compatibility. By logical extension, Wollstonecraft suggests that the middle-class women with whom she is most interested need to identify by class, not gender—to understand that they belong with similarly ranked men.

Were such women to forgo the appeal of other women, recognize their allegiance to men, and develop the similarities that make the sexes more compatible, motherhood would prosper. In negative terms, women's exaggerated mental and physical differences inhibit good parenting; as Barker-Benfield puts it, "the female equivalent of . . . an abrogation of manhood is the loss of motherhood" ("Mary Wollstonecraft" 109). "Weakness of body will not permit [women] to suckle their children, and weakness of mind makes them spoil their tempers" (*VRW* 179; see also 10, 139, 151, 174). In positive terms, women's access to masculine attributes would solve the problem: "By the exercise of their bodies and minds women would acquire that mental activity so necessary in the maternal character, united with the fortitude that distinguishes steadiness of conduct. . . . Make women rational creatures, and free citizens, and they will quickly become good wives, and mothers" (*VRW* 178; also see 4, 64, 68, 174).

At its best, mothering fosters marital compatibility by promoting gender similarity. "The woman who strengthens her body and exercises her mind will, by managing her family . . . become the friend, and not the humble dependent of her husband" (*VRW* 29). Parenting has the potential to bring out the kind of resemblance between the sexes on which marital happiness is based. "The man and woman often meeting on account of the child, a mutual interest and affection is excited by the exercise of a common sympathy" (*VRW* 138; also see 6, 142, 178).

As time and again Wollstonecraft opposes any emphasis on the exclusive value of the body, a logical corollary of the need to minimize sexual difference is the need to minimize erotic expression.[14] An ideal marriage is chaste, she insists, for "a master and mistress of a family ought not to continue to love each other with passion" (*VRW* 30; also see 73, 138). Similarly, good motherhood and sexual activity are opposed. Like scores of contemporary medical authors, for instance,

Wollstonecraft argues that lustful husbands—unwilling to share their wives' bodies with their children—are generally responsible for most women's failure to breastfeed (*VRW* 73). "Drawn from their duty by the [lasciviousness and] admiration of men," women are unable "to acquire sufficient understanding to know how even to nurse their babes" (*VRW* 176–77). Passages like these have understandably led scholars to accuse Wollstonecraft of "reinscrib[ing] . . . the mutually exclusive nature of sexuality and maternity" (Perry, "Colonizing" 217).[15]

It is worth noting, however, that Wollstonecraft's promotion of female chastity also challenges what she sees as the systematic objectification of women in the service of male desire. In urging mothers to nurse rather than supply their husbands with "wanton tricks" (*VRW* 142), she insists that a woman's body should be more than a source of male pleasure.[16] She is perhaps not so much unwilling to promote female sexual enjoyment as convinced of its preclusion by the economy of women's objectification. Maternal breastfeeding, she reasons, would foster marital happiness because it promotes the sexual abstinence on which gender parity and heterosexual compatibility depend.

Given the current state of society, however, the actual benefit of mothering is that it compensates women for heterosexual disappointments. Since men continue to view women as sexual objects and since "love . . . as an animal appetite, cannot long feed on itself without expiring," husbands are bound to be unfaithful. With such inevitabilities a woman's only real comfort is to "transf[er] her fondness to her children" (*VRW* 73). Arguing that "the neglected wife is, in general, the best mother" (*VRW* 31) and that in "the exercise of their maternal feelings providence has furnished women with a natural substitute for love" (*VRW* 152), Wollstonecraft assumes that child care offers women greater affectionate gratification than heterosexual romance.[17] Three years later she looked to her own child for such gratification, ironically telling the unfaithful Imlay that "no lover was ever more attached to his mistresses, than [Fanny] is to me" and that nursing Fanny is "my only solace," "my only pleasure" (Wardle 281).

In one arresting passage in the *Rights of Woman*, Wollstonecraft implies that when their marriages are most disappointing, mothers will produce more daughters than sons, as if marking their dissatisfaction with heterosexuality by reducing the number of men. Quoting from John Reinhold Forster's *Observations Made During a Voyage Round the World,* she describes how African mothers generally produce girl children because their polygamous husbands do not have the energy to regenerate their own sex (*VRW* 70). Deprived of the "physical love" (*VRW* 70–71) they would enjoy in a monogamous society, African wives develop a vigorous and hot constitution, which, according to Forster, leads to the conception of more girls, since the sex with greater vigor and heat reproduces itself. The pregnancy myth complements those explored in chapter 1; Caroline Belmont, for instance, who married a man with at least one illegitimate child, also gave birth to a girl.

Most important in Wollstonecraft's case, though, is the suggestion that the failure of heterosexuality might lead to a female society—exactly the kind of world that begins to materialize in *The Wrongs of Woman*. In the *Rights of Woman*, Wollstonecraft goes no further, pointing out that in Europe the "males born are [slightly] more numerous" than the females (*VRW* 71). Since, like African men, European husbands regularly "weaken [their] constitutions" with multiple partners (*VRW* 6), the population distinction must originate in the relative coolness and sexual sobriety of English wives. In dividing English and African wives, Wollstonecraft again suggests that for women difference inheres not in gender but in some other category—in this case nationality and race.[18]

But because Wollstonecraft repeatedly accuses English men of being unfaithful, and because she so often portrays all women as slaves, the African woman appears to embody the English woman's discontent. If the African mother can be "irritable" (*VRW* 70) and desirous because she is different from the English mother, her unhappiness with male infidelity indicates that despite what Wollstonecraft claims elsewhere, women of all backgrounds also have something in common.

The Wrongs of Woman; or, Maria

Appearing six years after the *Rights of Woman, The Wrongs of Woman; or, Maria* features a range of English women who give birth to daughters only. The unhappily married Maria, for instance, wishes "for my own consolation, to be the mother of a daughter" (*WW* 160), who can serve as romantic replacement for her exploitative and unfaithful husband and offer her "something still to love" (*WW* 81). But though she gives birth to a girl, Maria, like virtually every other mother depicted in the novel, is prohibited from caring for her child. In *Evelina* and *The Italian* mother-daughter separation is a narrative inevitability, but in *The Wrongs of Woman* it becomes the subject of political interrogation.

Denied property in every sense of the word—the right to own money or land, to have custody of their children or authority over themselves— all women are homeless; treated as prisoners and lunatics, they become motherless, daughterless slaves.[19]

In the *Rights of Woman*, Wollstonecraft de-emphasizes the significance of bodily sexual difference to argue that women are entitled to the same educational opportunities as men. In *The Wrongs of Woman*, she concentrates on legal inequities—something she had promised to discuss in a second volume of the *Rights of Woman* that was never produced. The turn to the law requires a reconsideration of her earlier argument, since the law strictly separates the female from the male body, making no allowances for woman's manly potential or maternal obligations. In a society where fathers have the exclusive right to child custody, motherhood has no legal existence.

Confronting the law on its own terms, Wollstonecraft accepts as a given the importance of women's difference from men, but she uses this difference to stress the law's failure to acknowledge and protect women's separate experiences. As Claudia Johnson explains, "the specificity of the female body, far from being the strategic nonissue it was in Wollstonecraft's political tracts, here is its starting point" ("Mary Wollstonecraft" 162). Making a range of unusually explicit references to sexuality, pregnancy, miscarriage, abortion, labor, birth, breastfeeding, and weaning, Wollstonecraft showcases the bodily basis of woman's maternal roles and ultimately implies that the mother's physical attachment to her children entitles her to have legal access to them.

The *Rights of Woman* promises that if middle-class men and women were to become more similar heterosexuality would improve. *The Wrongs of Woman* suggests that given current inequities, hetero-sexuality cannot work and that women are more likely to find satis-fying companionship with members of their own sex. In both works, compatibility depends on similarity, but the terms of similarity shift; whereas *Rights* urges gender parity, *Wrongs* stresses women's affinities with each other regardless of class. "Waiting-women" and "ignorant servants" (*VRW* 127) pose a bodily threat to middle- and upper-class women in the *Rights of Woman*. In *Wrongs*, the privileged heroine must learn that her most valuable companion is Jemima, her prison guard and housekeeper. Maternal breastfeeding, which in *Rights* facil-itates heterosexuality, marks the need for victimized women to unite in *Wrongs*.

It is tempting to view the differences between the *Rights of Woman* and *The Wrongs of Woman* in biographical terms, especially because there is a lot of autobiographical detail in the novel. After writing the *Rights of Woman,* Wollstonecraft had an affair with Imlay, experienced pregnancy, childbirth, and breastfeeding, and learned how it felt to be abandoned. The novel's preoccupation with maternal biology and its pessimistic account of heterosexuality can be read as her response to her failed romance, even though she was working on the book while enjoying apparent contentment with William Godwin.[20]

But I will focus instead on the political implications of Wollstonecraft's remodeling of the female body. The difference in strategy between the *Rights of Woman* and *The Wrongs of Woman* raises one of the most basic questions of feminist debate: is it more productive to claim that women deserve certain rights because of their similarity to men or to stress how women's bodily differences create different needs?[21] Wollstonecraft's alternate perspectives of the female body and heterosexuality in *Rights* and *Wrongs* reveal her utilitarian interest not in a stable concept of woman, but rather in the manipulative potential of representation. Like the discourse on breastfeeding discussed at the opening of this chapter, her divergent images suggest the extent to which the maternal body could be adjusted to serve various political ends.

In *The Wrongs of Woman,* Wollstonecraft's insistence on the inequities of property is pronounced. But instead of blaming aristocratic inheritance patterns for the objectification of the female body, as she does in the *Rights of Woman,* Wollstonecraft focuses on the way the law differentiates between men and women regardless of class, positioning the female body as a form of male property and making it impossible for women to have property of their own. The novel features a number of middle-class male characters who care only about material status, endorse primogeniture, and are hardly different from the aristocrats about whom Wollstonecraft had earlier complained.

Thus, George Venables, a failed businessman, marries Maria because she has been designated her uncle's heir, while her eldest brother (like James Harlowe in *Clarissa*) rages at Maria for depriving him of their relative's wealth (*WW* 180). Even her uncle, distinguished by his unconventional willingness to leave a woman his estate, tries to persuade Venables to marry Maria by secretly offering him five thousand pounds. It is partly because her market value has already been established that later Venables proposes to prostitute Maria to his friend on the principle "that every woman ha[s] her price" (*WW* 161).

The uncle's role in marketing Maria indicates his own problematic interest in her. Like Evelina with Mr. Villars, Maria calls him "My more than father!" (*WW* 156), indicating the sexual complexities of their bond. Indeed, Maria's uncle begins doting on her after the woman he loves forsakes him. Maria recounts how "I . . . became a favourite. . . . My uncle's increasing affection led him to visit me often" (*WW* 128). That the uncle decides to leave his niece the fortune he earned to impress his would-be wife suggests Maria is rewarded for becoming a substitute lover. That the fortune itself is the result of his business ventures in India points to the imperialist roots of English women's plight, something novels like *Belinda* and *Adeline Mowbray* explore in greater detail.

The personal history Maria's prison guard, Jemima, reports reads as an exaggerated version of Maria's experience and draws, as in the *Rights of Men* and the *Rights of Woman,* on the image of West Indian slavery. Illegitimate and impoverished, Jemima describes herself as having been "born a slave, and chained by infamy to slavery during the whole of existence" (*WW* 106). After being abused by her father, she is bound as apprentice to a "master," who beats, rapes, impregnates, and disowns her. "A slave, a bastard, a common property" (*WW* 109), she has no economic alternative but to become a prostitute. When she finally acquires work as Maria's prison guard she feels fortunate.

Her husband never hits her (*WW* 163), so Maria is spared the physical abuse Jemima endures, but both women suffer from maternal deprivation.[22] Each has lost the chance to mother and be mothered, and in each case the loss is rendered as thwarted breastfeeding. The novel opens shortly after Maria's daughter is kidnapped, apparently by her husband.[23] "Tortured by maternal apprehension," Maria feels her "burning bosom . . . bursting with the nutriment for which [her] cherished child might now be pining in vain" (*WW* 75). Maria's inability to feed her child mirrors her alienation from her own late mother, who sent her out to nurse (*WW* 130).

Jemima's history differs in degree but not in kind. When her master rapes and impregnates her, she decides to ingest the "infernal potion" (*WW* 107) he procures to produce an "abortion" (*WW* 109) after he says that if she goes to term, he will "get a nurse for the brat I laid to him" (*WW* 108). Though the explanation is imprecise, it seems likely that Jemima's decision is based in part on her realization that she will not suckle her child, who may then repeat her own history of neglect. When her mother died in childbirth, Jemima was consigned "to the cheapest nurse my father could find," a woman who left her "in dirt, to cry with cold and hunger till I was weary" (*WW* 103). It follows that as soon as she learns of the theft of Maria's nursing baby, Jemima offers to help find her, and "the woman awoke in a bosom long estranged from feminine emotions" (*WW* 80). If in *Rights* maternal sentiment is not natural but habitual, in *Wrongs* it is innate (if sometimes repressed), as fundamental as the bosom itself.

Maria and Jemima's longing for breastfeeding is symptomatic of the hunger that opens between mothers and daughters in a world where their separation abounds. The daughter of Maria's former wet nurse gives her daughter to Maria, and even Venables's dead mistress's child is a girl. Like Jemima's father, Venables sends his illegitimate daughter to the poorest wet nurse available. He openly hopes she will starve, just as he appears willing to let his legitimate daughter starve when he arranges for her to be taken from Maria's breast.

Above all, mother-daughter separation signals woman's loss of reproductive authority. Wollstonecraft's prefatory complaint that novel heroines generally appear to "come forth highly finished Minervas from the head of Jove" (*WW* 73) speaks not just to the problem of literary production but also to men's general appropriation of female generative power. Read against the later account of Jemima's abortion and Maria's "confinement" in a madhouse, for instance, Wollstonecraft's fear that her novel will be seen as an "abortion of a distempered fancy" (*WW* 73) marks the difficulty of bringing any creation to term in a society that grants woman no rational control over her own fertility, be it artistic or biological.[24]

Thus, it is specifically when Maria is pregnant that Venables tries to prostitute her to his friend, and Maria's subsequent decision to leave him puts her at risk of "a miscarriage" (*WW* 171)—especially because Venables has her "hunted out" (*WW* 173). Childbearing marks a dangerous and sometimes lethal form of male dominion for a variety of marginal female characters: Venables' mistress and Jemima's mother die upon being deserted by the fathers of their illegitimate children; Jemima encourages a patron to abandon his pregnant mistress, who subsequently commits suicide (*WW* 116); and one of the residents of the asylum, abused by the "rich old man" to whom she was married "against her inclination . . . during her first-lying in, lost her senses" (*WW* 88).

Venables' newspaper advertisements threatening "any person harbouring" his pregnant wife "with the utmost severity of the law" (*WW* 172) points to the source of the problem in men's property rights. Literally the owners of women, children, and fetuses, men rule reproduction and child rearing, and they can exploit both to their material advantage. After recognizing his mistake in encouraging Maria's marriage, Maria's uncle tries to circumvent Venables's property interest by leaving his fortune to the daughter instead of Maria and making Maria the custodian. Were the fortune to pass directly to Maria, Venables would be entitled to it by his right as husband, but so long as it belongs to the child and Maria is simply the guardian, it initially appears that Maria can be "mistress of [her uncle's] fortune, without putting any part of it in Mr. Venables' power" (*WW* 180).[25]

When it comes to defending male greed, however, the law is foolproof. Though he cannot acquire the uncle's fortune directly, Venables draws on his right of custody, warning Maria that he will "claim the child" if Maria does not give him "the greater part of the property" (*WW* 182). It thus becomes legally impossible for Maria simultaneously to retain her daughter and her uncle's property (which she would need to support the child). When she refuses to give him money, Venables kidnaps their daughter and has Maria incarcerated— also fully within his rights. As the author of the Bill for Infant Custody would complain forty years later, if a mother refused to yield a child to its father he could have her "sent to prison, there to remain until she [should] yield or until she [should] die" (*Great Britain Parliamentary Debates*, vols. 39–41, col. 1082).

Though on the surface an improvement over her husband, Darnford, the male inmate with whom Maria has a romance, also has property interests that interfere with Maria's maternity. He speaks "of the loss of her child, as if it had been his own" (*WW* 187–88). But though in several versions of the novel's fragmented ending Maria is impregnated by Darnford, in most of these the pregnancy ends in miscarriage. One of the fragments suggests the possibility that the termination of the pregnancy occurs after Darnford takes Maria's money to travel to France to reclaim his own fortune (*WW* 192) and then abandons her upon learning that she has lost her fortune (*WW* 201, 202). By deserting her when her property value diminishes, he causes her to miscarry.

The impossibility of a mother's breastfeeding a daughter is directly linked to the problem of property, for the privileging of male inheritance feeds on maternal devotion to sons. Maria's mother sends Maria and her sisters out to nurse but breastfeeds their older brother, for whom she consequently develops an "extraordinary partiality" (*WW* 130). It follows that at her death she leaves him her own "little hoard" (*WW* 136), even though Maria was the one who nursed *her* during her final illness.[26] The suckled son is treated not as a form of property but as an individual worthy of privilege. It is because the mothering of daughters might mark woman's comparable importance that, for the short period during which Maria retains her nursing daughter, she also retains control over her uncle's property.

But such a state cannot last in a world where men's advantages begin at the breast. After Maria loses her daughter, she can only write a memoir for her, a poor substitute for material connection (as Lacan would have it). Not only does Maria never name her daughter, but throughout the period she is writing to her she engages in an epistolary "intercourse" (*WW* 91) with Darnford that takes precedence: "to write [him] letters was the business of the day, and to receive them the moment of sunshine" (*WW* 91). Maria hopes the memoir will "instruct her daughter, and shield her from the misery, the tyranny, [she] knew not how to avoid" (*WW* 82). But when she believes her child is dead, she gives the manuscript to Darnford, who draws on it to seduce her (*WW* 187–88).

Irigaray argues that language fails woman because "representing oneself . . . is in some ways *taken away from [her] at the outset*" (*Speculum* 83). As a token of exchange, woman cannot direct linguistic currency, and her subjective experiences have no representational value. It is symptomatic that relatively few cultural narratives and myths exist to symbolize what mother-daughter attachment might mean (Whitford 120). A daughter has "no right to play in any manner whatever with any representation of her beginning [because she is offered] no specific mimicry of [her maternal] origin" (Irigaray, *Speculum* 78; also see 33, 71, 83). If woman were able to represent her relationship to her mother, Irigaray implies, she might construct a subjective position that would help detach her from circulation.

It is typical of psychoanalytic theory to focus on the daughter's and not the mother's experience. Wollstonecraft, in contrast, charts the mother's futile attempt to communicate with her daughter, not the reverse. But like Irigaray, she points to the impossibility of representing the mother-daughter bond in a world where women are commodified. Under such circumstances, the mother-daughter relationship is doomed, and language cannot compensate. Thus Maria's memoir does not even reach her daughter.

Along similar lines, when, in court, Maria invokes maternity to answer her husband's charges of adultery, she is legally unintelligible. Speaking without the aid of counsel, she describes caring for her husband's abandoned bastard daughter: "though I could excuse the birth, I could not the desertion of this unfortunate babe" (*WW* 195). The contrast between her maternal feeling and the biological father's indifference supports a larger argument. Maintaining that she has a right to divorce Venables and choose another lover, Maria "exclaim[s] against the laws which . . . force women, when they claim protectorship as mothers, to sign a contract, which renders them dependent on the caprice of the tyrant, whom choice or necessity has appointed to reign over them" (*WW* 195). Describing a maternal sympathy that transcends biological and marital bounds, she divides a mother's claim to protectorship from a wife's position as property and approaches the radical conclusion that the law needs to distinguish maternity from marriage as a separate domain.

The force of Wollstonecraft's formulation should not be underestimated. Though she divides maternity and marriage in the *Rights of Woman* when implying that the best mother is the neglected wife, here she suggests more: that motherhood be accorded a form of independent legal protection. Were it logically extended, the argument might include a defense of the mother's right to child custody.

Opposing any measure that could enable an "adulteress to enrich her seducer" (*WW* 199), the judge dismisses Maria's charges against her husband partly to protect Venables' property interests.[27] All subsequent evidence suggests that Maria loses at least part of her inheritance, either because it "is thrown into chancery" court (*WW* 201) or because damages are awarded to Venables (*WW* 202). Most important, the judge makes no reference to Maria's discussion of motherhood, bringing into stark relief its legal nonexistence.

Offering no clear corrective for the problem of property distribution, Wollstonecraft ends by suggesting that women's only recourse is to reject the family that enslaves them, forgo heterosexual relationships, and unite around their shared need to mother and be mothered.[28] In the fragmented conclusion, Maria must replace her love for Darnford with the longing to promote "a mother's tenderness [and] a mother's care" (*WW* 121) that she and Jemima share. The narrative shift from heterosexuality to homosocial maternity is accompanied by Wollstonecraft's concerted attempt to symbolize the mother-daughter bond.[29]

The shift is complicated by Maria and Jemima's class difference. Having been abused by her upwardly mobile stepmother and her first mistress, Jemima is suspicious of higher ranked women. But since Maria is the first to acknowledge her as "a fellow-creature" (*WW* 119), Jemima becomes deeply attached to her. Her "horror of men" (*WW* 110) notwithstanding, Jemima mediates Maria's affair with Darnford and has a kind of vicarious romance with the heroine; she helps the couple exchange books and letters, is present at their first kiss (*WW* 100), and cries with "pleasure" upon hearing their "accents of tenderness" (*WW* 101).

As if instructed by the *Rights of Woman*, Maria defines her allegiances not by gender but by class. Preferring not to think of the urban poor "as my fellow-creatures, as if an ape had claimed kindred with me" (*WW* 168), she tolerates Jemima, who appears to be "superior to her class" (*WW* 78), but takes more interest in the similarly ranked Darnford. He cultivates Maria's snobbery, sparing her an account of his dalliance with prostitutes because they "were of a class of which you can have no knowledge" (*WW* 94; see also 97). He is, of course, wrong: Jemima is a former prostitute and Maria has herself been sexually marketed.

But it is not until Darnford deserts her, in the outline of the fragmented conclusion, that Maria finally begins to recognize the futility of heterosexuality.[30] Though the murkiness of the fragments prohibits a definitive reading, the most elaborate and commonly discussed finale is clear on some points: a pregnant Maria learns of Darnford's desertion, attempts a combined suicide and abortion by swallowing laudanum, but then vomits when Jemima enters with the reputedly dead daughter, who, thanks to Jemima's coaching, says "Mamma!" Maria catches the child "to her bosom," rests her beside her "on the bed[,] . . . remain[s] silent for five minutes, crossing her arms over her bosom," and then exclaims: "The conflict is over!—I will live for my child!" (*WW* 203).

Wollstonecraft had written these exact lines shortly after her own suicide attempt following Imlay's desertion: "The man on whom I relied with the utmost confidence has betrayed me . . . yet I will live for my child" (Wardle 330). In both texts the "conflict" is between heterosexuality and maternity—between dying from a heartbreak and living to raise a daughter. When Maria brings her child to bed, clutches her to her breast, and chooses to live, she privileges female kinship over male companionship. In contrast to *The Italian*, which ends with marriage and the dismantling of the mother-daughter bond, Maria is not reunited with her daughter until she overcomes heterosexuality.[31]

The transition affords singular representational power. In *Evelina* the mother's imprint on her daughter is posthumous, and in *The Italian* mother and daughter are alienated when their kinship is articulated. But when Maria's daughter says "Mamma" and Maria catches her "to her bosom" (*WW* 203), language and body meet; the naming of their bond marks the moment it is physically established. It is a testament to the utter unconventionality of this moment that the narrative abruptly ends.

Precisely because it is fragmented, the conclusion exemplifies the difficulty of symbolizing the mother-daughter relationship. Granted, Wollstonecraft failed to complete *The Wrongs of Woman* because she died after childbirth, the eerie consequence of which was that her own daughter would never know her (and would, in *Frankenstein*, offer one of the most haunting accounts of motherlessness). But the discrepancies among the notes Wollstonecraft left indicate not just a lack of time but a profound indecision. In some projected endings, Maria has a miscarriage; in others she does not. The finale concluding with her suicide is followed by one in which she lives for her child. Wollstonecraft's uncertainty about ending the novel with Maria's pregnancy or with her discovery of her daughter indicates the social difficulty of establishing these plots as acceptable narratives.[32]

Given these constraints, the simple attempt to symbolize the mother-daughter bond has a certain radical promise. For all her class difference, it is Jemima who revives Maria's daughter and reunites mother and child, performing the exact opposite service of *Roxana's* Amy. Having taught the girl to say "Mamma," she seals their linguistic and material bond. As Claudia Johnson reminds us, Maria had promised to reward Jemima with the role of "second mother" should she discover the girl (*WW* 121; "Mary Wollstonecraft" 169). The family that results from her success redefines the domestic world. The hope for middle-class heterosexuality in the *Rights of Woman* yields to a maternal partnership between a mistress and her maid, who may soon have two children (in this version of the ending Maria's suicidal abortion has been averted). "The emancipated, sturdy, parentally purposive, and rationally loving republican couple that Wollstonecraft spent her career imagining is, finally, a female couple" ("Mary Wollstonecraft" 170).

The vision complements Maria's argument for a legal distinction between motherhood and marriage. Venables may have lawful control over Maria's daughter, but Jemima and Maria are driven to find her because they share a sexually determined desire for a child and a superior capacity to care for her. Maria's "burning bosom" (75) proves both the specificity of a mother's suffering when she loses an infant and the infant's special need for her. Similarly, even as she performs an abortion, Jemima experiences "the sensations of new-born life . . . with indescribable emotion" (*WW* 109). In the novel, mother and child are so mutually dependent that their separation poses the risk of death. Thus, Maria's daughter is reported dead and Maria attempts suicide. It is only when Maria recovers her child in the fragmented conclusion that both of them live.

The Infant Custody Bill

For modern readers, Wollstonecraft's universalization of the desire to mother may smack of essentialism. It is telling that the novel's repeated references to abortion stress not a woman's right to refuse maternity but rather the desperation she feels when prohibited from conforming to it, powerful enough to make her terminate her pregnancy. But however compromised Wollstonecraft's position may now seem, in her own day she radically anticipated the parliamentary arguments for maternal custody. *Evelina* and *The Italian* each celebrate the natural basis of the mother's authority; *Evelina* even does so in the context of legal inequities. But *The Wrongs of Woman* does more: it considers the possibility of using the naturalness of maternity to challenge the law—something *Evelina* aims simply to circumvent.

The subject of custody had been on Wollstonecraft's mind at least since 1794, when she lamented to Imlay: "Considering the care and anxiety a woman must have about a child before it comes into the world, it seems to me, by a *natural right*, to belong to her. . . . [But] it is sufficient for man to condescend to get a child, in order to claim it. —A man is a tyrant!" (Wardle 242). Contrasting the father's legal proprietorship with a maternal "right" to custody that begins with pregnancy, the complaint anticipates the tensions in *Wrongs*.[33] Maria, like all mothers, is legally "dependent on the caprice of a *tyrant*" (*WW* 195; my emphasis), who claims their daughter.

The ultimate passage of the Infant Custody Bill in 1839 was an event of immense legal importance for English women. The bill established that, under certain circumstances, a separated mother had the right to visit with and in some cases even retain the custody of her children, especially young ones. In granting this authority, Parliament both attached legal status to the act of mothering and legally distinguished married women from their husbands for the first time in British history.

As Burney intimates in *Evelina* and Wollstonecraft makes clear in *Wrongs,* before the establishment of the bill, a father had exclusive parental rights, regardless of the children's ages or his own deserts. Trial records of the period routinely conclude that the "father is entitled to the custody of his children, to the exclusion of their mother"—even if the children are "within the age of nurture" (R v Greenhill [1836], *Digest* 233) or if the father is "living in adultery" (Ball v Ball [1827] and R v Greenhill, *Digest* 232, 233).

One notorious case from 1804 bears remarkable similarity to *The Wrongs of Woman.* In R v De Manneville, a father who had kidnapped his child from the mother "to compel a disposition of property in his favour" (C. Norton 104) was permitted to retain the infant because "the father of a child is entitled to the custody of it, though an infant [be] at the breast of its mother" (*Digest* 228). When Serjeant Talfourd introduced the Infant Custody Bill in 1838, he referred to the De Manneville case: "The husband by stratagem or force, obtained admittance to the house where [the mother] had taken refuge, seized the child at the breast, and carried it off, almost naked, in an open carriage" (*Great Britain Parliamentary Debates,* vols. 39–41, col. 1083).

Like the account of Mr. Venables' behavior in *The Wrongs of Woman,* the argument stresses both the father's egregious indifference to the baby's health (it is "almost naked in an open carriage") and the violence involved in separating the child from the mother's breast. The villainous husband described by John Leader, another parliamentary proponent of the bill, also resembles Venables: "A man who may be drunken, immoral, vicious, and utterly brutalized [*sic*], may place his wife, who seeks to live separately from him, in [the] cruel dilemma" of having to choose between remaining with him or giving up her child (*Great Britain Parliamentary Debates,* vols. 39–41, col. 1090).

The similarity between Mr. Venables and the abusive husbands and fathers described in the parliamentary records suggests just how well Wollstonecraft had begun to formulate the terms for challenging paternal custody. Her account of the mother's natural importance to her child is also apt. Talfourd argued that when the mother is "prevented from bestowing upon [her children] in their early infancy those solicitudes of love . . . nothing can compensate" (*Great Britain Parliamentary Debates*, vols. 39–41, col. 1082–83). *The Wrongs of Woman* extols "a mother's tenderness, a mother's self-denial" (*WW* 75) and emphasizes the childhood suffering that results from maternal absence and neglect, particularly in Jemima's case.

Talfourd and his supporters were more direct than Wollstonecraft about the paradox of the mother's legal irrelevance. Talfourd argued that "if nature were suffered to interpose, the chain of argument [that establishes paternal rights] would be severed, and the legal spell dissolved" (*Great Britain Parliamentary Debates*, vols. 39–41, col. 1085). Similarly, John Leader noted that

> It may be admitted that the wife is the fitter person to have the care of the early education of her children, to form their habits, to minister to their childish wants[,] to soothe them in trouble, and to tend them in sickness. All this may be admitted; but the law sternly refuses to listen to the pleadings of natural sympathies and affections, [and] gives to the husband the charge and possession of the children, and denies even the sight of them to the beloved and loving mother. (*Great Britain Parliamentary Debates*, vols. 39–41, col. 1090)

Perhaps because she wrote when it was still important to prove the naturalness of maternity, Wollstonecraft could not take full rhetorical advantage of the legal ironies that emerged once this naturalness was assumed. Nevertheless, by juxtaposing her defense of maternity with an attack on the law, she assembles the pieces of argument on which the parliamentary proponents for maternal custody would come to rely.

Even as they sought to capitalize on the child's need for the mother, the supporters of the Infant Custody Bill finally rested their case not on the grounds of what was best for the child (whose needs were recognizable but whose rights were not) but on the grounds of what was best for the mother. Stressing the special importance of visiting privileges, Talfourd explained, "I do not seek to restore to infants those habitual influences of maternal love . . . but I do ask some mitigation of the mother's lot—some intervals in which forsaken nature may be cheered and waning strength repaired by the sight of the objects of farlooking hope" (*Great Britain Parliamentary Debates*, vols. 39–41, col. 1089). Caroline Norton, who helped spearhead the Infant Custody Bill and solicited Talfourd's support, gained national attention for her expressed desire to reclaim her children on the basis of *her* best interest, not theirs. "Against the inflicted and unmerited loss of her children," Norton wrote in a widely published pamphlet, a woman "*cannot* bear up" (C. Norton 11). Unconventionally organizing her novel around the mother's—not the daughter's—suffering and painting Maria as a woman of "waning strength," Wollstonecraft makes almost the identical point.

Perhaps most impressive is Wollstonecraft's anticipation of the need for a legal distinction between marriage and maternity. Opponents of the Infant Custody Bill were quick to point out the domestic dangers of just this division. One parliamentary dissenter, Sir Edward Sugden, complained that if women attained legal rights as mothers, marriages would be weakened. Although he accepted as given that "men had very little notion of the intensity of a mother's affection for her children," Sugden insisted that "the question to be considered was whether the Bill . . . would not present a motive to induce separations between husbands and wives" (*Great Britain Parliamentary Debates*, vols. 39–41, col. 1091; see also vols. 42–44, col. 1050). Immediately before the bill's passage, he warned that "Under the present law, parents, mothers especially, had a great inducement, from the natural love and affection they bore to their children, to put up with many petty trifling differences and annoyances [they experienced with their husbands] which there were no means of remedying, because the marriage tie remained unbroken." Should the bill be passed, he feared that "in many cases, separations, followed by divorces, would ensue, simply because of the facilities afforded mothers of indulging their natural love, by access to their offspring" (*Great Britain Parliamentary Debates*, vols. 48–50, col. 160).

Revealing the marital value of denying motherhood legal status, Sugden reasons that because its natural basis guarantees its continuity, maternity should reinforce marriage, which is implicitly less stable and less desirable for women. The defendants of the Infant Custody Bill inverted such logic. Assuming that under certain circumstances separations and divorces were tolerable, they granted the mother an independent right to her children on the grounds of the naturalness of her love.

The idea that there should be a legal distinction between motherhood and marriage, which Wollstonecraft begins to formulate in her final work and upon which the passage of the Infant Custody Bill necessarily depended, is not in evidence in *A Vindication of the Rights of Woman*. Although Wollstonecraft is critical of the workings of heterosexuality in the *Rights of Woman,* she is anxious to repair them. Calling for men and women to develop greater similarities, she describes motherhood as a source of heterosexual compatibility. The shift in conception from the *Rights of Woman* to *The Wrongs of Woman*—from a maternal body that marks gender parity to one that signals sexual difference and female interdependence—is historic. In reflecting and shaping a growing discourse about the natural, universal, and sexually specific basis of maternal desire and behavior, Wollstonecraft formulates the bodily argument that will establish a married woman's legal individuality. For all the problems this argument continues to present for feminists, it has also had a concrete political utility.

Chapter 4

The Maternal Bosom

Sexual and Colonial Difference in Belinda

WOLLSTONECRAFT'S SHIFTING interpretations of the sexual and social meaning of the maternal bosom suggest something of the flexibility of the mother's image. That suckling can signify masculine, middle-class virtues in the *Rights of Woman* but expose the fallacy of male power and class difference in *The Wrongs of Woman* indicates its remarkable capacity to incorporate varying and even conflicting political concerns. In Maria Edgeworth's *Belinda,* the maternal bosom is at the center of such conflict. Wollstonecraft changes the meaning of breastfeeding when changing texts, but Edgeworth assembles competing values in one book, simultaneously exposing the ideological promise and the instability of the mother's body.

In many ways, *Belinda* rehearses familiar problems. It is pre-occupied with the objectification of women and the hazards of their exchange among men. Though homoerotic relations offer escape from this traffic, permanent respite proves impossible. Insisting both on the universality of women's oppression and the need to maintain class difference, the novel brings the tension between gender and rank into stark relief. What distinguishes *Belinda* from the earlier novels, however, is its attention to the overarching impact a commercial and specifically colonial economy has in shaping these problems. Though colonialism supports both Evelina's London pleasures and Maria's inheritance, it remains in the background of narrative concern. *Belinda* openly examines the exchange between domestic maternity and empire, each of which influences the other.

In so doing it brings questions about sexual, class, and colonial distinctions into the kind of juxtaposition that characterizes Dr. Cadogan's, Dr. Buchan's, and Rousseau's descriptions of breastfeeding. More than in the earlier novels I discuss, the mother in *Belinda* is the source of new citizens, the space where reproduction is either harnessed or infected. She determines which class and race will predominate in an increasingly integrated society, where people from the colonies are as apt to make their way to England as those in England are to go to the colonies. Like Thomas Malthus in his extraordinarily influential *Essay on the Principle of Population* (1798), Edgeworth suggests that the female body is the site for controlling human increase.[1]

But even as she positions maternity in the service of national and imperial interests, Edgeworth is critical of the attendant commodification of the female body. Alert both to the endurance of aristocratic values and to women's role in consuming and displaying the spoils of empire, *Belinda* suggests that aristocratic materialism and colonialist venture converge in women's objectification. The good mother's value inheres in the internal qualities of love and dedication and in what *Belinda* describes as her detachment from "the selfish solitary votaries of avarice and ambition" (216). But as an institution motherhood supports the very gender and colonial economies that contradict this by prizing bodies as external assets.

Belinda breaks into two overlapping narratives, the first domestic and the second colonial, which are linked by events involving the central maternal figure and the titled heroine's patroness, Lady Delacour. When the novel begins, Lady Delacour has rejected motherhood and is suffering from what she believes is a fatal pistol wound to her breast. The "hideous spectacle" (32) of her injury signals both her maternal failure and her sexual ambiguity. She received the wound when she was a cross-dressed participant in a duel provoked by the aptly named Harriet Freke, a transvestite who was then her best friend.[2] Before the book is two-thirds complete, Lady Delacour breaks from Harriet and reveals her enduring desire to return to domesticity, and her injured breast is healed. Like *The Wrongs of Woman*, *Belinda* suggests that sexual difference and maternal longing are intrinsic. Lady Delacour's natural self is her domestic one, and as soon as she recognizes this, her bosom—the penultimate symbol of femininity—recovers.

In the second narrative, which begins in the second third of the novel and continues until the end, Lady Delacour turns to the colonial arena, playing the pivotal role in extraditing Belinda's Creole suitor from Jamaica. The Creole blurs the boundaries of nation and race much as the breast injury blurs sexual difference, but Lady Delacour reduces this confusion by positioning him on the other side of the line that defines England. Yet because she also supports the plantocratic class in Jamaica, which profits from the joint commodification of English women and African slaves, Lady Delacour collapses some of the national and racial distinctions she otherwise promotes. In the end, the objectification of women she sanctions returns value to their material surface, undercutting her earlier idealization of maternity. When Lady Delacour recovers from the breast injury motherhood emerges as woman's internal essence. But the colonial activity maternity promotes contradicts this by commercializing the female body.

Maria Edgeworth and Colonialism

Critics generally agree that in eighteenth- and nineteenth-century English literature, femininity is portrayed as both similar to and different from colonial otherness in ways that destabilize the English woman's relation to empire. When Jenny Sharpe suggests that Jane Eyre's subjectivity "is constituted through a complex system of tropes . . . which cannot be reduced to the simple binarism of colonizer and colonized" (29–30), she encapsulates a theoretical consensus about the complex role the British woman writer or female character plays in shaping—as well as defining resistance to—colonialism.[3] Typically identified as the first Irish novelist, Edgeworth has become a visible subject of feminist and colonial inquiry. Though long recognized for her Irish interests, she has begun to appeal for her broad concerns with domestic and imperial authority. Several scholars, for instance, have commented on the role the West Indies plays in the resolution of *Belinda*'s marriage plot.[4]

Edgeworth's volatile history in Ireland highlights the ambiguity of her colonial affiliations. In 1782, when she was fourteen, her father, Richard Lovell Edgeworth, moved the family from England to Ireland so that he could preside over his estate there. In Parliament, Richard Edgeworth was considered a Protestant defender of Catholic interests, but as a landlord he was in enough danger during the peasant uprising in 1798 to flee with his family to a Protestant stronghold, where he was then nearly lynched by a Protestant mob (M. Butler, *Maria Edgeworth* 137–38).[5] Two years later, offended by the bribery used to pass the Act of Union that joined the Irish and English Parliaments, Richard Edgeworth voted against the measure even though he supported it (M. Butler, *Maria Edgeworth* 181–83; M. Butler, introduction 35).

Just as it is difficult to fix Richard Edgeworth's political behavior, critics have debated his daughter's beliefs. While some emphasize the development of her "Colonial Office mentality" (Hurst 86–87), others, including her noted biographer Marilyn Butler, argue that Edgeworth's conservative sympathies are balanced by "progressive, at times even radical" critiques of the Anglo-Irish landowners (*Maria Edgeworth* 125; see also her introduction, and Dunne).

Ireland's legislative absorption into the English Parliament followed in the wake of the American Revolution, the first great splintering of the empire. The formation of the United States produced enormous anxiety about the fate of the Caribbean remainder of the "American Empire," anxiety that was compounded by the long war with France and the slave agitation roused by the French Revolution (especially in San Domingo). Jamaica, a crucial source of the sugar that fueled the British economy, had begun to decline in prosperity by the end of the eighteenth century, in part because of business interruptions during the American Revolution, devastating hurricanes in the 1780s, and England's raising of sugar import taxes to support the war against France (Patterson 27).[6] In addition, both the plantocracy and the slave population in Jamaica were notoriously rebellious. The plantocrats supported the American Revolution, resented the British government's demand that they help fund their own defense, and declared the sovereign right to determine their laws (Burns 511, 517–18, 538, 551–52, 558–59, 600), while the slaves instigated conspiracies, revolts, and near revolts at least ten times between 1776 and 1815 (Burns 511, 599; Burt 141; Patterson 271–73). With the abolition of slave trading in 1807 and the growth of competitive sugar markets in

Brazil, the French West Indies, Cuba, and the East Indies (Patterson 28), the value of the "first" empire in the West Indies would decline as the importance of the "second" one in the Far East began to rise (Burt 3–169; Fieldhouse 55–83; Patterson 15–51).

Belinda is, on the one hand, concerned with the maintenance of Jamaican wealth but, on the other, also anxious to distinguish Jamaican from English boundaries at a moment when the colony was becoming a potential liability. At the same time, the novel associates national ambition and national identity with maternity and heterosexual propriety. Lady Delacour prevents Belinda from marrying the Jamaican Creole only after her intrinsic maternity is revealed in a move that also marks the eradication of female homoeroticism. In *The Italian*, homoerotic desire between mother and daughter spares the heroine for marriage and is ultimately compatible with patriarchal politics. But in *Belinda*, homoerotic desire occurs outside the family among unrelated women and is subversive. The novel links the need to demarcate the boundaries of gender difference on which heterosexuality, marriage, and maternity depend with a need to imagine national boundaries impervious to racial mixing, presenting female homoeroticism and miscegenation as analogous dangers.[7]

Sexual Ambiguity and the Maternal Cure

Edgeworth's Belinda has the same name as the mock epic heroine of Pope's *The Rape of the Lock*. But in the first portion of *Belinda* it is the fashionable Lady Delacour who actually resembles the poem's protagonist, as she herself notes when she quotes Pope to describe her dependence on "the cosmetic powers" that mask her injury and its symptoms (34; Pope 1.124). Both women need to have their faces "completely repaired" every morning (*Belinda* 34; Pope 1.141), and both texts make clear that the makeup on which women rely is likely to be derived from colonial products.[8] Pope's protagonist artfully "[n]ourish[es]" her lock (2.20) and teasingly withholds it from the man who would cut it, while Lady Delacour (terrified of the mastectomy she believes is her only cure) paints to prevent people from discovering the need to cut off her breast.[9] Whereas the domestic woman is supposed to be intrinsically female and to have a depth of character "far more valuable than her surface" (Armstrong 76), Pope's heroine and Lady Delacour depend on material self-display.

Lady Delacour's wounded—and now apparently diseased—breast stands as punishment for her rejection of domestic values, particularly that of good motherhood. Before receiving the injury, she was addicted to dissipation, epitomized by her refusal to be confined during her first pregnancy; everyone in the novel, including Lady Delacour, believes this is why her baby was stillborn. Following the birth of her second child, she yielded to the "fashion . . . for fine mothers to suckle their own children" (42) and failed. "After the novelty was over, I became heartily sick of the business; and at the end of about three months my poor child was sick too" (42). This child also died.

Though her third child, a daughter, survived, Lady Delacour was by then so thoroughly convinced of her maternal inadequacy that she neglected her: "I sent it off immediately to the country, to a stout, healthy, broad-faced nurse, under whose care it grew and flourished" (42). When the book opens, the girl is living at boarding school, and Lady Delacour is alienated from her child. "I am convinced that she hates her daughter," her husband's aunt exclaims. "Why she never speaks of her—she never sees her—she never thinks of her" (103). To the aunt, Lady Delacour is a "monster" (102) of a mother, a word obviously designed to remind the reader of the now "hideous spectacle" of her bosom (32).

Though some of the blame for her familial failures falls squarely on Lady Delacour, her aristocratic husband and his relatives foster the materialism that undercuts domesticity and maternity. Lord Delacour, a gambler and alcoholic, married her to acquire her fortune and settle his debts. Lady Delacour recounts the history by describing herself as a commercial product: "the heiress lozenge is a specific in some consumptions" (36). Like cosmetics, drugs were often derived from colonial imports and were aggressively advertised and widely consumed at the turn of the century, along with a host of other fashionable (and frequently foreign) items to which the novel refers—including plants, pets, and razor blades (McKendrick, Brewer, and Plumb 146–94, 316–27).

New commercialism and old aristocratic values conspire to objectify women. Even as Lord Delacour marries her for her market value, his relatives insist on their age-old property rights in Lady Delacour's production of male heirs. In keeping with aristocratic tradition, they expect to oversee her first pregnancy and supervise the birth (42).[10] Convinced that the paternal family's interest in the child exceeds the mother's attachment to it, the "old dowager" behaves as "chief mourner"

(42) when the second baby dies. And instead of simply being happy when the third infant survives, Lord Delacour is so concerned with patrilineal descent that he cannot "bear the child, because it [is] not a boy" (42). His discontent influences Lady Delacour's decision to send the child out to nurse.

When she rejects her husband and his family and becomes involved with Harriet Freke, Lady Delacour appears to seek an escape from both commercial and aristocratic dehumanization. Wearing men's clothing and sporting "the character of a young rake" (47), Harriet stands enough outside the traffic in women to redirect it by courting girls in distress and provoking duels between ladies.[11] By pointing to the instability of gender boundaries, Harriet's ambiguity undercuts the foundation of sexual difference on which women's objectification necessarily depends. As the famous Reverend James Fordyce explained in the mid-eighteenth century, the female transvestite challenges "the distinction of form, which the Almighty had established in creation" (qtd. in Atkinson and Atkinson 104).[12]

Transvestites raise "the specter of homosexuality" (Epstein, "Either/Or" 124) since they are potentially the same sex as their romantic partners. As Lisa Moore contends, Harriet's "male-parodic behavior" marks "the possibility of a female [homo]erotic agency" ("'Something More Tender'" 505). Lady Delacour says that she turned to Harriet to fill the "'aching void' in my heart" and calls her a "bosom friend" (13), evoking both the part of her body she withholds from her children and the injury resulting from her duel in Harriet's honor. Lady Delacour also twice calls herself an amazon (34, 194), alluding not simply to her imagined need for a mastectomy but also to her sexual deviance; her first reference follows directly upon a quotation from *The Rape of the Lock,* in which the queen of the Amazons encourages Belinda to reject men.[13] Regardless of whether her relationship with Harriet is actually consummated, Lady Delacour's heterosexual routines are clearly confounded.[14] Like the neglectful mother described in Dr. Buchan's treatise on breastfeeding, she becomes detached from her husband, and her claims to "fidelity, modesty, [and] chastity" are thrown into serious doubt (Buchan 170).

Although Harriet becomes her enemy shortly after the novel begins, Lady Delacour continues to reserve her bosom for women only, forbidding her husband or any male doctor to enter her "boudoir" and see her undressed. Certain that she is dying of breast cancer, she depends for care on her masculine and sadomasochistic waiting-woman Marriott (note the name's assonance with Harriet), who rules her with a "rod of iron" (20).[15] As in Wollstonecraft's *Rights of Woman*, in which "ladies and their waiting-women" are "more [grossly] familiar with each other than men" (*VRW* 127), Lady Delacour's relationship with Marriott marks the interface between sexual and class confusion. Though she will "not yield an iota of power to her husband," Lady Delacour submits "herself to [Marriott's] every caprice" (20). Bound to a crisis in rank, Lady Delacour's resistance to heterosexuality confirms Susan Lanser's intriguing suggestion that women's same-sex relations were most apt to be defined as sexually transgressive when perceived as "threat[s] against status" (185).[16]

Belinda helps restore domestic and maternal order and cure Lady Delacour by displacing both Marriott and Harriet. She assumes partial responsibility for Lady Delacour's dressing and informs Marriott that her mistress will no longer "suffer herself to be treated with disrespect" (160).[17] At the same time, Belinda replaces Harriet in Lady Delacour's affections. Though Lady Delacour is tempted to pursue a homoerotically charged relationship with her ("What was Harriet Freke in comparison with Belinda Portman? . . . Oh, Belinda! how entirely have I loved! trusted! admired! adored! respected! revered you!" [183]), Belinda resists this in the interest of heterosexuality and maternity. She is assisted by the hero, Clarence Hervey, who vows to "wean" (124) Lady Delacour of dissipation and see her "happy in domestic life" (165).[18]

Clarence and Belinda arrange for Lady Delacour to be reintroduced to her daughter Helena, who, like the heroines described in chapter 1, bears an "astonishing resemblance" to her mother (175). The physical similarity conventionally facilitates their reunion (Clarence orchestrates the meeting after identifying Helena by her looks), and Helena's enduring love proves that Lady Delacour has not "forfeited [her] natural [parental] claim[s]" (123). When Lady Delacour recognizes "her daughter as part of herself," she is "inclined to be pleased with her" (175), confirming Lady Anne Percival's insistence on the instinctive basis of maternal sentiment: "Such a being" as an unfeeling mother cannot "exist in the world" (103). Inspired by her example, Lord Delacour overcomes his aristocratic preoccupation with male heirs and takes an interest in the girl.

With her renewal of maternal sentiment, Lady Delacour is finally inclined to submit to the mastectomy she thinks will save her life. Earlier, she resists the procedure because she believes it will objectify her, explaining that the doctors will not "perform such an operation for a wife, without the knowledge, privity, consent, &c. &c. &c. of her husband" (179). But, after insisting that Lord Delacour has "the strongest claim to be consulted" about the operation, Belinda persuades Lady Delacour to welcome him to her dressing room and expose herself (179, 267). For the first time in years Lord Delacour sees his wife undressed, and the heterosexual impact is immediate. As soon as he witnesses the injury, Lord Delacour's love revives "in full force" (269), as if all he required were the opportunity to exercise his viewing rights. Once his authority is reestablished, there is no longer cause to prevent the surgeons from operating, and without even mentioning Lady Delacour's consent, the novel describes her preparations for the procedure.

When it occurs, the operation confirms Lady Delacour's interior femininity and maternity while paradoxically insisting on the necessity of the objectification that led her astray. As soon as they undress her, the doctors discover that Lady Delacour has no disease, just a festering bruise, readily curable so long as she "leave[s] off the terrible quantities of laudanum" (313) she takes. In finally allowing her body to be circulated among men, Lady Delacour learns that her breast is fundamentally normal. The organ's purity rectifies the system of sexual difference the wound had challenged, proving that unfeminine behavior cannot change a woman's internal essence; but the revelation ironically depends on male control of her material surface.

For the most part this contradiction is muted as the emergence of the "real state" (314) of the breast confirms earlier intimations that Lady Delacour's "real character" (292) is a domestic one. The peeling away of her body's surface injury completes the process of disclosing her inner womanhood and maternity, which, it now appears, was never in jeopardy but only obscured. At last, Lady Delacour has "no secret to keep—no part to act; her reconciliation with her husband and his friends restored her mind to ease and self-complacency. Her little Helena was a source of daily pleasure; and no longer conscious of neglecting her daughter, she no longer feared that the affections of her child should be alienated" (316). Like the dedicated mother in the medical manuals, Lady Delacour becomes the center of a political stability based in sexual and class order. With her own gender ambiguity resolved, Lord Delacour restored as husband, and Marriott in submission, everyone seems to have found the proper place.[19]

This includes Harriet Freke, who, on the night before Lady Delacour's cure, is caught in a "man trap" (311) that mangles her leg so badly "she would never more be able to appear to advantage in man's apparel." In a symbolic substitution, Harriet's leg is "cut" moments before readers learn that Lady Delacour's breast will not have to be removed. Whereas the "bruised" leg cannot heal (312), apparently because Harriet Freke never had a biological right to wear pants, Lady Delacour's "bruise" is reparable (314). Marking woman's natural difference and maternal instinct, the breast emerges unscathed.

Miscegenation and Colonial Boundaries

In the second narrative, the need to define and secure internal integrity returns on a national scale with the entrance of two West Indian characters who seek sexual control over English women. Mr. Vincent, a Creole from Jamaica, comes to England to be educated and falls in love with Belinda, who is enamored of Clarence Hervey. Mr. Vincent's fate is intertwined with that of Mr. Hartley, a middle-class Englishman who made a fortune in Jamaica and, having narrowly survived a slave rebellion, has returned home to marry off the daughter he deserted. As Mr. Vincent's and Mr. Hartley's stories converge, the problems of homoeroticism and gender ambiguity are gradually replaced by questions about heterosexuality, nation, and race. Does the Creole born abroad have as much right to Belinda as her countryman Clarence Hervey? And should Mr. Hartley, who abandoned his family in England to become a bigamist slaveowner in Jamaica, be allowed to bequeath his English daughter—tellingly named Virginia—to the man of his choice? Published soon after the Act of Union with Ireland, during a period when England was both anxious about how to preserve the remains of the American empire and concerned about the empire's economic instability, *Belinda* raises questions about how the boundaries between England and the West Indian colonies should be drawn.[20]

Whereas earlier Belinda mutes Lady Delacour's sexual subversion, now it is Belinda's sexuality that presents potential dangers, which Lady Delacour ultimately resolves. Emboldened by the breast cure that fixes her maternal identity, she arranges for both Belinda and Virginia to marry and reproduce with native Englishmen. In the process she helps extradite the Creole and reward the plantocrat, justifying the maintenance of national difference without sacrificing the English pursuit of colonial wealth. But even as motherhood thus becomes the basis of colonial success, the oppression of English women is increasingly linked with that of African slaves.[21] Although the trope of the English woman as slave capitalizes on an emotionally charged history while erasing the specific cruelty of slavery, the analogy simultaneously disrupts the national and racial distinctions on which justifications of slavery and colonialism depend.

Arriving from Jamaica and bearing the name of another rebellious English colony,[22] Mr. Vincent disrupts distinctions of nationality and race much as Lady Delacour's breast injury and Harriet's transvestism confuse sexual difference. In the eighteenth century, the term "Creole" was ambiguous, referring to persons born in the colonies whose parents were of European or of African descent, including island-born slaves (R. K. Richardson 57). Even a Creole who was a wealthy landowner of pure European roots presented "a historically unique political" challenge to the process of imagining a national homeland, according to Benedict Anderson, for the Creoles "constituted simultaneously a colonial community and [a Europeanized] upper class" (58). Rich West Indian Creoles, like Mr. Vincent, who came to England and pushed "upward into the ranks of the landed gentry," were seen as threats to English social order (Sypher 504).

Boundaries were erected, Anderson suggests, by "the convenient, vulgar deduction that creoles, born in a savage hemisphere, were by nature different from . . . inferior to," and implicitly racially other than "the metropolitans" (60). Edward Long's influential *History of Jamaica* (1774) identifies Creoles as an alternative species, "descended from British ancestors" but "stamped with . . . characteristic deviations" (262), some of which, according to other authors, were the effect of their "contamination [by] the negroes" (qtd. in Sypher 515). Mr. Vincent's arriving for an English education guarantees nothing about his racial purity, for as Long complains, "many Mulatto, Quateron, and other illegitimate children [are] sent over to England for education . . . where . . . they pass under the general name of West Indians" (274). Accordingly, Mr. Percival asks Mr. Vincent if he plans to "turn savage," and Lady Delacour likens him to "Caliban" (234, 339).[23]

To complicate matters, Mr. Vincent has a "black servant," Juba, who has journeyed with him to England because "the poor fellow begged so earnestly to go with young massa" (219).[24] Perhaps named after the African prince in Joseph Addison's popular play *Cato* (1713), Juba is a selfless, willing, and happy assistant, described by Lady Anne Percival as "the most grateful, affectionate creature I ever saw" (239).[25] But according to Edward Long (427), Juba was also a popular

African name for a woman, and it is in keeping with the troubles cross-gendering raises earlier in the novel that the servant is easily influenced by Harriet Freke. After Harriet convinces him that he is haunted by an obeah woman, Juba, like Lady Delacour before, becomes ill and recovers only with Belinda's help (221–22).[26] The reference to the religious practice of obeah, a widely feared source of slave resistance, is a reminder that slaves throughout the West Indies, and especially in Jamaica, are engaging in deadly rebellions like the one later alluded to in the novel.[27] Indeed, if Juba's eagerness to follow Mr. Vincent to England proves the reciprocal value of the master-slave relationship, the place Juba insists on going to is one where in theory, if not in fact, he can be legally free.[28]

Although Juba functions in part as a foil to make his master appear more European and civilized, the novel also draws attention to the kinship between Mr. Vincent and "negroes." Mr. Vincent acquired his fatal addiction to gambling in the West Indies when "day after day" he played, "with eagerness, at games of chance, with his negroes" (422). He also identifies himself with African men when he reads Belinda *The Dying Negro* (347), the enormously popular antislavery poem written by Thomas Day, Richard Edgeworth's good friend. The poem describes how "a Black, who a few days before, ran away from his master . . . with intent to marry . . . a white woman, being taken, and sent on board the Captain's ship, in the Thames; took an opportunity of shooting himself through the head." Mr. Vincent apparently sympathizes with the African speaker in the poem, who, like him, discovers the supposed superiority of European female beauty. Later Mr. Vincent attempts to shoot himself in the head, when he realizes that his relationship with Belinda is doomed (431).[29]

To the extent that Mr. Vincent is identified with the dying Negro, his desire to marry Belinda presents the threat of miscegenation, which repeats the problems raised by homoeroticism in the first portion of the novel. Both are sexual dangers that confuse binary categories of difference, and both threaten maternity: homoeroticism because it is not reproductive, and miscegenation because when it *is* reproductive the maternal body becomes the site of a racial and national blending that threatens population control. The concern about the national effect of reproductive relations between black men and white women is typified in Long's complaint that "English blood will become so contaminated with this mixture . . . till the whole nation resembles the Portuguese and *Moriscos* in complexion of skin and baseness of mind. This is a venomous and dangerous ulcer, that threatens to disperse its malignancy far and wide, until every family catches infection from it" (qtd. in Shyllon 104–5).[30] From this perspective, the threat of miscegenation in *Belinda* complements Lady Delacour's breast disease.

Edgeworth was clearly mindful of miscegenation. She allowed Juba to marry a white country girl in the first edition of *Belinda* (1801) but omitted this event when she revised the text for inclusion in Anna Barbauld's British Novelists Series (1810), explaining, "My father says that gentlemen have horrors upon this subject, and would draw conclusions very unfavourable to a female writer who appeared to recommend such unions" (M. Butler, *Maria Edgeworth* 495). As Kathryn Kirkpatrick points out, Edgeworth apparently worried that Belinda's relationship with the Creole posed a similar challenge, for she also dampened the romance between Belinda and Mr. Vincent and deleted the proposal scene in the revision (introduction xxviii–xxxii).

In both versions, Belinda rejects Mr. Vincent when she discovers that he has been borrowing money from a Jew to support his enduring "negro" habit of gambling. Produced at a time when "to judge from their public complaints most [West Indians] were well on the way to bankruptcy" (Ward 45), the representation of Mr. Vincent's gaming and of his dependence on the proverbial Jew may reflect fears about the Jamaican drain on the English economy.[31]

For Lady Delacour, Mr. Vincent's money marks a national difference that makes him undesirable as a husband and reproductive partner for Belinda. She tells the heroine that Clarence Hervey, her other suitor, "might do as well . . . considering, that an English member of parliament is, in the eyes of the world . . . a better connexion, than the son of a West India planter" (358). Lady Delacour reinforces the insinuations about Mr. Vincent's unfamiliar race when she reminds Belinda that it was a fight between the Jew and the (homonymic) Juba that revealed the Creole's gambling losses: "Without that wrestling match of theirs, the truth might never have been dragged to light, and Mr. Vincent would have been this day your lord and master" (451). Drawing on an image of interior exposure reminiscent of the unmasking of her own femininity and maternity, she implies that Mr. Vincent is too much like Juba and the Jew to possess the heroine.[32] The domestic role she assumes in securing Belinda's sexual and reproductive borders represents a form of national and racial border patrol as well.

Lady Delacour's desire to have Belinda marry Clarence Hervey (the "English member of parliament" [358]) instead ultimately aligns reproductive purity with colonial ambition, proving that the extradition of the Jamaican Creole need not compromise England's access to Jamaican profits. Initially, Clarence cannot marry Belinda because he is pledged to Virginia (the abandoned daughter of the Jamaican plantocrat), whom he has educated in seclusion to be his future wife as suggested by Rousseau's *Émile*. In addition to referring to J. H. Bernardin de Saint-Pierre's *Paul et Virginie* (1796), Virginia's name evokes the lost American colony that had ranked with Jamaica as one of the most valuable properties of the American empire before the Revolution (Fieldhouse 58).[33] Clarence accordingly treats her as property. Not only does he sport a lock of her hair (139) like the baron in Pope's poem, but Virginia is constantly worried that she does not feel sufficient gratitude toward him (382, 383, 386, 388, 389, 400, 466)—a sentiment customarily expected of a good slave like Juba (239).[34]

When he tires of Virginia after meeting Belinda, Clarence decides to try to market her. On learning that her father has returned home from Jamaica to find the daughter he deserted, Clarence searches for him, hoping that Virginia's colonial wealth will attract a host of admirers. Positioning the girl to become an "heiress lozenge" (36) like Lady Delacour earlier, Clarence now hypocritically wants "the fashionable world in all its glory . . . [to] be before" Virginia (395), even though he had previously insisted on secluding her from material corruption. In addition to publicly exhibiting her portrait, he inserts "proper advertisements in all the papers" (393), reminiscent of an earlier moment when Belinda is described as having been brought to market by her aunt and been "as well advertised, as Packwood's razor strops" (25). Alluding to the "strops" used to beat West Indian slaves, Packwood's famous advertisements sometimes featured black characters as promoters.[35]

When Clarence locates Virginia's father, Mr. Hartley is so overwhelmed with "gratitude for the kindness, which Clarence had shown to [his daughter], he protested that he should look upon her as a monster, if she did not love him" (407). As when Lady Delacour is called a "monster" of a mother, the term signifies a freakish departure from gender norms at the same time that the patriarchal basis of those norms is critiqued. Mr. Hartley's investment in a system of exchange and entitlement based on "gratitude" may spring from his sentimentalization of his own benevolence as a slaveowner, but the fact that he barely survived "a rebellion of the negroes on [his] plantation" indicates that his slaves hardly felt thankful toward him (476);[36] his name is likely ironic.

Lady Delacour, who bears the French version of the same name, arranges for Mr. Hartley to exchange his daughter to greatest colonial advantage despite the evidence of his abusiveness. Discovering that Virginia secretly loves Captain Sunderland, the man who rescued her father during the slave revolt, Lady Delacour brings the couple together. The union frees Clarence Hervey to marry Belinda and secures Mr. Vincent's permanent removal—Lady Delacour's overt goals. But, more ominously, it also ensures that Virginia will serve as "payment" of her "father's debt of gratitude" to Sunderland (476), as Lady Delacour cheerfully explains.

Lady Delacour first meets Captain Sunderland when he rescues Juba in a scene reminiscent of the one in which Harriet cuts her leg. Juba's head is "terribly cut," and his ankle sprained, in a battle with a baronet and his dog (437), and Sunderland brings "the disabled negro" to the Delacour home to be treated with a "quack" balsam (474) discovered by a slave named Quassi (75). Sunderland's interest in the "bleeding negro" may suggest his sympathy for slaves (438). But the name Quassi or Quashee (historically associated with the "stereotype of the lying, lazy, thieving male slave" [Bush 53]) signals slave subversion, which Sunderland had contested when he rescued Mr. Hartley.

Lady Delacour manipulates the coincidences to ensure that, like the cut lock that forces Pope's Belinda into the heterosexual economy, the "cut" black man will remain available for circulation. By ascertaining that Juba's savior is also Virginia's hero, and by bringing the two lovers together, she guarantees that Sunderland will inherit some of the black slaves he suppressed on behalf of Virginia's father. The marriage affirms that English male rights to reproduce on a virgin body and to possess a colonized land worked by slaves are parts of the same privilege. If Virginia can be read as the sundered land of a former colony, Sunderland, who has already proved his ability to contain rebellion in a remaining colony, enacts a myth of reclamation.

Lady Delacour completes this picture of national success by inducting Belinda into the colonial system. Moments before announcing Clarence's "right to Belinda's hand" (478), she suggests that their marriage be delayed so that the hero can accompany Captain Sunderland on another "cruise" (477), most likely to Jamaica. There Clarence will presumably follow his predecessor in "making a fortune . . . to render the object of his affections independent" (475). This likelihood raises multiple ironies, one being that the status of woman as both "object" and consumer (with a fortune to dispose of) reproduces the terms of commodification that once compelled Lady Delacour to reject domesticity. Another is that by this point in the novel, the process of commodification has been linked to the slave trade, which the domestic woman endorses but which her own exchange resembles. As this resemblance grows, the national and racial differences Lady Delacour constructs in condemning Mr. Vincent and supporting Captain Sunderland's slave inheritance become meaningless.

Her vision of heterosexual stability in the final pages is equally precarious. In a theatrical scene that she directs, Lady Delacour petitions the remaining characters to

> let me place you all in proper attitudes for stage effect. . . . Captain Sunderland—kneeling with Virginia, if you please, sir, at her father's feet. You in the act of giving them your blessing, Mr. Hartley. . . . Clarence, you have a right to Belinda's hand, and may kiss it too. Nay, miss Portman, it is the rule of the stage. . . . My Lord Delacour . . . should be embracing me, to show that we are reconciled. . . . Helena, my love, do not let go your father's hand. There! quite pretty and natural! (478)

Arranging Belinda, Virginia, and her daughter Helena to greatest patriarchal effect, Lady Delacour epitomizes good motherhood. She prepares the girls to reproduce according to an idea of racial purity she has helped define in support of a "national economy" that devalues them (39). And yet the final line of the passage highlights the artificiality of a moment that must be staged to seem "natural." Concerned only with appearances, Lady Delacour mockingly proclaims, "What signifies being happy, unless we appear so?" (478). Earlier Lady Delacour's breast was cured when her heterosexuality and maternity were interiorized, but now heterosexuality becomes a surface image, and the internal stability of the final pose she directs is challenged. If Belinda is forced to let Clarence kiss her by "the rule of the stage," what are her "real" desires, and how legitimate are the colonialist maneuvers based on her compliance? Judith Butler suggests that when the "performative" basis of sexual difference and desire is revealed, the notion of "a true gender identity" is exposed as a "regulatory fiction" (*Gender Trouble* 141). When Lady Delacour claims to "finish the novel" (477), character and author merge in a play on performance implying that neither of them trusts the "pretty" picture.

The picture, of course, suggests that motherhood is the basis for stability *"Abroad and at Home"* (479). Lady Delacour's maternal reformation inspires her colonial authority, and both license her role in creating a new generation of English mothers. But if that role also requires a commodification of the female body that directly contradicts the interior virtue on which maternity is supposedly founded, then the image is actually chaotic—and the restored breast just another version of disease. Showing that motherhood promotes and depends upon the very commercial objectification it appears to oppose, *Belinda* ends with the same kind of confusion it initially sought to resolve. Even as motherhood is deployed for imperial interests, the value of those interests is undercut and the novel can end only with Lady Delacour's intractable riddle: "Our *tale* contains a *moral,* and, no doubt, / You all have wit enough to find it out" (478).

Chapter 5

Mother, Daughter, and Mulatto

Women's Exchange in Adeline Mowbray

THOUGH OF all the novels studied in this book Amelia Alderson Opie's *Adeline Mowbray, or The Mother and Daughter* has received the least critical attention, it is one of the most thematically inclusive maternal narratives of the period. Opie designed the novel as a fictionalized and cautionary account of the life of Mary Wollstonecraft, whom she knew and admired, but, like many women writers of the period, she felt obliged to denounce.[1] Ultimately, however, *Adeline Mowbray* moves beyond loose biography to examine the impossibility of mother-daughter love in a commercial and colonial world. It is attentive to the problem of language and desire, to the hazard of women's exchange among men, and to the imperial economy that frames their circulation. Particularly interested in the family romance of racial differentiation, *Adeline Mowbray* offers an ideal opportunity to return to psychoanalytic theory and to consider it in direct relation to the politics of maternity.

The novel breaks into two related narratives, the first of which concerns the heroine's early upbringing and heterosexual induction.

Unlike the common heroine, Adeline has the distinction of being raised in the same household as her parent. The problem of maternal absence persists, however, since Mrs. Mowbray neglects her daughter to pursue her own intellectual ambition. If *Evelina* links maternal absence with the necessity for language and *The Italian* links it with the construction of desire, *Adeline Mowbray* ambitiously does both. Anticipating the psychoanalytic case study in its emotional scrutiny, the novel suggests that Adeline's hunger for her mother shapes her sexual as well as her linguistic development.

As in *Belinda*, the second narrative begins with the entrance of a racially differentiated colonial character, who establishes the narrative terms for the novel's resolution. Savanna, an escaped mulatto slave, appoints herself as Adeline's servant and, in the process, becomes her surrogate mother. To the extent that Adeline's sense of deprivation can be diminished, Savanna provides relief. Bound to Adeline with a material reliability Mrs. Mowbray never provides, Savanna offers support precisely because her racial difference makes her economically dependent and her slave history equips her for servitude. Savanna also helps return Adeline to the privileged social position she lost when divided from her mother. As the ultimate representative of the dark underclass, the servant provides a point of contrast against which Adeline's superior status can be distinguished.

In introducing a mulatto servant to solve the heroine's maternal deprivation and identity confusion, *Adeline Mowbray* offers an opportunity to envision what Hortense Spillers describes as "the not quite thinkable . . . meeting ground between race matters and psychoanalytic theories" ("'All the Things'" 135). Psychoanalysis has long served feminist interrogations of female subjectivity, but as Jean Walton notes, until recently, few feminists questioned "the historically determined whiteness of the [psychoanalytic] models they employ[ed]" (246)—models that, among other things, take the bourgeois European family as their norm.[2] It is one of the many ironic values of psychoanalysis that its theory about repression has enabled readers to uncover the institution's own unacknowledged investment in racial and colonial difference. Viewed from a historical perspective, psychoanalysis is inextricably tied to the imperial context from which it emerged and can be analyzed accordingly.[3]

But psychoanalysis also provides adaptable tools for cultural analysis. Its interest in the social formation of subjectivity, particularly as constituted by the symbolic order of language, can be adjusted to interpret the very problems the institution conventionally resists discussing. As Spillers explains, "the subject's profound engagement with and involvement in symbolicity is everywhere social" ("'All the Things'"142), meaning that language and identity are as tied to problems of nation, class, and race as to gender and sexuality. "What requires radical rethinking," Judith Butler writes, "is what social relations compose this domain of the symbolic" ("Passing" 279), or, as Helene Moglen puts it, "how the profound complexity of psychic life is historically formed and historically enacted" (216).

If postcolonial theory can probe the racial history of psychoanalysis and psychoanalysis can help explain the construction of racial subjectivity, *Adeline Mowbray* is revealing on both counts. The novel indicates that the family romance—on which psychoanalysis depends and which includes mother-daughter separation as a staple feature—is based in part in a colonial economy. At the same time, the role the mulatto plays in resolving both mother-daughter loss and the heroine's identity confusion suggests that race and colonialism are inextricably tied to the production of desire and subjectivity. As the pivotal figure of the family triangle, the dark woman in *Adeline Mowbray* points to the imperial roots and complexity of the preoedipal and oedipal narratives.

The glorification of maternity never obviated the need for motherly servants. Even when they chose to nurse their own infants and prided themselves on their maternal solicitude, women of means commanded assistance in caring for their children. The rise of maternal ideals was also inevitably accompanied by evidence of inadequate mothers like Lady Delacour and Mrs. Mowbray, and by the requirement for a class of surrogates to labor in the middle- and upper-class mother's absence.[4] The predictable unavailability of good mothers helped confirm the need for nannies. Colonial women were among the likely candidates for such positions. In the West Indies, slave women customarily performed as nursemaids and nannies (though most female slaves did field work). By fashioning Savanna as a surrogate mother, *Adeline Mowbray* suggests the psychological value of adapting a West Indian practice to English domestic life. As Carol Howard puts it, Opie imagines "a *maternal* system of domestic fealty to take place on English, rather than colonial, shores" (364).[5]

Opie herself was an abolitionist Quaker who described her "ever-increasing zeal in the cause of emancipation" as the product of "the kindly emotions which I was encouraged to feel for . . . [the African] race" beginning in childhood (Brightwell 13). In many ways

Adeline Mowbray derides slavery, but because it also sentimentalizes a maternal servitude grounded in racial difference, the political outcome is ambiguous. Like *Belinda*, whose progressive implications belie Edgeworth's colonial sympathies, *Adeline Mowbray* confounds expectations based on the author's personal history.

The Mother and Daughter

Adeline Mowbray's psychological acuity stems in part from its adjustment of the conventional maternal narrative. Because the mother is neglectful but not physically absent during the daughter's childhood, the novel is free to scrutinize Adeline's experience of rejection. Drawing on the increasingly standardized ideal of the good mother, the book anticipates psychoanalysis in its insistence on the emotional damage wrought by a bad one. As the evidence of Mrs. Mowbray's "self-love" (257) and Adeline's suffering accumulates, the advantage of selfless "maternal affection" (104) appears indubitable.

At the same time, however, *Adeline Mowbray* also indicates that Mrs. Mowbray's detachment is symptomatic of larger social ills. For all her wariness of Wollstonecraft, Opie evokes her in suggesting that mother-daughter separation is the inevitable by-product of woman's objectification. Especially interested in the overlaps between the traffic in women and that in colonial goods, Opie shows that female kinship is prohibited by women's inability to exchange commodities—including language and love—among themselves. Instead, mothers and daughters compete as sexual rivals for the dubious privilege of being transacted among men.

From the opening of the novel, Mrs. Mowbray's maternal inadequacy is politically vexed. A self-proclaimed genius who neglects her child to pore over "abstruse systems of morals and metaphysics, or new theories in politics" (2), she exemplifies the dangers of Wollstonecraft's call for female education by demonstrating the incompatibility of intellectual pursuit and maternal duty.

But even as Mrs. Mowbray marks the failures of liberalism, she also signals the hazards of hierarchy. After her husband dies, she becomes head of the household, which she "govern[s] . . . with despotic authority" (3). Adeline—who is subject to her educational experiments and "tormented . . . like an animal in an exhausted receiver" (3)—is Mrs. Mowbray's prime victim. For instance, arguing the health benefits of ascetic practices, Mrs. Mowbray deprives Adeline of shoes and restricts the child's diet to plain vegetables and water, while "her own table was covered with viands fitted for the appetite of opulence" (4). Such exercises in humility teach Adeline to govern "her faculties so meekly, that she never wounded the self-love of any one, by arrogating to herself any superiority" (16).

Mrs. Mowbray's unavailability and authoritarianism have dire emotional consequences. Overwhelmed by feelings of inferiority and deprivation, Adeline craves "unremitting attention" (6) and loves her mother with "a tenderness of a most uncommon nature" (165) because her love is largely unrequited. Only once, when Adeline is gravely ill, does Mrs. Mowbray feel "herself a mother" (6) and nurse her child back to health. For Adeline, who accuses herself of being "so ungrateful sometimes as to think [my mother] does not love me sufficiently" (7), the illness becomes a mental landmark and source of guilt. "When, as she advanced in life, she was sometimes tempted to think her [mother] deficient in maternal fondness, the idea of Mrs. Mowbray bending with pale and speechless anxiety over her sleepless pillow used to recur to her remembrance, and in a moment the recent indifference was forgotten" (6–7).

Adeline's memory features her mother as present and silent, the exact reverse of Mrs. Mowbray's ordinary position. Intent on proving her literary sophistication, Mrs. Mowbray is obsessed with words, which she erects as barriers between herself and her daughter. Adeline is "almost banished [from] her presence," for instance, because Mrs. Mowbray, like Walter Shandy, is busy producing a "voluminous manuscript" for her child's improvement (which proves useless because Adeline, like Tristram, outgrows its completion) (257). Evelina's mother bridges the signifier and the signified, but there is no such utopian referentiality for Mrs. Mowbray, whose language is so vacuous that "her practice was ever in opposition to her opinions" (3).[6] Though she boasts of having read all of John Locke's *Essay Concerning Human Understanding*, Mrs. Mowbray ironically epitomizes the linguistic abuse he condemns: "the using of words, without clear and distinct ideas; or, which is worse, signs without anything signified" (437).

Oblivious to Mrs. Mowbray's linguistic insincerity, Adeline hopes that by emulating her mother's reading and discourse she can gain the attachment she misses. Thus, Adeline "was resolved to try to make herself more worthy of her [mother], by imitating her in those pursuits and studies on which were founded Mrs. Mowbray's pretensions to superior talents" (13). Propelled by this longing, Adeline ironically develops a belief in the material referentiality of language that directly contrasts with Mrs. Mowbray's imprecision. Mrs. Mowbray never abides by her philosophies, but Adeline expects word and referent to meet in compatible theory and practice.[7] "While Mrs. Mowbray expended her eccentric philosophy in words . . . Adeline carefully treasured up hers in her heart" (13).[8]

However misguided, Adeline's literalism makes considerable psychoanalytic sense. Freud describes the preoedipal period as a time of symbiotic attachment between mother and child. Lacan stresses the preoedipal child's prelinguistic status, meaning not simply that the child cannot talk but also that there is no need for language because he experiences no physical separateness from his mother (and other objects). Language only becomes necessary when the unity with externalities like the mother's breast, gaze, and voice is lost. As Kristeva describes: "Through the mouth that I fill with words instead of my mother whom I miss from now on more than ever, I elaborate that want, and the aggressivity that accompanies it, by *saying*" (*Powers* 41).

In shifting from duality to the division that inaugurates language, the Lacanian subject moves into the symbolic order—a world of communication by signs that are radically disconnected from the "real" objects to which they refer. Language is predicated on the gap between subject and (maternal) object (the breaking of a preoedipal sense of unity) that parallels the gap between referent and word. Language, by definition, is nonrepresentational and thus the mark of absence. "The signified is always provisional . . . it is never 'resolved back into a pure identification of the real.' . . . [L]anguage isolates the subject from the real, confining it forever to the realm of signification" (Silverman, *Subject* 165–66).[9]

Adeline's mother epitomizes the vacuum of language, both because she marks the relation between words and maternal absence and because her own words have no material consequences. Like the Lacanian subject, Adeline is doomed to mourn this loss. But she is distinguished by her refusal to accept it. Endlessly searching for a way to return to her mother, Adeline rejects the linguistic code predicated on absence and continues to imagine that word and referent can meet.[10]

The fantasy places her beyond the reach of social customs. When the Lacanian subject enters the symbolic order he must accept his fixed position in a cultural system. Adeline resists this system, ultimately becoming "a stranger to the rules of general society" (177). The resistance is at the root of her affair with Mr. Glenmurray, the author who resembles William Godwin and whose work excites her "enthusiasm for a new order of things" (14). Tellingly, Adeline first reads Glenmurray because Mrs. Mowbray praises him, and then she becomes "completely his convert on her own conviction" (13).

Adeline is especially drawn to the text in which Glenmurray, like Godwin in *Political Justice,* attacks marriage, drawing "so delightful a picture of the superior purity, as well as happiness, of an union cemented by no ties but those of love and honour" (14). After she meets and falls in love with Glenmurray, Adeline refuses to marry him, following his text in insisting on the meaninglessness of social custom and the literalness of a simple declaration of love. Even when Glenmurray himself urges her to reconsider, Adeline characteristically objects on the grounds that his theory and practice must meet. [11]

Though Mrs. Mowbray is appalled by the impropriety of her daughter's affair, her disapproval is also the consequence of sexual competition, a subject that becomes increasingly important in the novel. Like the mother described in the *Rights of Woman,* who is "lost in the coquette, and, instead of making friends of her daughters, view[s] them with eyes askance, for they are rivals" (*VRW* 49), Mrs. Mowbray tells Adeline, "I assure you, there are people who think the mother handsomer than the daughter!" (43). Her competition points to the larger obstacles to mother-daughter affection and is a microcosm of the contest for bodily superiority that pits all women against each other. Many of the minor female characters—from Mrs. Norberry and her daughters (17–18, 94) to the Maynard sisters (74–76, 233) to Adeline's servant Mary (205)—are either threatened by the heroine's good looks or ready to fault her for their own sense of physical inadequacy. [12]

None of them recognizes the larger problem of women's position as male property. Only the narrator can explain that

> the true . . . [male] lover is always a monopolizer, always desirous of calling the woman of his affections his own . . . because it gives him a right to appropriate the fair treasure to himself,—because it sanctions and perpetuates the dearest of all monopolies, and erects a sacred barrier to guard his rights,—around which, all that is respectable in society, all that is most powerful and effectual in its organization, is proud and eager to rally. (38–39)

What Lacan would call the symbolic order ("all that is respectable in society, all that is most powerful and effectual in its organization") is in *Adeline Mowbray,* as in *The Wrongs of Woman* and *Belinda* before it, partly based in men's right to "erect" "barrier[s]" of ownership on the female body. The dynamic is sustained by women's competition with each other and blindness to their own objectification.

Mrs. Mowbray's marriage to Sir Patrick O'Carrol, who lusts after Adeline, encapsulates the problem. When Sir Patrick tries to rape Adeline, tells Mrs. Mowbray about his affection for her daughter, and then dies in a drunken stupor on a journey to claim her, Mrs. Mowbray holds Adeline entirely to blame: "I never, never will forgive her" for "being the object of that cruel preference" (102). Shortly after, she banishes Adeline with an extraordinary curse:

> mark my words: I solemnly swear . . . that until you shall have experienced the anguish of having lost the man whom you adore, till *you* shall have been as wretched in love, and as disgraced in the eye of the world, as I have been, I never will see you more, or pardon your many sins against me—No—not even were you on your death-bed. Yet, no; I am wrong there—Yes; on your death-bed . . . Yes, there; there I should—I should forgive you. (109–10)[13]

For the first time in the novel Mrs. Mowbray actually means what she says, tellingly when calling for Adeline's disappearance. Though Adeline still manages to hold Mrs. Mowbray's "head to her bosom, and [to kiss] her pale lips with almost frantic emotion" (111) before she leaves, it is impossible to sustain such love.

Irigaray suggests that the exchange of women among men renders the mother-daughter bond inexpressible. Because woman becomes a symbol of man's desire for origin, she cannot "represent 'her' relation to 'her' origin. . . . She is left with a *void,* a *lack* of all representation, re-presentation, and even strictly speaking of all mimesis of her desire for origin" (*Speculum* 42–43; see also 60, 68, 71, 78, 83, 84, 124). In *Adeline Mowbray* the mother can represent her alienation from her daughter in her curse, but when she later tries to locate Adeline through newspaper advertisements she fails, and all of Adeline's letters to her miscarry.

What gradually becomes clear is that women's inability to engage in what Locke calls "the commerce of thoughts" (*Essay* 315) is based especially in the relation between their objectification and the colonial market. Men's rights to erect "barrier[s]" of ownership on the female body are paralleled by their "monopolies" over slaves and colonial land (39). Indeed, "all that is most powerful and effectual in [social] organization" (39) stems from men's overlapping sexual and imperial control, meaning that a wide variety of goods, including "women, signs, commodities, and currency always pass from one man to another" and cannot pass among women themselves (Irigaray, *This Sex* 192).

Thus, Sir Patrick O'Carrol marries the rich Mrs. Mowbray not only to have greater sexual access to Adeline but also to support his "encumbered [Irish] estate" (27). Similarly, when Glenmurray grows fatally ill, he wants to "bequeath" (158) Adeline to his cousin Charles Berrendale, along with the promise that she will "manage his [colonial] affairs" (151). Berrendale, whom Adeline marries after Glenmurray's death, lives off an annuity from his former wife's Jamaican inheritance. When Adeline does not prove profitable enough, he returns to the West Indies and bigamously marries one of his first wife's rich relations.

Though Glenmurray hopes Adeline will shed the stigma of their own affair by marrying Berrendale, she remains tainted by her sordid past, which the novel very explicitly depicts as a problem of color and materiality. Identified by her illicit sexuality, Adeline bears the burden of the body (the ironic correlate to her literalism) and is categorized as a dark outsider. As Felicity Nussbaum puts it, "[in] the language of the novel, refusing to marry is a 'savage' decision" (42). Thus Dr. Norberry tells the heroine "[your mother] has whitewashed herself and blackened you" (113), just pages after Mrs. Mowbray calls Adeline a "shame to [my] race" (108). The mother-daughter dynamic is again paradigmatic, as a variety of rivalrous female characters delight in disproving Adeline's claims to "fair perfection" (75). That the heroine is described as having an "exquisitely fair" (74) complexion cements their jealousy, since fairness signifies both the external beauty and the internal goodness that determine female worth in the sexual market: after all, every man wants to "appropriate" a "fair treasure to himself" (39).

Losing her place in the world, Adeline is increasingly associated with the underclass. In Adeline's childhood, the servants fed her the delicacies her mother withheld and pledged eternal friendship. But now Mary, her serving maid, calls her a "black mawkin" (179) and thinks "herself authorised to insult [Adeline], and to raise herself to her level" (120). When Mary later infects Adeline with smallpox by throwing her arms around her and "parr[ying] all Adeline's endeavours to break from her" (208), their inextricability is literalized and Adeline's skin becomes permanently marked. It is partly to "recover my rank in society" (175) that Adeline marries Berrendale, but he makes the situation worse by remarrying in Jamaica.

The Mulatto

Savanna's entrance midway through the novel is pivotal in Adeline's restitution. Often referred to as "the mulatto," Savanna satisfies the heroine's emotional and physical needs while enabling Adeline to acquire exactly the colonial and commercial power by which she is otherwise victimized. Though the novel condemns slavery, it also suggests the value of importing West Indian women to England to perform the material and psychological work biological maternity cannot guarantee.

At the same time, Savanna becomes Adeline's alter ego, in ways that evoke and revise the mirroring and maternal roles servants like Amy (in *Roxana*) and Jemima (in *The Wrongs of Woman*) play.[14] Both roles align Savanna with materiality; Savanna performs the physical work that Adeline's mother neglected and bears the burden of the colored body, relieving Adeline of this stigma.[15] As servant and colonial other, the mulatto stands for the underclass and racially differentiated women with whom Adeline has been unfavorably compared, marking a point of contrast against which the heroine can be distinguished and re-categorized as a member of the "fair sex."[16]

Savanna's role as surrogate mother points to the historical part race and servitude play in the bourgeois family romance. Though Freud's texts never directly address the centrality of the maternal servant, she insistently emerges to trouble his oedipal model. Thus, Jane Gallop notes that "the family never was, in any of Freud's texts, completely closed off from questions of economic class. And the most insistent locus of intrusion into the family circle . . . is the maid / governess / nurse" (144).[17]

Colonial slavery guaranteed that at least some of these "intruders" would be women of color. This is particularly true of the American South, where the mammy became an iconic figure. Though there was no commensurate role for black women in England, Savanna's mulatto heritage evokes the English plantation system that delegated house (as opposed to field) work to lighter-skinned female slaves, for whom the role of nurse was a coveted position. Opie's own mother had a black nurse, and families from America and the colonies routinely brought their black nurses with them on trips to England.[18] Savanna's maternity prefigures the "racialized history of child care" that grew out of colonial slavery, reminding us, as Walton explains in another context, that "the tasks of the 'mother' so typically described in psychoanalytic accounts of early development (nursing, cleaning, eroticizing certain zones of the body, assisting in the acquisition of language, mediating in the mirror stage) were [likely to be] . . . undertaken by black women in the white slave-owning or servant-employing household" (225–26).

Savanna's role in absorbing the burden of abjection that formerly hampered the heroine can be linked to her maternal function. In her frequently cited essay on the subject, Kristeva links abjection to the child's original loss of the mother: "The abject confronts us . . . with our earliest attempts to release the hold of the *maternal* entity. . . . It is a violent, clumsy breaking away, with the constant risk of falling back under the sway of a power as securing as it is stifling" (*Powers* 13; also see 5, 10). The loss of the mother, experienced as the division that inducts individual identity, propels the creation of an excluded Other. Though subjectivity is defined in opposition to the Other, there is always danger of collapse since the very need for expulsion evokes the earlier moment of cohesion. "I expel *myself*, I spit *myself* out, I abject *myself* within the same motion through which 'I' claim to establish *myself*" (Kristeva, *Powers* 3; also see 10).

A number of critics have invoked Kristeva's theory of abjection to describe the mechanism of racial differentiation and degradation.[19] Frantz Fanon long ago suggested that "the real Other for the white man is and will continue to be the black man" (161 n. 25). In *Adeline Mowbray*, the heroine finds maternal satisfaction in the black *woman*, and then undergoes the process of division by which her own identity is constituted. Savanna bears the burden of all Adeline must expel, including the hazards of the sexual female body.[20] As befits abjection, which is associated with the move from the preoedipal to the oedipal period and thus "coextensive with social and symbolic order" (Kristeva, *Powers* 68), the division enables Adeline to find her linguistic place in the world. But abjection is also a tentative "border" that "above all" signals "ambiguity" (Kristeva, *Powers* 9). "A blood vessel who could be described as being neither black nor white, yet also as both white and black" (Brody 16), the mulatto figure stands in between, suggesting the simultaneity of similarity and difference.[21]

Savanna first appears when Adeline is still living with Glenmurray, who is dying. Glenmurray begs Adeline to buy him a pineapple, an extravagant West Indian import the couple can ill afford. Just as she is about to purchase the fruit, Adeline sees the "mulatto woman" crying in the street as her husband is dragged to debtors prison; their child, "the tawny boy," cries and clings to her apron. The creditor refers to Savanna as an "'ugly black toad!' Adeline till then had not recollected that she was a mulatto; and this speech, reflecting so brutally on her colour,—a circumstance which made her an object of greater interest to Adeline,—urged her to step forward to their joint relief" (141).[22] Predictably attentive to language, Adeline is so struck by the reference to color that she overlooks Glenmurray's desire for a pineapple and, heeding her own "irresistible impulse" (141), gives Savanna their last guineas. When he later learns of the exchange, Glenmurray condemns Adeline for depriving him "of the only pleasure he may live to enjoy!" (143).

Thus, Savanna's racial difference displaces the demands of heterosexuality and offers Adeline the power of colonial consumption for the first time in the novel. Formerly viewed as an object of currency among men, the heroine now bears her own currency, dispensing it for the woman whose blackness has made *her* "an object of . . . interest." The next day, Savanna brings her son to Adeline's home and explains that her heart will break "if you do not take my service." Genuflecting with the tawny boy, Savanna makes the child "vow wid me to be faithful and grateful to this our mistress, till our last day; and never to forsake her in sickness or in sorrow! I swear dis to my great God" (147–48). The oath is the exact reverse of Mrs. Mowbray's vow never to see Adeline again.

The narrative sentimentalizes Savanna's bond, calling it "the service of the heart" (157) and presenting it as her voluntary marriage and fealty, but this hardly disguises the commercial implications. Interpreting the behavior as volitional enslavement, Adeline later refers to Savanna as "my property" and tells her that "you have given me a right to claim your life as mine" (195). Carol Howard's explanation is apt: "the paltry sum intended for Glenmurray's pineapple ultimately buys Savanna's unwavering devotion and annuls her freedom" (Howard 366). The purchase will bear fruit for generations. When Adeline's daughter is born, "the mulatto . . . [sends] for the tawny boy to come and see his new mistress, and vow to her, as he had done to her mother, eternal fealty and allegiance" (185).

In this way charity, the exemplary work of the "fair" sex, becomes a colonial and commercial investment, a form of giving that returns as profit.[23] When Adeline awakens to Savanna's gaze "the idea of the mulatto, and of the service which she had rendered her, recurred to her mind, and diffused a sensation of pleasure through her frame. 'There is a being whom I have served,' said Adeline to herself" (157). The confusing referents (who is "she" and "her"?) reflect the reversal, for Savanna will repay Adeline's service by serving her "pleasure," an exchange made possible by "the idea of the mulatto."

Notably one of the profits Adeline receives is food, of which her mother deprived her in childhood. When Adeline gives money to "the little tawny boy" he purchases cakes and apples to give to her (160–61). Similarly, when Berrendale encourages Adeline (then pregnant) to curb her appetite so he can satisfy his own, Savanna buys her expensive sweetmeats "wid mine nown money," despite her "slender wages" (184). From Mrs. Mowbray's "indulgencies of the palate" (4) to Glenmurray's desire for pineapple to Berrendale's interest in "the delicious things for the table which Jamaica afforded" (194), good food is defined as a commercial (and often West Indian) luxury—one Adeline lacks until Savanna arrives.[24]

Sickness has equal psychological resonance and social significance. Except for the one time her mother nursed her in her youth, Adeline typically tends to the ill. After she cares for her grandmother, she nurses the dying Glenmurray (reversing what actually happened with Wollstonecraft, who predeceased Godwin). The gouty Berrendale marries Adeline in part to enjoy her "bending over his restless couch" (176). Like access to good food, the right to be nursed is determined by the hierarchical relegation of luxuries—a privilege Adeline finally experiences when Savanna nurses her during her depression and her later bout with smallpox.

In feeding and nursing Adeline, Savanna offers her the physical comforts Mrs. Mowbray withheld, filling the gap of maternal loss; servitude proves a more reliable source of nurture than kinship. The difference between Mrs. Mowbray's "vow" (110) never to see her daughter until the latter is dying and Savanna's "vow . . . to be faithful and grateful to" Adeline until her own death (147–48) is, above all, the difference between absence and presence. Reified by her own racial status as property, Savanna's bodily availability offers the heroine the kind of material connection for which she has longed. Mrs. Mowbray only once bends "with pale and speechless anxiety over her [daughter's] pillow" (6), but Savanna maintains a constant watch with her "formidable eyes" (272). It is only by "meet[ing] every day the eyes of [this] one being fixed with never-varying affection on hers" that Adeline can overcome the sense that she is "alone in the universe" (196).

That Opie specifically imagined Savanna as a replacement for maternal loss is suggested by the autobiographical significance of the character's name. Opie's mother, Amelia Briggs, who died when Opie was fifteen, lost her own parents when she was a toddler living in Bengal; she was subsequently sent to England, accompanied by a "black" nurse named "Savannah."[25] Opie opens a poetic memorial to her mother by describing Savannah as a slave:

> An orphan'd babe, from India's plain
> She came, a faithful slave her guide!
> Then, after years of patient pain,
> That tender wife and mother *died.*
>   (Brightwell 9)

Standing apart from the mirrorlike reflections of maternal death (the author's mother was an orphan and now she is dead), the "faithful slave" emerges as the "guide" when the mother, who once had such "power to . . . guide" is gone (Brightwell 10). Ironically, the family materials Opie left for her memoirs make clear that in actuality, Savannah decided she would never "be reconciled to England" and insisted on returning to Bengal (Brightwell 8). That Opie revised this history twice—by presenting Savannah first as a "*faithful* slave" in the poem and then as a self-created slave in the novel—indicates just how important it was for her to imagine the black woman as a willing and loyal maternal surrogate.

In *Adeline Mowbray,* Savanna also figures as a substitute for the heroine herself, who becomes increasingly ill and physically absent, as if fated to be as unavailable to her dependents as her own mother was to her. When she tells Savanna she will "claim your life as mine" (195), Adeline marks the extent to which her rights of ownership establish the narrative grounds for an exchange—or blending—of their characters. As Adeline becomes invisible, Savanna assumes the burden of her previous experiences. Adeline suffers from her mother's absence and Glenmurray's death, but Savanna worries about losing Adeline. When the heroine briefly disappears after being contaminated with smallpox, the servant reacts to her "absence" with "strong hysterics" (214). And when it is subsequently clear that Adeline is dying, Savanna pleads with her to live (270), much as Adeline urged Glenmurray before (153).

It is consistent with the exchange that Savanna endorses linguistic literalism as Adeline ironically replicates Mrs. Mowbray's indifference to material referentiality. Having once offered a principled denunciation of marriage, Adeline now overlooks her misery with Berrendale and suggests that "marriage . . . has a tendency to call forth

and exercise the affections, . . . control the passions," and discour-
age "unbridled licentiousness" (243). Commencing "a declaration of
war" (184) against Berrendale, Savanna insists that words reflect reality. While Adeline silently accepts Berrendale's complaints about her
housekeeping, Savanna tells him: "Home was very comfortable till you
come" (193). Later she confronts Berrendale in Jamaica, denouncing
his bigamy with a "torrent of reproaches that trembled on her lip" (202).

But even as Savanna criticizes Berrendale, her erotic interest
in men and shady sexual past shift the stigma of sexual abjection away
from the heroine. If, earlier, Adeline's sexual freedoms "blackened"
her (113), the mulatto now bears the burden of promiscuity.[26] She has
been married at least twice, perhaps bigamously to her second husband,
William, who is possibly white. (He and Savanna produced "the tawny
boy," and, unlike Savanna and the child, who are generally labeled by
their colors, William is always referred to by his Christian name.)

The intimation reminds us that "the mulatto" may be the
product of a master's miscegenetic rape, but the emphasis is less on
such abuse than on Savanna's suspect behavior. Though she later turns
against Berrendale, for instance, Savanna is so intimate with him during
the early months of Adeline's marriage that the heroine worries about
their "familiarity" (174) (much as Mrs. Mowbray had worried about
Adeline and Sir Patrick). When Colonel Mordaunt pursues Adeline
after Berrendale deserts her, Savanna tells him that he is "a charming
man, and infinitely handsomer than Berrendale, though she must own
he was very good to look at" (216).

It is in keeping with her heterosexual interests that, when she
learns her husband is languishing in Jamaica, Savanna asks Adeline for
a release from her vow so she can go to nurse him. The dependent
Adeline puts conditions on the departure: "You shall go to Jamaica,
Savanna. . . . You shall see and try to recover William . . . and then
you shall return to me" (195). As in *Belinda*, Jamaica exists offstage as
the place that reorganizes English life. But whereas the colony supports
domestic marriage in Edgeworth's novel, in *Adeline Mowbray* it marks
the severing of heterosexuality. When Savanna arrives in Jamaica, her
husband is dead, and Berrendale eventually dies from guilt over his
bigamy (230). With Savanna's and her own husband gone, Adeline
reclaims her servant and is freed from her marriage.

Adeline's release from heterosexuality and recovery of Savanna
are followed by her improved relation to language. Savanna returns with
the story of Berrendale's infidelity, and Adeline, accompanied by the

tawny boy, approaches a lawyer to prove her marriage. (This does not affect the dismissal of heterosexuality, since Berrendale dies; nevertheless, Adeline needs to prove she was not his mistress.) The lawyer—a disreputable character, who has taken Adeline's former servant Mary as his mistress—doubts Adeline's marriage to Berrendale. But the tawny boy insists, "I went to the church with them, and my mother cooked the wedding-dinner. . . . Did you never hear the story of the pineapple? . . . I know what I say" (210).

If, in *Evelina*, the mother's signature on her daughter and letter yoke word and thing, establishing the validity of her marriage, the tawny boy's linguistic certainty has a similar effect for different reasons. As a colonial subject of precarious status, the tawny boy substantiates Adeline's superiority, certifying that she *was* married to Berrendale and is not a mistress like Mary or sexually suspicious like Savanna. Words, goods, and people all circulate to Adeline's advantage, for the "*story* about the pineapple," the wedding dinner, and Savanna's servitude jointly substantiate the heroine's authority.

Savanna continues the mediation that makes linguistic commerce possible when she, and not Adeline, receives the "evidence" and "attested certificate" of Adeline's marriage to Berrendale (217). Soon after, she orchestrates Adeline's reconciliation with her mother. By the novel's conclusion, the term "mulatto" becomes a code for this kind of intermediacy, and it is precisely because Savanna stands between them that mother and daughter reunite.

The Exchange Between Women

After Berrendale dies, the terms of Mrs. Mowbray's vow are completed to the letter, and the text is narratively positioned to resolve the mother and daughter's estrangement. Having been abandoned by her husband (like her mother before her), Adeline is "forsaken, despised and disgraced!" (203). Weakened from smallpox and her general depression, she is approaching the "death-bed" where Mrs. Mowbray promised to see her again (109–10). In fact, Mrs. Mowbray "had long forgiven her [daughter] . . . pined after her . . . [and] sought, though in vain, to procure intelligence of her" (247). She finally locates the languishing Adeline in a cottage on her own estate.

It is there that Savanna oversees the mother-daughter reunion. "Grasping Mrs. Mowbray's arm with frightful earnestness," she hands her a letter Adeline has just written, exclaiming "read that—'tis for you!" (268), upon which Mrs. Mowbray "clasp[s] [Adeline's] unconscious form" (268).[27] As when the tawny boy tells "the story of the pineapple," Savanna validates Adeline's privileged identity (in this case, her high birth). Finally arranging for Mrs. Mowbray to receive one of her daughter's letters, she both establishes the foundation for mother and daughter to communicate (much as Jemima does when she teaches Maria's daughter to say "Mamma") and closes the gap between language and body, prompting Mrs. Mowbray's long-sought embrace.

Adeline's letter includes her wish to "bequeath" both Editha (her daughter) and Savanna to her mother's "care and protection" (264, 266). Reminiscent of the way the dying Glenmurray had "bequeathed" (222, 229) Adeline herself to Berrendale, the transactions evoke the enduring problem of human exchange. Ultimately, however, Editha profits from the circulation while Savanna alone is commodified.

This difference partly stems from Adeline's different relation-ship with Editha, whom she tellingly names for her own missing mother. Though she suckles the child in infancy, she quickly delegates her to Savanna, and like her mother before her substitutes language for presence (244–45). Wollstonecraft's Maria writes a memoir because she is forcibly divided from her daughter, but Adeline writes because she is convinced Editha will benefit from her absence. Whereas Maria decides to "live for my child" (203), Adeline claims that "were it possible for me to choose between life and death, for my child's sake, the choice would be the latter" (244).[28]

If, as Irigaray suggests, mothers and daughters cannot forge a signifying "commerce among themselves" (*This Sex* 196) because they are rival commodities, the problem is partly based in their inability to develop the distinct subject positions upon which any transaction necessarily depends. "There is no possibility whatsoever, within the current logic of sociocultural operations, for a daughter to situate herself with respect to her mother: because, strictly speaking, they make neither one nor two, neither has a name, meaning, sex of her own, neither can be 'identified' with respect to the other" (*This Sex* 143). Margaret Whitford explains this as the problem of women's "forever competing for the unique *place* occupied by the mother" and of their not being able to "differentiate themselves from their mother" (117).

Indeed, Adeline's bequest of her daughter to her mother lacks distinction. Adeline worries that Mrs. Mowbray will be "disgust[ed]" with the child because she looks like Adeline herself (264). And though

Mrs. Mowbray responds favorably to her namesake, she egotistically says that the girl "shall be dear . . . as my own soul!" (269). Either way, the positions of mother and daughter collapse. It is symptomatic of the inadequacy of the commerce that Adeline "vainly [tries] to speak her wishes, as Savanna put[s] the sleeping girl in Mrs. Mowbray's arms" (269).

As with her transmission of the letter, Savanna here serves as the bodily conduit of exchange between Adeline and Mrs. Mowbray, a position reinforced when she herself is passed between them. Though unintelligible when transmitting her daughter, Adeline announces the gift of Savanna, telling her mother "to your care, I bequeath her" (270). Pledging to transcend the mother-daughter bond, Mrs. Mowbray responds: "I will love her as my child . . . and behave to her better" (270).

Again Irigaray is helpful. In considering how women might effect "the break" from being *"objects of exchange"* to having "a language, and a currency of exchange . . . of their own" (Whitford 119, 117), Irigaray extends Freud's suggestion that the daughter desires to impregnate her mother by imagining a mother and daughter generating their own female child: "Engendering a girl's body, bringing a third woman's body into play, would allow [the daughter] to identify both herself and her mother as sexuate women's bodies. As *two* women, defining each other as both like and unlike, thanks to a third 'body' that both by common consent wish to be 'female.' This would attenuate the lack of differentiation between the daughter and the mother or the maternal function" (*Speculum* 35–36).

I submit that in *Adeline Mowbray*, Savanna is the third female body that facilitates mother-daughter connection precisely because her racialized position licenses her own continued objectification. The very nature of exchange requires that someone (or something) be available for traffic, and Savanna best meets this need. At the same time, her mulatto status and designation "as both like and unlike" the English women among whom she circulates defines the overlaps and the differences on which community depends.

Whereas their exchange among men positioned Adeline and Mrs. Mowbray as bodily rivals, their competition is now defused by their mutual control over the servant. Identified by her earlier and literal status as property, the former slave forges their bond by her unique capacity to be bound between them. Adeline depicts the gift of Savanna as a form of charity and repayment, telling Mrs. Mowbray, "I owe that faithful creature more than I can express" (270). But as when she bought Savanna's servitude for the price of a pineapple, charity remains part of a feedback loop that enables English women to profit from colonialism while appearing morally superior to it.

This kind of exchange makes it possible for little Editha to become the novel's primary beneficiary. Not only is the child slated to receive Mrs. Mowbray's substantial property (which now includes Savanna), but the penitent Berrendale left a will acknowledging her his "only heir." The "very considerable fortune" Berrendale leaves Editha (and not his son from his first marriage) is composed entirely of his Jamaican profits (230).

Despite the bleakness of Adeline's death, the novel's conclud-ing vision of female kinship is one of the most optimistic of the period. The gift of Savanna leads to the creation of a community of women. Adeline's Quaker friend, Mrs. Pemberton, tells her: "I give thee my word, that I will never leave thy mother, and that Savanna shall be our joint care" (274). The image of Mrs. Mowbray, Mrs. Pemberton, Dr. Norberry (sobbing like "an old woman" [272]) and little Editha collected at Adeline's deathbed when Savanna is transferred from one woman to another suggests that the impediments to female bonding have finally been overcome. No other novel studied here is so hopeful about female kinship. Even *The Wrongs of Woman*, which also resists the conventional marriage finale, offers only an ambivalent and fragmented vision of such connection.

Many of the novels point to the difficulty of establishing and symbolizing the mother-daughter bond in an economy based in women's exchange. Presenting women's alienated commodification as an inevitability, they ask whether and how mothers and daughters can ever return to each other. Only *Adeline Mowbray* anticipates feminist theories like Irigaray's in imagining a commerce that might resolve women's alienation. But commerce, by definition, requires a currency. With remarkably little self-consciousness, the novel sacrifices Savanna. In *Belinda* maternity emerges as a colonial enterprise of dubious moral worth, but *Adeline Mowbray* idealizes the matrilineage forged around human property.

Perhaps there is some acknowledgment of the problems of this arrangement in the novel's final words. Suggesting that she might not be able to temper her jealousy were Adeline to survive, Mrs. Mowbray tells her dying daughter "never, never were you so dear to me as now!" (275).

Not enough has changed if Mrs. Mowbray loves her daughter most because she is about to expire. Despite her previously expressed desire to die in her mother's arms, Adeline silently turns to the only figure who offers unconditional bodily support. She brings "Mrs. Mowbray's hand to her lips," but she lays "her head on Savanna's bosom" to die (275).

Chapter 6

The Riddle of Emma

Maternity and the Unconscious

EMMA IS the fifth major novel in Austen's opus and the first in which the heroine's mother is dead. The detail is notable in its own right, but especially so given Austen's resistance to the popular narrative conventions of the period, among which (as we have seen) the motherless heroine was one of the most predictable. Austen opens the famously antiformulaic *Northanger Abbey* by announcing that Catherine Morland's mother "had three sons before Catherine was born; and instead of dying in bringing the later into the world, as any body might expect, she still lived on—lived on to have six children more—to see them growing up around her, and to enjoy excellent health herself" (1). The narrator's delight in defying her reader's expectation; for a dead mother is palpable.

Maybe because she is more confident of her own originality, Austen seems less fearful of formulaic implications when she writes *Emma*. In this chapter I argue that part of her artistic triumph is her modernization of the absent mother plot. If novels like *Evelina*,

The Italian, and *Adeline Mowbray* develop what are now recognizable details of the psychoanalytic family romance, *Emma* incorporates some of these along with what would become one of the most trenchant tenets of psychoanalysis: the idea that there is an unconscious that frames individual desire and behavior and that is constituted, in part, by the centrality of the mother and the inevitability of her loss.[1] Though (as with many of the details that follow) I am hardly the first reader to stress the importance of maternal absence in *Emma,* I am not interested in the exclusive value of such an interpretation but in the historical significance of its very availability.[2]

Unlike all the other novels discussed here, *Emma* devotes no overt attention to the mother's absence, which is nonchalantly dismissed as a possible problem in the second paragraph: Emma's "mother had died too long ago for her to have more than an indistinct remembrance of her caresses" (5). Otherwise, Emma shares none of the overt difficulties that plague the conventional heroine. Instead of being unfairly disinherited and homeless, she is "rich, with a comfortable home" (5). Emma even differs from other Austen heroines in her singular freedom from the threat of impoverishment.[3] In opening with the announcement that Emma is both unmoved by her mother's loss and financially secure, the novel creates the necessity for a new narrative focus. Since *Emma* has no obvious external troubles, her story has to be about something else.

I argue that it is about her internal troubles, which stem from the very motherlessness nobody acknowledges as a problem;[4] the lost mother is, as Frances Restuccia puts it, *Emma*'s "unspeakable or nearly unspeakable theme" (451). Drawing on the convention of maternal absence but refusing its trappings, *Emma* both logically extends and recasts the mother-daughter story. Like *Adeline Mowbray, Emma* suggests that the loss of maternal attention is damaging to a child's mental health. But unlike this or any other previous novel, *Emma* insists that such damage is registered not in clearly visible suffering but in the inarticulate subtlety of emotional distress. The moment of mother-child connection is so obscure in *Emma* that it escapes intelligibility but so fundamental that its loss can never be directly overcome, the preoedipal paradigm at the heart of psychoanalysis.

Another way to understand this difference is to consider how, in every other novel studied here, mother-daughter separation is inextricably tied to some form of dramatic social degradation. In most, the daughter loses status by losing her mother; Evelina appears to be illegitimate, Ellena seems a poor orphan, and Adeline becomes an outcast. In *The Wrongs of Woman* and *Belinda* it is the mother who suffers; Maria is incarcerated when her baby is kidnapped and Lady Delacour is stigmatized for sending her infant out to nurse. While in some of these texts (especially *Wrongs* and *Adeline Mowbray*) the psychological pain of mother-child separation is also pronounced, it never overshadows the heroine's compromised social status, and the solution depends on her ability to resolve the latter: in *Evelina* and *The Italian* the heroines gain paternal legitimation; in *The Wrongs of Woman* the heroine seeks access to private property; and in *Belinda* and *Adeline Mowbray* the heroines exert colonial control.

In many ways, *Emma* is also about the heroine's socioeconomic problems, although Emma's financial stability requires an unconventional focus. If other heroines worry about poverty, Emma worries about maintaining her privileges. In the changing world of Highbury, where middle-class moneymaking and ideals are becoming increasingly powerful, Emma's own genteel values and status are under attack. Much of the novel revolves around Emma's anxiety about commanding upper-class authority in a society that no longer automatically sanctions it—an anxiety with which critics generally assume the novel sympathizes.[5]

But whereas in earlier novels mother-daughter separation and social degradation are mutually dependent narrative problems, in *Emma* the heroine's social fears can be read as an expression of her distress about her mother's death. Though obviously important in the novel, Emma's concern about losing social status appears contingent on the original loss of her mother—an exacerbation of a prior condition. The novel intimates that Emma might be less provoked by social neglect if she had the comfort of a mother's undivided attention.[6]

Psychoanalysis is often accused of "isolating the family from society" (Tate 16) and thereby obscuring the social, political, and economic dynamics of human behavior and desire.[7] To the extent that *Emma* subsumes the socioeconomic narrative in the maternal one it might be said to anticipate this effect. It is in keeping with this mystification that unlike *Belinda*, *Adeline Mowbray*, or even Austen's own earlier *Mansfield Park*, *Emma* pays minimal attention to the colonial industry that fuels the economic changes with which Emma struggles.[8] From this view, what makes *Emma* modern is the success with which it conceals socioeconomic and political problems behind the illusion of "private" experience, a concealment that arguably characterizes the novel form Austen herself helped perfect. The valorization of privacy is not popular, and, like the novel in general, Austen has been vulnerable to charges of ideological complicity.[9]

What is lost in such criticism is an appreciation of the historical change Austen represents. If current readers can criticize *Emma*'s prioritization of the personal and domestic experience, this is only because the value of individual psychology has become so entrenched that we are now provoked to challenge it. Though it is important to admit the limits and hazards of this ideology, it is also important to investigate the context of its induction. In revising the standard features of the mother-daughter story and internalizing the heroine's suffering, *Emma* brings the family romance to psychological fruition. Modern motherhood rises from its dead mother plot.

Austen's Mothers and Narrative Perspective

There is a remarkable evolution in Austen's depiction of maternity. Defying the popularity and sentimentality of the missing mother trope, her earliest novels emphasize the mother's existence. But with each successive work, the female parent grows more absent. It is as if Austen is compelled to confront the convention she resists—as if with each completed novel she is further emboldened.

Austen's first unpublished novel, *Lady Susan* (1795), resembles *Adeline Mowbray* in attending to the sexual rivalry between mother and daughter. But unlike Adeline, who longs to reunite with her parent, Frederica is so oppressed by the brutal Lady Susan that she must struggle to escape her. It is not the mother's absence but her presence that frames the daughter's distress.

Northanger Abbey (1803, pub. 1818), as noted, commences with the announcement that Catherine Morland's mother is alive. In this novel about the need for new narrative plots, the more predictably positioned Eleanor Tilney—whose mother died in mysterious ways—is only a secondary character. Schooled in popular novels, Catherine is obsessed with Mrs. Tilney's death, but her interest proves misguided. It is not so much that Catherine is wrong to imagine that General Tilney has injured his wife, as that her preoccupation with the dead mother is too limited. Thus, her own story of misunderstanding and desire takes precedence over Eleanor's struggle with maternal absence.

In the three novels that follow *Northanger Abbey*, each heroine finds it increasingly important to detach herself from her parent. Of all Austen's living mothers, Mrs. Dashwood of *Sense and Sensibility* (1811) most conforms to the cultural model of emotional devotion and is best loved by her daughters. But her tenderness is linked to her sensibility and romantic imagination, which Marianne emulates in disastrous ways, and which the more rational Elinor attempts to reject.[10]

In *Pride and Prejudice* (1813), the less tender but anxiously matchmaking Mrs. Bennet is, as critics note, plagued by realistic concerns about women's economic disadvantages; her "total want of propriety," however, is deplored, and Elizabeth and Jane rise because they are distinguished from her. As Darcy tells Elizabeth, "let it give you consolation to consider that, to have conducted yourselves so as to avoid any share of the like censure, is praise no less generally bestowed on you and your eldest sister than it is honourable to the sense and disposition of both" (198).

Fanny Price's situation in *Mansfield Park* (1814) is even more extreme. At age ten, she is taken from her throng of siblings and overwrought mother, for whom she is named, and sent to live in her uncle's upper-class home. There, Fanny develops the genteel values that make it impossible for her and her mother to remain close. A frequently quoted passage about the one time Fanny visits her original family makes the estrangement clear:

> [Fanny] must and did feel that her mother was a partial, ill-judging parent, a dawdle, a slattern, who neither taught nor restrained her children, whose house was the scene of mismanagement and discomfort from beginning to end, and who had no talent, no conversation, no affection towards herself; no curiosity to know her better, no desire of her friendship, and no inclination for her company that could lessen her sense of such feelings. (390)

Having moved the daughter further away from the mother in each successive novel, Austen takes the logical next step in *Emma,* opening with the announcement that the mother is long dead. In *Persuasion* (1818), Anne Elliot's mother is dead as well. But unlike in *Emma,* Anne's mother did not die "too long ago for more than an indistinct remembrance," but rather when Anne was conscious enough to miss her: "Anne had gone unhappy to school, grieving for the loss of a mother whom she had dearly loved . . . and suffering as a girl of fourteen, of strong sensibility and not high spirits, must suffer at such a time" (152). Fourteen years more have passed, but Anne is still pained as she continues to think of the place where her mother "had been used to sit and preside" at Kellynch-hall (126); she maintains a steady dislike of Bath, arising, Lady Russell believes, from Anne's "having been three years at school there, after her mother's death" (14).

It is the contrasting nonchalance about the mother's death in *Emma* that interests me, for this novel is arguably as much about loss as *Persuasion*. Readers have noted, for instance, that Emma's apparently inappropriate attachment to Harriet Smith can be explained if interpreted as Emma's compensation for the marriage and thus loss of Miss Taylor (now Mrs. Weston). Such a reading helps make sense of the heroine's subsequent need to prevent Harriet's engagement to Mr. Martin. While Emma herself illogically insists that Mr. Martin is not highborn enough for her illegitimate friend, it seems more likely that she is actually driven by the fear of losing another companion to marriage.

What even such a brief foray into the novel makes clear is how easy it is to psychoanalyze Emma—how appropriate it seems to assume that her behavior with Harriet is motivated by painful feelings she herself does not understand (the word "blind," for instance, recurs frequently [112, 149, 203, 411]). Emma, in other words, appears to have an unconscious. The illusion of such depth neatly parallels Austen's first full engagement of maternal absence.

The historical importance of *Emma*'s evocation of the unconscious can hardly be overstated. That characters in a range of genres from ancient to modern times appear to have hidden depths and to be driven by irrational and unacknowledged feelings is indisputable. From *Roxana* to *Clarissa* to *Adeline Mowbray* to Austen's own earlier works, the novel is particularly deft at presenting such a possibility. But I would argue that *Emma* is the first English novel in which the existence of an unconscious seems indubitable—the first in which the heroine's misunderstanding of her own mind is the subject of the story.[11] Distinguished by its unprecedented combination of intimacy and irony, *Emma* develops the unique capacity to render Emma's thoughts and their inaccuracy simultaneously. Readers know what Emma thinks *and* we know that what she thinks she thinks is incomplete. By their very dissonance, Emma's thoughts must mask others she cannot access.

The differences between Samuel Richardson's epistolary intimacy and Henry Fielding's sweeping satire have conventionally encapsulated the polar possibilities of the early novel's points of view.[12] Pamela's letters, for instance, which, as one contemporary reader puts it, seem to be "written, under the immediate Impression of every Circumstance which occasioned them" and to capture "the fair Writer's most secret Thoughts" (4) are sentimental, personal, and interior.

This is exactly what Fielding sought to counter in the ironically detached and picaresque *Joseph Andrews,* in which he parodies *Pamela* and famously seeks to describe "not men, but manners; not an individual, but a species" (159). Pamela is confined to increasingly contained domestic spaces from which little is left to narrate but her "Passions of the Mind" (4). But we know almost nothing of the mental workings of Fielding's main characters, who, in their romp through the country, meet people from all walks of life, many of whom (including a hilarious new version of Pamela herself) serve not as psychological subjects but as universal examples of human selfishness and affectation. Burney, who admired both Richardson and Fielding, incorporated each of their narrative strategies in *Evelina,* developing an epistolary *and* picaresque novel that sometimes offers an interior view of the traveling heroine's thoughts and feelings and sometimes presents a detached and satiric account of the society she observes.

Austen's trademark is, as Ian Watt explains, to have "combine[d] into a harmonious unity the advantages both of . . . the internal and of the external approaches to character" (297).[13] Whereas *Evelina* and works by later writers such as Lewis and Edgeworth vacillate—often disjointedly—between sentimental and satiric moments, Austen's satirical narrator has steady access to the characters' sentiments. Many have suggested that Austen's greatest technical achievement is her original deployment of free indirect discourse— the art of "rendering a character's thoughts in his own idiom while maintaining the third-person reference" (Cohn 100).[14] Moving between discursive positions—sometimes offering detached estimations of human fallibility, sometimes presenting the heroine's feelings in free indirect style—Austen's narrator deftly balances ironic distance with interior insight.

Nowhere does the combination prove more fruitful than in *Emma,* where the narrator joins both perspectives in her treatment of the heroine and her "blunders" (another recurrent word [112, 296, 348]). The fun of *Emma* is that the narrator often makes fun of Emma's mistakes and misperceptions while nevertheless remaining sensitive to her interior view.[15] Thus, when Emma's brother-in-law correctly suggests that Mr. Elton is in love with her and not Harriet, as Emma has planned, "[Emma] walked on, amusing herself in the consideration of the blunders which often arise from a partial knowledge of circumstances, of the mistakes which people of high pretensions of judgment are for ever falling into; and not very well pleased with her brother for imagining her blind and ignorant, and in want of counsel" (112). The free indirect style works to marvelous effect here as the narrator steers the reader close enough to witness Emma's thoughts and far away enough to detect her ironic inaccuracy. We are thereby poised to understand what Emma cannot: that she herself is guilty of the blunders and foibles for which she blames John Knightley.

Granted, Emma is not the first Austen heroine to be treated with irony or to misinterpret her world. Both Catherine Morland and Marianne Dashwood develop misperceptions based on literary fantasies. Though not misled by popular novels, Elizabeth Bennet misunderstands Darcy's value and wrongly accepts Wickham's account of Darcy's past. But unlike *Northanger Abbey* and *Sense and Sensibility*, which signal the heroines' problematic perspectives from the outset, it is not until Elizabeth recognizes her mistake about Darcy's character that the reader is likely to do the same. On a first reading of *Pride and Prejudice*, our understanding rarely outstrips Elizabeth's; so when she reads Darcy's letter and exclaims "till this moment, I never knew myself" (208), we are apt to share at least some of her surprise.

Emma's blunders are at once more convoluted and complicated than Catherine's or Marianne's and more obvious and excessive than Elizabeth's. While the reader is often as ironically detached from Emma as from Catherine and Marianne, her misunderstandings and fantasies cannot be so easily explained. Emma shares Catherine's and Marianne's fallacious literary expectations;[16] her assumption that Harriet will prove highborn, for instance, suggests her taste for the popular novels Harriet admires (like Roche's *Children of the Abbey* [29]) in which such conclusions are conventional. But ultimately, the problems of reading and romance cannot fully account for the variety of Emma's fantasies and mistakes.

At the same time, Emma is distinguished from Elizabeth Bennet by the ironic perspective that shapes the reader's interpretation of her. Whereas in *Pride and Prejudice* we are rarely distanced enough to comprehend an event before Elizabeth does, the clues to Emma's wrongheadedness are abundant. Thus, Emma grows increasingly perplexed by Elton's apparent interest in her even before he proposes to her, and Knightley tells Emma he thinks Jane and Frank are involved long before their engagement is made public. So too, Emma persists in making mistakes for most of the novel while Elizabeth becomes somewhat more clear-sighted after reading Darcy's letter.

It is the combined complexities of Emma's fantasies and mistakes and the ironic presentation of them that makes the novel so psychologically rich. Given Emma's exceptional intelligence, the very persistence and variety of her blunders beg for an explanation. In a book that makes continuous reference to riddles, the biggest riddle is Emma herself: why does she make the mistakes she does? The answer, we can deduce from the novel's ironic tone, is unlikely to be available to Emma. Because of her propensity for error, Emma's own account of her behavior is suspect. We as readers, on the other hand, having been offered both insight into Emma's inner thoughts and ironic distance from them, are left with the impression that we can understand Emma better than Emma herself. The possibility of using Emma's thoughts to explain her behavior even though she has no access to this explanation creates the illusion of the unconscious; Emma appears to have a hidden mental source of behavior, detectable only by careful interpretation. Because its irony encourages the reader to understand Emma as she herself cannot, *Emma* might be said to anticipate the role of the modern psychotherapist.

Emma makes four major errors in the novel. Her first mistake concerns her fantasy about Harriet's marrying Mr. Elton. Her next, more elaborate fantasy involves Jane Fairfax, who Emma believes is having some kind of secret affair with Mr. Dixon, Jane's best friend's husband. Emma's worst blunder occurs when she insults Miss Bates at Box Hill—the moment that marks the climax of the novel. She makes her final mistake when she fears that Mr. Knightley loves Harriet, only then realizing that she has long wanted him for herself.

Though there are a wide variety of ways to account for Emma's mistakes, what interests me is the way each can be explained as her unconscious reaction to her mother's absence. The abundance of other motherless children in the novel—Harriet Smith, Frank Churchill, and Jane Fairfax—points to the symbolic weight and frequency of a condition that is rarely discussed.[17] Far from being a source of visible hardship as in many earlier novels, in *Emma* motherlessness is repressed. Its influence is identifiable only if readers assume that what is hidden and denied is more meaningful than overt action. Precisely because it encourages such assumptions, *Emma* proves a useful register of social change.

Emma and Loss

Because it offers one of the only references to the dead mother, it is worth quoting the opening paragraphs of *Emma* at length.

> Emma Woodhouse, handsome, clever, and rich, with a comfortable home and happy disposition, seemed to unite some of the best blessings of existence; and had lived nearly twenty-one years in the world with very little to distress or vex her.
>
> She was the youngest of the two daughters of a most affectionate, indulgent father, and had, in consequence of her sister's marriage, been mistress of his house from a very early period. Her mother had died too long ago for her to have more than an indistinct remembrance of her caresses, and her place had been supplied by an excellent woman as governess, who had fallen little short of a mother in affection. (5)

The account of Emma's fundamental happiness, though not presented as a direct rendition of her interior consciousness, appears to capture both Emma's own sense of self and her society's estimation of her.[18]

Given its possible proximity to Emma's perspective, however, we might ask how accurate this portrait is. The ensuing pages of the novel, like much else in *Emma,* offer reasons to reconsider the evidence—and even to wonder if the opening is ironic. Emma's "indulgent" father is also "nervous" and "easily depressed" (7). His hatred of marriage and preoccupation with illness speak to a larger anxiety about loss, particularly the loss of women. Several women have parted from him; these include Isabella and Mrs. Weston, both of whom he describes as "poor" (though they are likely happier away from him), and, of course, his wife. He mentions the latter only once, when complimenting Emma on a riddle for Harriet's book: "It is no difficulty to see who you take after! Your dear mother was so clever at all those things!" (78).

In contrast to novels like *Evelina,* in which maternal resemblance resolves the father and daughter's estrangement, in *Emma* it is the source of their problematic attachment. As mistress of her father's household, Emma becomes her mother's marked replacement. This may explain why Mr. Woodhouse includes his daughter among those he worries will grow ill, though to all others Emma appears "the complete picture of grown-up health" (39). As if recognizing her value as substitute wife, Emma is determined to spare her father further loss, resolving never to marry so that she will "never [have] to quit" him (264).

The possibility that her mother's death may have also affected Emma is, as previously noted, initially dismissed. Not only does Emma barely remember her mother, her "place had been supplied by an excellent woman as governess." But the implication that missing people are easily replaced is quickly undercut. Though Miss Taylor has "fallen little short of a mother in affection" (itself a pointed qualification), she falls seriously short in other respects. She has never exercised parental "authority" over Emma, and the familial relationship theirs resembles is not that of mother and daughter but rather that of "sisters" (5).

Indeed, the "unperceived" danger facing Emma is directly related to her lack of supervision: "The real evils . . . of Emma's situation were the power of having rather too much her own way, and a disposition to think a little too well of herself" (5). The description points to the liabilities of Emma's intelligence and self-assurance, about which Knightley complains a few chapters later: "Emma is spoiled by being the cleverest of her family" (37). Specifically linking Emma's permissive upbringing and her grandiosity, Knightley lays the ground for considering whether she would have been less prone to problems had her attentive mother lived. "In her mother she lost the only person able to cope with her. She inherits her mother's talents, and must have been under subjection to her" (37).

Moreover, the cavalier suggestion that a dead mother—or any absent person—can simply be replaced by someone else is belied by Emma's reaction to Miss Taylor's loss: "Such a friend as Mrs. Weston was out of the question. Two such could never be granted" (26). Rendered from Emma's perspective, the observation acknowledges what the opening paragraphs deny: certain losses are irrevocable. Thus *Emma* refutes the solution offered by a novel like *Adeline Mowbray*, in which the servant becomes an ideal surrogate parent. In commencing with the removal of the servant figure, *Emma* forecloses the possibility of using her to rectify Emma's struggle with maternal absence. Significantly, Mrs. Weston soon becomes pregnant (Anna Weston is born at the novel's end), thereby preparing to become somebody else's parent.

The loss of Miss Taylor is only the most recent in the sequence of losses that begins with Emma's mother's death and continues with her sister's marriage.[19] What distinguishes Miss Taylor's marriage from these earlier separations is its association with conscious pain. For Emma, "it was Miss Taylor's loss which first brought grief." The evening after the wedding Emma had "only to sit and think of what she had lost" (6).

Emma turns to Harriet Smith as a stopgap measure, choosing her as a walking companion because "in that respect Mrs. Weston's loss had been important" (26). Otherwise there is a fundamental difference between her former governess and new friend: "Mrs. Weston was the object of a regard, which had its basis in gratitude and esteem. Harriet would be loved as one to whom she could be useful. For Mrs. Weston there was nothing to be done; for Harriet every thing" (27). The comparison suggests just how excluded Emma feels from Mrs. Weston's life, even though she brags about having "made the match" (11) between the Westons.

Harriet is comforting because, unlike Mrs. Weston, she seems needy. The association is the first of many indicating Emma's growing socioeconomic anxiety. The only way Emma can imagine securing Harriet's allegiance is by being "useful" to her—a word she will use again when describing her relations with people "a degree or two lower" than the yeomanry (29). Mrs. Weston's former loyalty, however much enhanced by love and intimacy, had been founded in her dependence as governess. Now that she is married and there is "nothing to be done" for her, Emma has no structural means of enforcing their bond and must rely exclusively on the persistence of good feeling. The extent to which Mrs. Weston falls "a little short of a mother in affection" may consequently prove significant. Looking for a new and more reliable form of patronage, Emma seizes on Harriet, whose need for help and improvement appears reassuringly extensive.

Critics interpret Emma's subsequent orchestration of and fantasies about Harriet's romantic future in various ways. On the one hand, Emma treats Harriet as an alter ego, providing her with the motherly care and romance she herself lacks. On the other, Emma appears to be in love with Harriet and afraid of losing her to a man. Like *The Italian*, the novel can be read for its homoerotic implications and the tie between these and the daughter's original mother-love. More generally, *Emma* replicates many earlier novels in suggesting that heterosexuality involves a painful break in relations between women—first between Emma and Mrs. Weston, and then between Emma and Harriet. As Mrs. Weston tells Knightley, "no man can be a good judge of the comfort a woman feels in the society of one of her own sex" (36).[20]

Clearly, Emma is determined to avoid losing Harriet, like Miss Taylor before her, and, by implication, her mother before that. Harriet's potential engagement to Mr. Martin is especially threatening to Emma since he is not dependent on her ("a farmer can need none of my help, and is therefore in one sense as much above my notice as in every other he is below it" [29]). When Emma develops an elaborate plan to prevent the match, the illogic with which she defends it suggests that her actual motives escape her. Thus, Emma convinces Harriet to reject Mr. Martin for being too lowborn when it is Harriet who is illegitimate. And, despite her own recognition of the problems of substitution, she wants Harriet to replace Mr. Martin with Mr. Elton, even though Mr. Elton obviously expects to marry well.

The comedy that results when Mr. Elton proposes to Emma instead of Harriet proves just how effectively Emma has dampened Harriet's marital prospects. To offset Knightley's anger at her manipulations, Emma memorably tells him that she has not "set my heart on Mr. Elton's marrying Harriet . . . I only want to keep Harriet to myself" (66). She is consciously bluffing, but her words appear truer than she knows.

Almost immediately after her plans for Harriet backfire and Emma resolves to "[repress] imagination all the rest of her life" (142), she unwittingly develops a new fantasy—this one centered on Jane Fairfax, who has just arrived in Highbury to visit her aunt and grandmother, Miss and Mrs. Bates. Though she lacks wealth and social position, Jane is Emma's rival in beauty, intelligence, and talent, and the story Emma invents for her, which again has little basis in reality, seems to signal her unconscious anxieties about these advantages. Emma imagines that Jane is involved in a surreptitious romance with Mr. Dixon, who is married to Jane's best friend, the daughter of Mr. and Mrs. Campbell. The Campbells have raised and supported Jane from childhood and are now reluctantly parting with her so that she can become a governess.

The difference between Emma's fantasies about Harriet and about Jane is telling. Whereas Emma imagines she can patronize Harriet and supervise her romance, she believes Jane is independently involved in an affair that marks her fundamental ingratitude. If Jane were involved with Mr. Dixon she would be dishonoring the very people to whom she is most indebted.

Emma's fantasy about Jane is particularly significant for the socioeconomic disparities it registers. It is based on the possibility that a dependent woman might resent her position and be willing to put her own needs before her patron's interests. Jane and the Campbell daughter are raised as nominal sisters, but only the latter is guaranteed an inheritance and the husband wealth secures. The more beautiful and talented Jane is expected to earn her keep. When Emma assumes that Jane is willing to replace Miss Campbell in romance and power, she may be expressing a fear that her own socioeconomic privileges cannot prevent Jane from surpassing her in Highbury. The story also recapitulates Emma's loss of Miss Taylor in its frank acknowledgment of the disagreeableness of the job of governess.

Most novels of the period, including Austen's own, focus on a deserving heroine in financial distress and would put Jane at the center of the plot.[21] Nancy Armstrong argues that, as a genre, the novel typically elevates middle-class ideology by proving that a heroine's merit is more valuable than her birth. But *Emma* tells the more psychologically challenging story of a rich heroine trying to claim the rights of birth in a world where women like Jane have the merit to outdo her. When Mr. Knightley tells Emma that she sees in Jane "the really accomplished young woman, which she wanted to be thought herself" (166), he indicates Jane's capacity to challenge the very system on which Emma's self-importance is based. Having grown up with every expectation that she would be at the center of Highbury, Emma may well experience the mortification of marginality.

While their wealth establishes the Woodhouses as "first in consequence" in Highbury and "all look up to them" (2–3), they lack both the landed estate of the high gentry and the active connection to commercial life of the middle class. As Beth Fowkes Tobin points out, "all the characters but Emma and her father have economic ties to Highbury or Donwell" ("Moral" 239). Mr. Knightley's extensive estate, dating back to "Henry VIII's dissolution of the monasteries" proves his superior gentility and stature (Tobin, "Moral" 237). Meanwhile, Highbury's rising commercial class, impressed with its own activity, is increasingly indifferent to Emma's claims to grandeur (the Woodhouse wealth is probably based in trade, but Mr. Woodhouse does not work [Tobin, "Moral" 238]).[22] Emma is anxious to distinguish herself from the growing circle of "new money" families like the Coles and the Eltons. What Emma is not prepared for is their potential disdain for her, epitomized when she fears she will not be invited to the Coles's dinner party (207–8) and when the Eltons publicly snub Harriet—and by extension Emma—at the Crown Inn ball (327–30). At the ball's commencement, Emma finds herself having "to stand second to [the newly married] Mrs. Elton, though she had always considered the ball as peculiarly for her" (325).

Emma's social loss extends her loss of Miss Taylor and her mother before that. While her ambiguous status is troubling in its own right, it is especially so because it exacerbates a prior condition, becoming yet another means by which Emma finds herself less central. Her nuanced fantasy about Jane, whom she describes as "a riddle, quite a riddle!" (285), helps unravel the riddle of Emma's hostility toward her. The idea that Jane will steal love from Mrs. Dixon—a more privileged and less accomplished woman with whom Jane otherwise has much in common—precisely captures the threat Jane represents for Emma.

This threat is partly sexual; eating little but apples and epitomizing feminine weakness, Jane appeals to the only men Emma ever considers for herself: Frank Churchill and Mr. Knightley. But Jane also attracts a more generic attention from a variety of characters, who are moved by her disadvantages. Although as a motherless child Emma shares at least one of Jane's liabilities, she is not privy to the same compassion because she appears to have "little to distress or vex her." Of course, by rational standards, Jane's position is unenviable; when practiced by the likes of Mrs. Elton, for instance, compassion has condescension as its downside (the same can be said of Emma's treatment of Harriet[23]). But emotional factors may weigh heavily for Emma, who has the pain of watching people like Mr. Knightley and Mrs. Weston treat Jane with special care. Mr. Knightley worries about Jane's health, secures horses to take her to the ball, and sends her his last apples. Mrs. Weston fantasizes that Jane will marry Knightley (224), positioning Jane not only as Emma's rival for Mr. Knightley but also as a rival for her own interest. As a former governess, Mrs. Weston logically identifies with Jane and hopes Jane will follow her example in transcending the profession by securing a good husband.

Jane also enjoys exactly the kinship ties Emma lacks. Both girls are motherless, but Jane's maternal aunt and grandmother are happy to assume parental care. Though Miss Bates often embarrasses Jane, she is a more reliable mother substitute than a governess, who has independent familial attachments. Even Emma recognizes her own resentfulness of the Bates's "blinding" preoccupation with Jane, telling Frank "[I] was prone to take disgust towards a girl so idolized and cried up as she always was, by her aunt and grandmother, and all their set" (203). For all the Bates women's liabilities, Jane can be sure that she is their major point of interest. Emma has no such guarantee. Her doting father is also self-centered, and her older sister and *only* female relative is mother to five children (including one named Emma [99]), who command all her "maternal solicitude" (92).

Linked by their preoccupations with loss, Emma's fantasies about Harriet and Jane betray her insecurity about love and attention. Her desire "to keep Harriet to myself" (66) and her concern about Jane's social centrality point to the gap a devoted mother might have filled. It is not simply that Emma has the impossible task of compensating for an irrevocable absence. There is also a looming possibility that she herself is dispensable, first to Harriet (who may be in love with Mr. Martin) and then to the people of Highbury (who are in love with Jane). The absent mother may not be replaceable; but in a world where Harriet and Jane vie as her alter egos, Emma perhaps is.

Box Hill

The insult at Box Hill, which constitutes Emma's most pernicious blunder and marks the climax of the novel, bears all the earmarks of unconscious expression. Emma later says she could not "help saying what I did"—as if the outburst exceeded willful control. She is at first oblivious to the weight of her remarks, telling Knightley they were "not so very bad" and only recognizing their "full meaning" when he interprets them (374). When Emma finally comprehends her effect, she is more "depressed" than ever in her life, and tears run "down her cheeks almost all the way home . . . extraordinary as they were" (376). As when Elizabeth Bennet announces "till this moment I never knew myself," Emma has the shock and shame of recognizing that she is not the person she thought she was.

The insult is simple but devastating. Miss Bates responds to Frank's challenge for entertainment by promising to supply three very dull remarks, and Emma prohibits her from saying more than three dull things at once. Convinced that the general community (which here includes Mr. and Mrs. Elton, Jane, Frank, Harriet, Mr. Weston, and Mr. Knightley) shares her distaste for Miss Bates's verbosity, Emma tells Knightley, "Nobody could have helped it" (374). But he famously describes the insult as Emma's personal abuse of socioeconomic power:

> [Miss Bates] is poor; she has sunk from the comforts she was born to; and, if she live to old age, must probably sink more. Her situation should secure your compassion. It was badly done indeed!—You,

whom she had known from an infant, whom she had seen grow up from a period when her notice was an honour, to have you now, in thoughtless spirits, and the pride of the moment, laugh at her, humble her—and before her niece, too—and before others, many of whom (certainly *some*,) would be entirely guided by *your* treatment of her. (375)

If read in light of Emma's growing social anxiety, Knightley's remarks suggest that her need to "humble" Miss Bates—and, by association, Jane—is a compensatory measure, an impulsive and even desperate attempt to reassert communal authority.[24]

The context for Emma's remarks is also telling. Immediately before it, Emma and Frank Churchill are flirting (and thereby wounding Jane more than Emma can know). The prospect of a romance with Frank no longer brings Emma "any real felicity," but she does like "him for his attentions" (368). Meanwhile, their flirtation is at the center of the group's attention (369). Frank describes Emma as "presid[ing]" over the company, but she guiltily recognizes that most members of the group disapprove of her behavior (which is why Mr. Weston's and Harriet's thoughts of her are the only ones she "might not be afraid of knowing" [370]). Even if she likes being center stage, the moment is still compromised. When Miss Bates offers to speak—no doubt at length—she threatens to divert attention from Emma altogether. By silencing her, Emma's insult prevents this.

What gives the insult its climactic force, however, is its mean-spiritedness, stemming from Emma's long-term hostility toward Miss Bates. Nobody else resents Miss Bates as she does. Though this can partly be explained by Jane's association with her, Miss Bates also poses a threat of her own. Of all the characters in the novel, she and her mother are the focus of the greatest communal *attention*, a word frequently used in descriptions about them (194, 223, 375, 377). When Mr. Weston warns Frank that any "want of attention to [Jane in Highbury] should be carefully avoided" (194), he highlights the Bates's status as objects of compassion. People pride themselves on their generosity toward the family, which is why gratitude is nearly as central a subject in Miss Bates's monologues as Jane.

By most measures, gratitude is a degrading mark of subservience—a person is grateful when her social position prohibits other forms of repayment.[25] But Miss Bates "enjoy[s] a most uncommon degree of popularity" for the happy willingness with which she accepts her role. With unusual lack of irony, the narrator explains that "the simplicity and cheerfulness of [Miss Bates's] nature, her contented and grateful spirit, were a recommendation to every body and a mine of felicity to herself" (21). Emma, of course, is the significant exception; she finds Miss Bates's gratitude so annoying that when Mrs. Weston suggests that Jane will marry Knightley, Emma retorts, "How would he bear to have Miss Bates . . . thanking him all day long?" (225).

Perhaps Emma is uniquely bothered because Miss Bates has secured a communal affection she herself can never enjoy. Precisely because Miss Bates accepts her unenviable situation so willingly, she stands "in the very worst predicament in the world for having much of the public favour"; nobody has cause to "hate her" (21). The same cannot be said of Emma, who, as a "handsome, clever, and rich" young woman (5), appears her opposite; Miss Bates is "neither young, hand-some, [nor] rich" and has "never boasted either beauty or cleverness" (21). It is a testament to all women's oppression that Emma's wealth and apparent self-esteem necessarily cost her popularity; a man with similar privileges would not be so penalized. But given such inevitabilities, the humble Miss Bates has an important, if ironic, social advantage.

Emma feels her handicap particularly when, after she has sanctioned the prospect of a ball at Crown Inn, Mr. Weston and Frank still seek Miss Bates's endorsement. Emma lamely complains: "You will get nothing to the purpose from Miss Bates. . . . She will be all delight and gratitude, but she will tell you nothing" (255). But "delight and gratitude" are attractive in ways Emma is loath to admit. Though Frank secretly longs to see Jane, the narrator notes Miss Bates's independent value: "As a counsellor, she was not wanted; but as an approver (a much safer character,) she was truly welcome. Her approbation, at once general and minute, warm and incessant, could not but please" (256). Because of her self-importance and higher status, Emma has neither the inclination nor the power "to please" in the same way and can never be as well loved.

It follows that Miss Bates has a full range of social contacts, from which the snobbish Emma is excluded. Her monologues refer to a wide variety of people, from servants to merchants to landlords. Her longest speech not only invokes almost every character in the book but includes those who would otherwise go unmentioned (Patty, Mrs. Wallis, William Larkins, John Saunders, and Mrs. Hodges [236–39]). With her wealth of contacts—almost all of whom visit and assist her in some capacity—Miss Bates stands at the crossroads of the Highbury world.[26]

Because Emma's insult singles out the verbosity that proves Miss Bates's communal centrality and endearment, it seems rooted in the loss and deprivation that provoke her earlier fantasies. For all her liabilities, Miss Bates has secured a love and concern that the more fortunate Emma appears to neither want nor deserve. It hardly seems coincidental that Miss Bates is also the only female character who has a living mother—indeed, one who has survived to a ripe old age.[27] Measured against the spinster's hardships, Emma's motherlessness and related loneliness appear incidental, and they are treated with corresponding neglect. But her persistent anxiety about loss and attention suggest she has suffered more than anyone, including she herself, comprehends.

Mr. Weston's riddle, which immediately follows the insult, is ironically well-timed: "What two letters of the alphabet are there, that express perfection? . . . Ah! you will never guess. You, (to Emma), I am certain, will never guess.—I will tell you.—M. and A.—Em—ma.—Do you understand?" (371). Since the insult to Miss Bates demonstrates Emma's *im*perfection, the conundrum is literally a blunder. But if read as a clue to *Emma*'s blunder, the solution is apt. The two letters that sound Emma's name also spell the word "Ma." In failing to "understand" the riddle of her character, Emma misses her mother again.[28]

Mothering Heterosexuality

It is fitting that Mr. Knightley is the only character to chastise Emma for the insult. Distinguished from those like Mr. Woodhouse and the Westons, who find Emma "perfect," and from those like the Eltons, who openly dislike her, he both recognizes Emma's fallibility and cares about her. (Though not exactly the same, his perspective most closely resembles the reader's joint distance and intimacy.) As "one of the few people who could see faults in Emma Woodhouse, and the only one who ever told her of them" (11), he "blame[s]" and "lecture[s]" (430) her to prove himself her "friend by very faithful counsel" (375). Thus, in addition to reprimanding Emma for her abuse of Miss Bates, Knightley objects to her treatment of Harriet and Jane. He may not interpret them psychologically, but Knightley identifies the problematic relationships at the source of Emma's blunders.

It is, of course, around Knightley that Emma's final—but first male-centered—blunder revolves. She hints that Harriet should pursue Frank Churchill only to have Harriet fall in love with Knightley, who seems capable of returning her feelings. The biggest threat to Emma's importance springs from neither Jane nor Miss Bates but from the one woman over whom Emma never doubts her own supremacy. In befriending and elevating Harriet, Emma manufactures her greatest rival, perfectly encapsulated when Harriet tells Emma: "If Mr. Knightley should really—if *he* does not mind the disparity [in social positions], I hope, dear Miss Woodhouse, you will not set yourself against it, and try to put difficulties in the way. But you are too good for that, I am sure" (407). Having, in her fantasy about Jane, implicitly recognized the ambition that might drive a dependent woman to challenge her patron and friend, Emma is now in the mortifying position she had imagined for Mrs. Dixon.

Announcing both her hopes for social mobility and her understanding of how she might secure it via male desire, Harriet marks the limits of Emma's control. If Knightley loves Harriet, the "difficulties" the status-conscious Emma may "put . . . in the way" are surmountable. Like Elizabeth Bennet, who scoffs at Lady Catherine De Bourgh's disapproval of her rumored engagement to Darcy—telling her "the wife of Mr. Darcy must have such extraordinary sources of happiness necessarily attached to her situation, that she could . . . have no cause to repine" (365)—Harriet knows Knightley's power outweighs Emma's feelings.

Emma is thus reminded of her insignificance at the same time that she is again faced with loss. Overwhelmed by potential deprivation, she finally comprehends the depth of her attachment to Knightley: "Why was it so much worse that Harriet should be in love with Mr. Knightley, than with Frank Churchill? Why was the evil so dreadfully increased by Harriet's having some hope of a return? It darted through her, with the speed of an arrow, that Mr. Knightley must marry no one but herself!" (408). Asking and answering her own riddles, Emma encounters more, only to realize the extent of her self-deception: "How to understand it all! How to understand the deceptions she had been thus practising on herself, and living under!—The blunders, the blindness of her own head and heart!" (411–12). Determined "to understand, thoroughly understand her own heart," she initiates a process of self-analysis that enables her to recognize her long-term "affection" for Knightley, and the "sensation" is the only "part of her mind" that is not "disgusting" (412) to her.

In suggesting that Emma undergoes a mental journey, moving through stages of self-scrutiny and humiliation to discover long-obscured feelings for Knightley, Austen assumes as given that there is a "part of [the] mind" that can have a profound impact on an individual without an individual's having easy access to it. Emma must shamefully peel away the layers of her "blindness," working from one "question of inquiry" to another to gain "knowledge of herself" (412). The insult to Miss Bates is pivotal because its irrational cruelty forces Emma to recognize the mystery of her own behavior, preparing her to understand that there are aspects of herself she does not know.

If Emma's first insight about Knightley concerns her attachment to him, her next one involves the origin of this feeling: "Till now that she was threatened with its loss, Emma had never known how much of her happiness depended on being *first* with Mr. Knightley, first in interest and affection" (415). Knightley has made Emma happy by making her the center of his attention and love. Although Emma's hostility toward Jane and Miss Bates suggests she feels bereft of these comforts, the prospect of losing Knightley prompts her to believe that he has provided them all along—that even as he has taken a benevolent interest in other women, he has always cared for and about her the most.

Much earlier, when explaining to Harriet why she plans never to marry, Emma portrays her father's devotion in similar terms: "Never, never could I expect to be so truly beloved and important; so always first and always right in any man's eyes as I am in my father's" (84). But it is only in the account of Knightley that such attention is linked with "happiness" and broader possibilities for communal security. Thinking his daughter is "always right," Mr. Woodhouse offers a love that is hermetically sealed. Knightley monitors Emma's faults with an eye toward her social integration: "He had loved her, and watched over her from a girl, with an endeavour to improve her, and an anxiety for her doing right, which no other creature had at all shared" (415).

The other creature who might have shared this "anxiety" was Emma's mother, as Knightley himself points out when noting that "in her mother she lost the only person able to cope with her" (37). That Emma discovers Knightley's solicitude only when she fears his absence suggests the precision of this resemblance—both in the nature of Knightley's attention and in the threat of its loss. It is telling that Emma associates Knightley's marriage with the impending birth of Mrs. Weston's child, viewing the events as related "privations": "The child to be born at Randall's must be a tie there even dearer than herself; and Mrs. Weston's heart and time would be occupied by it. They should lose her" (422). Even more than her marriage, the birth of Mrs. Weston's child spells the end of her maternal interest in Emma. In the paragraph in which this passage appears, the word "loss" (or a variation of it) recurs four times; and in the paragraph that begins the next chapter, Emma is described as being lonely and "melancholy."

When Knightley surprises Emma by proposing to her instead of Harriet, he breaks the melancholic cycle. Because Emma tends to experience love only in relation to loss (even her affection for her father is tied to her fear of leaving him), Knightley's potential absence is pivotal in enabling her to identify her feelings for him. Once those feelings are established, and the danger of loss itself suppressed, Emma is poised to recover from the anxieties and blunders that have plagued her. Now convinced that Knightley has taken care of her since childhood and that she has always cherished him for it, Emma frames a past in which what seemed to be missing was actually available; loss turns to gain as Knightley's threatened absence proves his constant presence.

The explanation that Emma has unknowingly loved Knightley for a long time—that she has a "relenting heart . . . disposed to accept of his" (431–32) despite her many earlier protestations against marriage— is crucial to the novel's resolution. Emma's sudden romantic transformation is plausible only when readers believe that it is not sudden psychologically. She may recognize her interest in Knightley "with the speed of an arrow" (408), but we have to grant that the feeling itself has long been brewing "unconsciously" (the term Emma earlier uses in her fiction about Jane's love for Mr. Dixon [168]) to accept the conclusion as anything more than what Casey Finch and Peter Bowen describe as the "politically inevitable fulfillment of the most vigorously enforced social and novelistic expectations" (1).

Though the historical imperative of the marriage is never actually in doubt, Emma doubts it, and her ultimate acceptance of Knightley works partly because it is presented as the satisfaction of her long-unacknowledged and unfulfilled need to be mothered.[29] When Emma begins to see Knightley's criticisms as evidence of his care and attention—when she thinks back on how he has tried to guide her since childhood—the very characteristics she had once opposed become attractive for their tenderness. Knightley satisfies because he stands in the mother's place.[30]

Heterosexuality—which initiates Emma's crisis with Mrs. Weston and which she steadfastly resists throughout most of the novel—becomes the solution to maternal absence.[31] Whereas a book like *The Italian* emphasizes the heroine's struggle in moving from mother to man, *Emma* promises that marriage can be maternal. This is the same promise that Janice Radway has identified at the heart of the modern romance.[32] Obscuring the incompatibility of the daughter's mother-love and her compulsory heterosexuality, *Emma* offers a hero who is motherly and masculine. Thus Emma is drawn to Knightley's tenderness, but Mr. Woodhouse sanctions the match to secure Knightley's protection from chicken thieves. Significantly, Knightley sports the hero's characteristically invulnerable social status, even amid the new money families of Highbury. Alone, Emma lacks the socioeconomic wherewithal to command instant respect, but as a landowner's wife she is guaranteed more authority. If Emma's socioeconomic fears stem from her mother's death, Knightley's manly mothering solves both problems simultaneously.[33]

The solution is enhanced by its modulation of the threat of incest, which is evoked by Emma and Knightley's relations as brother- and sister-in-law, and which (though the relationship is not legally prohibited) constitutes such a steady concern that the two must assure each other they are not siblings before they dance at the Crown Inn ball (331). Knightley's willingness to move to Hartfield, so that Emma need never leave her father, recapitulates a tension that his role as surrogate mother reduces. From a psychoanalytic perspective, the pro-hibition of the incestuous desire the family provokes compels the search for familial substitutes, particularly for the mother, who is the original object of love.

Capable of completing the Woodhouse family by joining it, Knightley is kindred enough to fill the needs that originate with the mother's loss. But he is also sexually different from the mother and de-tached enough from the family to offer an exogamous exchange. Were he simply a substitute brother or father, the incestuous danger might linger—as in novels like *The Italian* or *The Monk,* where heterosexual incestuous implications are more hazardous than homoerotic ones. But as both mother and man, family member and friend, he offers precisely the flexibility to defuse the taboo while apparently fulfilling the desires it generates.

If the aesthetic control of the heterosexual conclusion masks the political trauma and irresolvability of maternal loss that earlier novels expose, it also logically extends their paradigmatic assump-tions about the mother's impact. Moving with some regularity from *Evelina,* in which the mother leaves a physical mark on her child, late eighteenth- and early nineteenth-century women's novels increasingly internalize the mother's imprint. By *Emma*, the imprint is mentally embedded enough to be nearly undetectable. Implicit in the problems Knightley solves is the idea that a child's need for the mother is so fundamental that it shapes all subsequent experience, yet so primal that it escapes rational comprehension and visibility. As in the psychoanalytic story of the preoedipal moment, in *Emma* the mother becomes an origin so remote and irrecoverable that the feelings associated with her can never be directly expressed or understood. Preceding language, the experience of maternal love and loss is lodged in the unconscious and requires an unconscious resolution.

Without challenging the unconscious basis of the mother's early imprint, *Persuasion* offers a more overt account of the trauma of her loss. Unlike Emma, Anne is openly depressed when her mother dies, and the very tone of the novel is characterized by sorrow. *Persuasion* presents as a given what *Emma* implies—that a child's love and need for the mother is monumental and that their separation— however inevitable—causes exquisite pain.[34] In part the difference between Anne and Emma is one of age. Emma is arguably so young when her mother dies that her only memories are "indistinct" (5) and unconscious. But it is also tempting to suggest that the shift between *Emma* and *Persuasion* is historically significant. Whereas in *Emma* the emotional problem of maternal loss must be decoded, in *Persuasion* it obviously frames the daughter's development. Certain about the mother's dual centrality and absence, *Persuasion* completes the model that anticipates a psychoanalytic age.

NOTES

Introduction

1. As E. Ann Kaplan writes, "mother-representations in any one period are . . . always contradictory, multiple, many-sided" (*Motherhood* 19). Christopher Flint makes a similar point about the eighteenth-century family, which was "an extremely elastic category, used strategically to make many different kinds of arguments, political as well as literary" (307). "Enlightened domesticity," says Mitzi Meyers, was "available for divergent uses and interpretations" (143).

2. Even Amanda Vickery, who challenges the idea that "motherhood as a social role was an eighteenth-century invention," notes the impossibility of denying "the sheer glamour of the images of tender motherhood which proliferated in eighteenth- and early nineteenth-century media" (92, 93). The 1970s witnessed the publication of several important studies about the consolidation of the nuclear family and the development of maternal ideals: Edward Shorter, *The Making of the Modern Family* (1975); Lawrence Stone, *The Family, Sex and Marriage in England, 1500–1800* (1977); Randolph Trumbach, *The Rise of the Egalitarian Family: Aristocratic Kinship and Domestic Relations in Eighteenth-Century England* (1978); Ruth H. Bloch, "American Feminine Ideals in Transition: The Rise of the Moral Mother, 1785–1815" (1978). Other important works followed, for example: Judith Schneid Lewis, *In the Family Way: Childbearing in the British Aristocracy, 1760–1860* (1986); John Demos, *Past, Present, and Personal: The Family and the Life Course in American History* (1986); John R. Gillis, *A World of Their Own Making* (1996). In contrast to scholars who document a major shift in maternal practice in the eighteenth century, in *Forgotten Children* Linda Pollock argues that there appears to be no "significant change in the quality of parental care given to or the amount of parental affection felt

for infants for the period 1500–1900" (235). For useful summaries of the debate about the historical development of the nuclear family, see Flint 4–9 and E. Ann Kaplan, *Motherhood* 18–19.

3. On changes in maternal breastfeeding see Bloch 109–11; Fildes, *Breasts* 116 and *Wet Nursing* 79, 116; Gelpi, "Significant Exposure"; Jacobus 207–30; Kowaleski-Wallace 101–4, 129–35; Perry, "Colonizing the Breast"; Scholten 71–73; Yalom 105–23.

4. See Hoffer and Hull 69, 83–85.

5. On the passage of the Infant Custody Bill see J. S. Lewis 59. For a fuller summary of the legal histories of both infanticide and custody see my introduction, *Inventing Maternity* 1–2.

6. For particularly good discussions of these changes see Davidoff and Hall, and Perkin.

7. See, for instance, Pollak, *Poetics* 27–35, and Poovey, *Proper Lady* 3–15. For an instructive account of the historical problems raised in locating the rise of domestic womanhood in the eighteenth century or in any particular period see Vickery 2–7.

8. Ros Ballaster provides a helpful review of the scholarly "inability to resolve the question of the novel's origin" (7–30). On the ancient roots of the novel see Doody, *The True Story of the Novel*. On the amorphous nature of early English novels, the complexity or fallacy of defining their origin, and/or the problem of nationality, see, for instance, Homer Brown, "Prologue"; Lennard Davis, *Factual Fictions*; J. Paul Hunter, *Before Novels*; Michael McKeon, *The Origins of the English Novel*; John Richetti, introduction, *Popular Fiction*; Clifford Siskin, "Epilogue: The Rise of Novelism"; William Warner, *Licensing Entertainment* 1–44. April Alliston describes the extensive interdependence of eighteenth-century English and French women novelists. *Reconsidering the Rise of the Novel*, a special volume (12) of *Eighteenth-Century Fiction*, offers an array of approaches to the problem of the novel's origin.

9. Also see Deidre Lynch's excellent *Economy of Character* (1998).

10. Also see Flint 62, 322n.

11. There are scores of books on women novelists; I list only those centrally concerned with interpreting their "rise." The vast majority of these were published in the 1980s, when there was particular interest in resurrecting women writers, but Cheryl Turner's book is more recent; also see Donovan, and Tompkins 116–71. For valuable discussions of changes in female readership see Ballaster 35–42, and Gallagher (who also discusses the rise of women authors) 219–21. On the early novel's use of "woman as its master signifier" see Backscheider, "Novel's Gendered Space" 29.

12. For a detailed discussion of the discourse on maternal breastfeeding, see chapter 3.

13. Marianne Hirsch says the same of nineteenth-century women's novels; see 43–67.

14. On the prevalence of paternal absence and weakness in the novel and its demographic significance see Brian McCrea, *Impotent Fathers*. By the end of the eighteenth century there was what Ludmilla Jordanova calls "a significant shift . . . away from associating children 'naturally' with their fathers and toward associating them 'naturally' with their mothers" ("Interrogating" 373). It is symptomatic of this change and of the general dissociation of patriarchy from paternity that procreation ceased to be described by the word "generation" (with its association with "genealogy") and was instead denoted by the more feminized term "reproduction." For more on the diminution of the father see my introduction, *Inventing Maternity* 8, 13–16, 24.

15. For an excellent discussion of some of the socioeconomic and ideological pressures at odds with maternal practice see Toni Bowers, who notes that "'natural' motherhood was not available to mothers without the leisure born of middle-class social privilege, or those who insisted on developing their own subjectivity according to the liberal, competitive and capitalistic models developing in Augustan England" (*Politics* 98).

16. *Oedipus* had both universal appeal and historically specific relevance for Freud. Whereas Teresa de Lauretis, drawing on Vladimir Propp, argues that the oedipal drama of incestuous desire and the exogamous exchange that depends on its prohibition is "paradigmatic of all narratives" (*Alice* 112), Sarah Winter shows that Freud's particular preoccupation with *Oedipus* was the logical outgrowth of his nineteenth-century classical education (38–40).

17. Freud himself had relatively little to say about the preoedipal domain that he "surmised" but left "tantalizingly unexplored" (Jacobus 130). Still, his speculation has had extraordinary influence. Freud "revolutionized nineteenth-century motherhood discourses," E. Ann Kaplan claims, because his theory of mother-child "*fusion*" and account of "how the baby comes to know itself as an entity separate from its mother ushers in the concept of subjectivity" (*Motherhood* 29). So, too, it is Freud's preoedipal myth, Mary Jacobus suggests, "that has generated some of the most influential contemporary attempts to provide a feminist version of . . . psychoanalysis" (9).

18. Dickens, for instance, read Radcliffe's novels (Ackroyd 129).

19. On Mary's evolution as maternal icon, see Gillis, *World* 28, 29, 156–57, 166. Shari Thurer writes of the nineteenth century that "human mothers had been honored before, but not in such an inflated manner. Flesh-and-blood mothers had never been held up to the standards of the Virgin Mary. Even the Virgin Mary had not been held up to her own standards" (186). "What distinguishes the eighteenth-century discourse

of motherhood from its predecessors," Vickery suggests, "is not a sudden idealization, but rather the overlaying of a range of secular celebrations on the ancient religious solemnizations" (93).

20. Barbara Gelpi interestingly suggests that it was specifically the late eighteenth-century "eroticization" of the mother and especially of the maternal breast, epitomized and articulated in Rousseau's *Émile*, that helped initiate Freud's theories about the fraternal bonding that grows out of sublimated incestuous desire ("Significant Exposure" 130).

21. See, for example, Bloch, Fildes (*Breasts, Wet Nursing*, and *Women as Mothers*), J. S. Lewis, Scholten, Theriot, and Yalom.

22. Thus, Carroll Smith-Rosenberg's pathbreaking article "The Female World of Love and Ritual" suggests that the mother-daughter relationship was at the center of nineteenth-century patterns of female bonding. Linda Kerber's and Mary Beth Norton's studies of women and the American Revolution popularized the idea of "Republican Motherhood." Also see Nancy Cott, *Bonds of Womanhood*.

23. Jordanova suggests that in eighteenth-century scientific and medical texts, wombs, ovaries, and breasts became "emblems of femininity" (*Sexual Visions* 51). In *Making Sex*, Thomas Laqueur argues that it was not until the eighteenth century that female reproductive organs were defined as incommensurably different from male organs and that the uterus came to be seen as determinative of women's "manner of being" (149). And Londa Schiebinger suggests that Carolus Linnaeus's coining of the term "mammals" (which literally means "of the breast" [40–41]) was made possible by the Western idealization of maternal breastfeeding (40–74).

24. For a good discussion of Freud's marginalization of the mother's perspective, including a summary of relevant criticism, see Sprengnether 1–10. For more on feminist discussions of mother-daughter love see chapter 2.

25. For a history of the publication and reception of *The Reproduction of Mothering* see Buhle 249–65. For a review of the criticism of Chodorow see chapter 2.

26. For brief summaries of the differences between feminist object-relations theory and feminist Lacanican theory see Buhle 320; Garner, Kahane, and Sprengnether 21–25; Minsky 206.

27. Following the publication of *The Reproduction of Mothering*, there was an outpouring of psychoanalytically informed literary studies of mother-daughter themes; see Buhle 260–61.

28. Warner persuasively challenges feminist efforts to "align the genre of the novel with the female gender," arguing that early novels by Behn, Manley, and Haywood "cannot be gendered" ("Formulating Fiction" 280–84); while I too distrust the tendency to view women's writing

as womanly, I would suggest that at least some late eighteenth-century women writers strove to be read this way. Catherine Gallagher's *Nobody's Story* and April Alliston's *Virtue's Faults* note the inaccuracy of charting a monolithic female tradition, but nevertheless they stress the self-consciousness with which some women authors sought to construct one (Gallagher xv, xviii; Alliston 9–10). *Mothering Daughters* confirms this dialectic.

29. See Doody, *True Story of the Novel;* Backscheider, "The Novel's Gendered Space" and "Rise of Gender as Political Category"; and Warner, *Licensing Entertainment* and "Formulating Fiction."

30. When her family tries to make her marry against her will, Clarissa urges her mother to help her resist; later, when she is dying, Clarissa begs her mother for a last blessing. In both cases, Mrs. Harlowe is deeply sympathetic but bound to reject her daughter out of allegiance to her husband and son. In *Pamela* (1740–42), the heroine's sexual struggle begins after her master's mother (who is Pamela's surrogate mother) dies.

31. At the end of *Joseph Andrews,* Joseph is identified by the strawberry birthmark that records his mother's desire for the fruit during pregnancy. *Tom Jones* is resolved when Mrs. Waters (formerly Jenny Jones) reports that she masqueraded as Tom's parent at the request of his real mother: Bridget Allworthy. I discuss *Joseph Andrews* in more detail in chapter 1.

32. Castle makes a similar point ("'Amy'" 82).

33. John Gillis notes that until the early nineteenth century "motherhood was still subordinated to wifehood" (*World* 158). On Defoe's attention to the economic constraints prohibiting motherhood see Bowers, *Politics* 101. Robyn Wiegman argues that Roxana's "narrative is contingent . . . on her transference of reproduction (Motherhood) to production (Whoredom)—woman's limited, dichotomized choices in a capitalist patriarchy" (35).

34. While other critics have noted that Susan's return defines maternity as what Richetti calls a "biological and psychological necessity" ("Family, Sex, and Marriage" 33; also see Maddox 684), they tend not to recognize the historical novelty of this kind of naturalization of motherhood. I think *Roxana* is remarkable for the gradual introduction of the necessity of maternity, for the way in which its inescapability emerges not as the text's unifying principle but almost as an afterthought that evolves as the novel proceeds. As was arguably true in the culture at large, psychological maternity begins to take shape in the novel, but it is not the agreed-upon standard against which Roxana is always measured. Bowers is eloquent on how critical readings of *Roxana* betray ahistorical "assumptions about acceptable maternal behaviors" (*Politics* 100).

35. On the novel's "construction of woman as currency, as the medium of exchange between men" see Wiegman 40.

36. Many note that in murdering Susan, Amy acts as Roxana's double. See, for instance, Castle, " 'Amy' " 92, and Bowers, *Politics* 120.

37. In some cases, though, secondary maternal characters are problematic or villainous, such as Madame Duval in *Evelina* or the Marchesa di Vivaldi in *The Italian*.

38. John Hay, the first critic seriously to raise the possibility of Tristram's illegitimacy, finally concludes that the hero is premature. J. Paul Hunter counters Hay with elaborate evidence of Tristram's questionable paternity; see "Clocks" 182–87. Doody states flat-out that Tristram "is not Walter Shandy's son" ("Shandyism" 453). Also see Ostovich 332. I would like to thank Virginia Mastromonaco, who influenced my reading of Tristram's possible illegitimacy.

39. Walter also embraces scientific, legal, and political accounts of male procreative supremacy. Thus, as Louis Landa notes, he resembles the animalculists, who believed that the fetus existed fully formed in the sperm. (For more on animalculism see chapter 1.) Walter listens eagerly when Kysarcius explains *"That the mother is not of kin to her child"* (324).

40. See Cash.

41. Other critics have also commented on the novel's attention to the insufficiencies of language and the relation between representation and sexuality; see Perry, "Words for Sex" 27; Stevenson 174; and especially King 296–99, 304.

42. Ross King argues that the male characters turn to language to compensate for their sense of physical deficiency.

43. Tristram, for instance, is nearly castrated by a window because Trim removes the sashes to make field pieces for Toby's fortifications. On the connections between Toby's fortifications and Tristram's injury, see Allen 668 and McNeil 425. Noting Toby's disappointment when the Peace of Utrecht is signed, McNeil points to the ironically destructive basis of Toby's response to his own physical suffering; see especially 411, 418, 420, 425–26. For more on the representational insufficiencies of Toby's battlefield see King 308.

44. On the continuous "analogy between eloquence and childbirth" in the novel see Lamb 158.

Chapter 1

1. The mother's resolution is similar in *Tom Jones*, for when Bridget Allworthy is finally revealed as Tom's real mother his apparent incest with Mrs. Waters is dismissed.

2. Burney may have deliberately drawn on Fielding's example. She praises Fielding in her "Preface" to *Evelina*, and the novel several times alludes

to his half brother, Justice Fielding. In the "Dedication" to *The Wanderer* (1814), Burney says the only novel her father ever owned was Fielding's *Amelia* (1751).

3. On classic resolutions of adultery and incest see Trenkner 61, 92–94. In Heliodorus's *Aithiopika* (C.A.D. 250–380), the mother's writing on a silken girdle "tells [her abandoned] child her identity and the real story of her (legitimate) birth" (Doody, "Beyond *Evelina*" 367–68; also see her *True Story of the Novel*, 89–105).

4. On recognition scenes in the classical novel see Hägg 36, 68; and Trenkner 36–39, 91–108. On the relation between recognition and familial instinct in French classical tragedy see Cherpack, especially 7, 21–26, 31.

5. In Cervantes's *La Gitanilla* (*The Little Gypsy Girl*) (1613), the heroine's mother identifies her child by the trinkets in the daughter's possession, a white mole under her left breast, and a piece of skin between the smallest toes on her right foot (91–93). As I discuss later in the chapter, moles were generally seen as maternal marks. In his *La Ilustre Fregona* (*The Illustrious Kitchen-Maid*) (1613) the dead mother is named when the daughter is identified by the matching links of a gold chain and the words on matching pieces of parchment (127–29). In Shakespeare's *Pericles* (1607–8) and *The Winter's Tale* (1610–11), Marina and Perdita bear striking resemblances to their absent mothers (*Pericles* [5.1.105–13]; *Winter's Tale* [5.2.30–40]). In the *Aithiopika*, the female parent's "intuitive recognition" of the daughter is central to her identification (Doody, "Beyond *Evelina*" 368–69).

6. The connection between maternal markings and legitimacy may be a new or especially emphatic preoccupation in the eighteenth-century novel. In Cervantes's *La Ilustre Fregona*, for instance, the maternal tokens document not the child's legitimacy but her mother's rape (129). James Saeger suggests that in Renaissance literature legitimate children are generally identified with fathers while bastards are culturally positioned "within a feminized space" (180–81).

7. McCrea's analysis of *Evelina* (145–53), which includes a critique of my own earlier work on the novel, is helpful. Challenging readings that feature Evelina's struggle with patriarchal authority, McCrea emphasizes the impotence of Sir John Belmont (Evelina's father). While I agree with his emphasis, I would add that the novel is also fundamentally concerned with the laws that empower Belmont despite his ineptitude.

8. There is some debate about whether Lacan attributes language acquisition to the particular absence of the mother or to the general loss of the illusion of a whole self. See Clement 87, Kristeva, *Desire* 289, and Rose, introduction-II 31 on language as compensation for the mother; see Sprengnether 221 and Silverman, *Subject* 168–69 for Lacan's greater

interest in the lost self. I tend to discuss language as a replacement for maternal loss because the theory has achieved a certain popular currency.

9. Julia Kristeva argues that there is a form of poetic language associated with the preoedipal mother, but that it is the language of insanity (*Desire* 196), particularly when it involves the female poet; see J. Butler, *Gender Trouble* 82–86, and Rose, *Sexuality* 36.

10. Some scholars point to the problem of suggesting that the child's induction into language depends on the father, for children raised by mothers actually tend to learn language from them; see Gelpi, *Shelley's Goddess,* especially 23, and Silverman, *Acoustic Mirror* 76.

11. Catherine Clement puts it well: "the child must have been separated from its mother's body—weaned—and must be able to turn around and see someone else. This is the action upon which all subjectivity is based, the moment in which the human individual is born. It is also the necessary condition for the existence of language. . . . This is also the moment in which culture is born" (87).

12. Many critics have been interested in names and naming in Burney's autobiographical narratives and/or in *Evelina.* See G. Campbell; Doody, *Frances Burney* 40–41; Epstein, *Iron Pen* 96; Fizer; Oakleaf; Pawl; and my own " 'Oh Dear Resemblance.' " Much can be made of the names in *Evelina:* "Orville" and "Villars" are virtually inversions of each other, and "Anville," the fictitious surname Villars chooses for Evelina, alludes to both of them. Also "Anville" is a virtual anagram of "Evelina," and all of the letters for "Anville" can be found in "Caroline Evelyn." For a more extensive discussion of Burney's use of the trope of "Nobody" here and elsewhere, see Gallagher 203–14.

13. Fizer makes a similar point (81, 85).

14. The emphasis on burning has autobiographical resonance: Burney claimed to have burned her first novel *Caroline Evelyn* out of respect for her father's distaste for novels ("Dedication" xxii); Evelina's father burns Caroline Evelyn's marriage certificate.

15. Pawl also notes the erotic overtones of Villars's behavior (287). For a summary of the changes in wardship instigated by Charles II and their implications for representations of guardian-ward incest see Ellen Pollak's "Guarding the Succession."

16. Lynch's attention to the reading of faces and the linkage between personal character and printed character (at a time when literature was becoming increasingly commercialized) is fascinating. Clearly *Evelina* and the novels I discuss in the chapter's conclusion present the individual face as "the somatic correlate of a proper name" (Lynch 33). Often associating the countenance with the recuperation of a crucial text, such as a letter or will, the novels celebrate the mutually dependent legibility of bodies and print.

17. Fizer's discussion of the incest threat in *Evelina* is excellent; see especially 79–80, 83, and 92.

18. It is in keeping with the seamless connection between Caroline's letter and Evelina's body that Belmont views them as superimpositions of each other. "Ten thousand daggers could not have wounded me like this letter!" (385), he says, and then: "Evelina! thy countenance is a dagger to my heart!" (386). Adapting Lacanian theory, Margaret Homans argues that nineteenth-century women writers privilege literal language as a linguistic trace of a (preoedipal) mother-daughter bond. Her suggestion that female characters bear language by carrying messages or letters (*Bearing the Word* 31) is especially relevant for Evelina, who bears her mother's signature in countenance and letter.

19. Also see Doody's discussion of the illustration (*Frances Burney* 32–33) and Gallagher's discussion of the dedicatory poem (217–18).

20. A number of other mothers in the novel are either suspect or powerless. It was because Madame Duval tried to force her daughter to marry someone else that Caroline eloped with Belmont in the first place (15). Both her "tyrani[cal]" (15) interest in dictating Caroline's marriage and the "hardness of heart" (125) she showed after Belmont's desertion suggest that Madame Duval has yet to be influenced by maternal love and feeling. (For a sympathetic reading of Madame Duval see Straub.) "Mamma Mirvan" (28) is more tender, but she can neither protect Maria from her father's sexual insults (38) nor protect Evelina from Willoughby's harassments. Mrs. Mirvan's mother, Lady Howard, must accept that her daughter's "principal study seems to be healing those wounds which her husband inflicts" on all around him (53).

21. Upon learning of Belmont's acknowledgment, Orville happily introduces Evelina by her "real name" and looks forward to presenting her "by yet another name, and by the most endearing of all titles" (381).

22. For instance, when a child was conceived after a private separation it was considered the husband's legal heir, and the onus was on him to prove otherwise (Stone, *Road to Divorce* 180). In England an act of king and Parliament could legitimate an illegitimate child, but it was not until 1926 that the subsequent marriage of the parents was deemed grounds for legitimation (Teichman 34–35). For a discussion of how "European society seems always to have classed the largest possible number of children as illegitimate" see Laslett et al. 7–12.

23. Blackstone repeats this passage later in the text, reminding readers that bastards "are held to be sons of nobody, *nullus filius*" (368). Susan Staves criticizes the reductive nature of Blackstone's *Commentaries* and points to popular interest in the complexities and contradictions of legal decisions that Blackstone ignores (14–16). Burney, however, alludes to very basic legal prescriptions, making Blackstone helpful.

24. Emily Gardner alerted me to the legal problems surrounding the Belmont marriage.
25. On the problems of validating marriages and the Hardwicke Marriage Act see Gillis, *For Better, for Worse* 190–92; Laslett et al. 9; Perry, *Women* 60–62; and Stone, *Road to Divorce* 96–120. Blackstone writes that "marriages celebrated by license, where either of the parties is under twenty-one, not being a widow or a widower, without the consent of the father, or if he be dead [as was the case for Caroline], of the mother or guardian, shall be void" (187).
26. "Our law has made no provision to prevent the disinheriting of children by will, leaving every man's property at his own disposal" (Blackstone 195).
27. In other scenes, the law is an accomplice to abuse. Captain Mirvan and Willoughby arrange for Madame Duval to receive a letter from a country justice falsely informing her of Monsieur Du Bois's arrest so that they can attack her and Evelina when they journey to help him (141). Similarly, the Branghtons heartlessly plot to bring legal action against the impoverished Macartney (185).
28. "A father may by deed or will, dispose of the custody of his child, born or unborn, to any person"—except, apparently, the mother (Blackstone 203, 196). It was even legal for a testamentary guardian appointed by the late father to deprive a widowed mother of custody of her child (Teichman 42). Fathers gained the right to "free testamentary disposal of the custody of their minor children" in 1660 when "Charles II legally abolished the Court of Wards" (E. Pollak, "Guarding the Succession" 223).
29. "The birthmark's origin came to be illustrated by the French word *envie*, which literally means *desire*" (Huet 16).
30. On Aristotle see Gasking 27–30, Laqueur 30–59, and Merchant 157–62. For a summary of generation debates from Aristotle to the eighteenth century see Huet 37–45.
31. On Harvey see Gasking 16–36; Keller; Laqueur 142–47; Merchant 155–63; and Pagel, especially 270–82, 316, 320–21.
32. See Gasking 48, 56, and Needham 163, 168–70, 175, 205–11.
33. Though Caroline's wish that her daughter not "look [like] thy unfortunate mother" (339) is dashed, her greater desire for legitimation is achieved.
34. *Fatherless Fanny* was published after Reeve's death, but John K. Reeves suggests that the novel was adapted from and includes a ghost story Reeve wrote in 1787: *Castle Conner—an Irish Story*. The novel has also been attributed to Thomas Peckett Prest. The 1833 edition names "the late Miss Taylor" as the author (Garside and Shöwerling 1811).
35. Roche's novel was issued in eleven different editions between 1796 and 1832 (Blakey 57–58). Coleridge called Bennett's seven-volume work of

over two thousand pages "the best novel me judice [*sic*] since Fielding" (Blakey 54). Also see Blakey, appendix IV.

36. *Louisa* and *Celestina* borrow names from *Evelina*. Louisa calls herself Louisa Villars, and her father is named Belmont; characters named Willoughby and Lady Howard play central roles in *Celestina*.

37. Louisa's problems stem from her mother's guardian, Mr. Rivers, who tries to seduce her mother, separates her from her husband, tells each that the other is dead, and sends Louisa out into the world as an orphan. In *The Beggar Girl*, the grandfather tells the heroine's mother that her husband and daughter are dead and then persuades her to marry again, making her "an innocent adulteress" (VI, 330); like the grandfathers in *Louisa*, *Celestina*, and *Fatherless Fanny*, he is responsible for the heroine's presumed orphanhood. Though in *Children of the Abbey* much of the blame for the heroine's suffering falls on the grandfather's second wife, Lady Dunreath, the various patriarchs are faulted for their impotence. *Fatherless Fanny* traces several generations of patriarchal abuse. The heroine's great-grandfather imprisons her grandmother and leaves her to die (72–75). After her daughter—the heroine's mother—marries against the ruling patriarch's wishes, he separates her from her husband and forces her to marry the Bluebeard of Ireland, who "shut[s] [her] up for days together, without provision . . . drag[s] her by the hair of her head from one apartment to another" (79), and tries to poison her.

38. On the dangers of childbirth see Rogers, "Eighteenth Century." For a broader summary of mother-daughter plots in English and French epistolary novels by women see Alliston, especially chapters 3 and 4.

39. In *The Beggar Girl*, Rosa is more than once described as looking exactly as her father did before his face was deformed by illness (II, 180 and 264), but he recognizes her on the basis of her similarity to her mother: "That you are mine, Rosa, I need no proof. . . . Your resemblance to your noble mother, and the sound of your voice, so familiar and precious to my aural faculties, first attracted and then rivetted my regard" (VII, 401). Celestina resembles her father (IV, 295), but she also looks and sounds like her maternal cousin (IV, 226) and is recognized by her birthmarks (IV, 294).

CHAPTER 2

1. For an excellent overview of Radcliffe's achievement and place in literary criticism see Deborah Rogers, introduction, *Critical Response*.

2. Also see Sprengnether 183, and de Lauretis, *Practice of Love* 172.

3. Although she maintains that "the fantasmatic relation to the mother and the maternal/female body is central to lesbian subjectivity and

desire" (*Practice of Love* 171), de Lauretis is otherwise critical of the "homosexual-maternal fantasy," arguing that it elides the differences among women, particularly the sexual differences that pertain to lesbianism (see esp. *Practice of Love* 53, 182–83, 185–86, 190, 195, 198).

4. Sedgwick criticizes Irigaray's use of "homosexual": the male "homosexuality [Irigaray discusses] turns out to represent anything but actual sex between men" (*Between Men* 26). For Sedgwick, homosocial relations include, but are not limited to, homosexual ones (*Between Men* 1–2).

5. Critics routinely note Freud's uncertainty about the daughter's rejection of the mother; see, for instance, Sprengnether, 159–61 and Rose, *Sexuality* 43–45.

6. The most famous of Freud's allusions to female homosexuality can be found in "Some Psychological Consequences of the Anatomical Distinction Between the Sexes" (183) and in a footnote to his analysis of Dora (*Dora* 142n). In "The Psychogenesis of a Case of Homosexuality in a Woman" Freud argues that female homosexual desire signals a woman's masculine orientation. "The essential thing" here, Irigaray writes, "is to show that the object choice of the homosexual woman is determined by a *masculine* desire and tropism" (*Speculum* 99; see also her *This Sex* 37, 43, 65). "Hence," J. Butler complains, "there is no homosexuality, and only opposites attract" (*Gender Trouble* 61); also see de Lauretis, *Practice of Love* 31, 43–45, 57. There are many discussions of Freud's treatment of Dora, among them Rose, *Sexuality* 41–47, and Sprengnether 41–54.

7. See de Lauretis, *Practice of Love* 195, and Roof 103–8. Other critics have questioned Chodorow's idealization of the preoedipal mother and her theoretical inability to challenge the terms of sexual differentiation; see Doane and Hodges 33–52; de Lauretis, *Practice of Love* 62n; Sprengnether 189, 193–94. What interests me most, however, is Chodorow's invaluable suggestion that the daughter's attachment to her mother complicates her entrance into heterosexuality. Other feminist theorists have been more explicit about the homoerotic implications of the daughter's love, but they are working with a similar premise.

8. Kristeva describes the lesbian dimension of mother-daughter love as a form of psychosis; see *Desire* 239 and 279. For critiques of Kristeva's account of lesbianism and mother-daughter relations, see J. Butler, *Gender Trouble* 84–88; de Lauretis, *Practice of Love* 72, 179, 197; and Roof 94–103.

9. See Castle, *Apparitional Lesbian* 71, 122.

10. See de Lauretis, *Practice of Love* 62–63, and Roof 108–18.

11. For a summary of the problems with Rich, see de Lauretis, *Practice of Love* 190–92.

12. Also see Haggerty; C. L. Johnson, *Equivocal Beings* 47–69; and Nussbaum 141–49.

13. Also see M. A. Doane 43–46.

14. Susan Lanser argues that many women writers of the period "represent the female body as the object of another woman's gaze" (192).

15. Mary Ann Doane describes female spectatorship as either trapped in "a kind of narcissism" (45) or locked in the "same logic" as the male gaze, performing a "male striptease" that "simply reinforces the dominant system of aligning sexual difference with a subject/object dichotomy" (44); also see 48.

16. See my summary of critical trends in "Veiled Desire" 73, 86–87n. 1. For a good example of recent attention to the role of maternal longing in the "female Gothic" see Haggerty 66–70.

17. I retain the problematic preoedipal/oedipal hierarchy in discussing *The Italian* because the novel represents Ellena's attachment to her mother as an early stage of development, occurring before familial terms and rules have been defined.

18. In her analysis of *The Italian*'s portrait of the old regime, C. L. Johnson notes a similar movement from a progressive to a conservative plot; see *Equivocal Beings* 123 and 128–29.

19. On the image of the veil, see C. L. Johnson's illuminating discussion of how the "recurrent gestures of unveiling and exposure work in intertextual counterpoint to Burke's *Reflections*" (*Equivocal Beings* 125–27); also see Broadwell, and Sedgwick, *Coherence* 140–75. For the multiple meanings of veils in eighteenth-century novels, see Nussbaum 124.

20. We learn only that "Ellena had been struck by the spirit and dignity of his air, and by his countenance" (9). We also know that the "pleadings of her . . . heart" urged her to receive him as an admirer (36). In both window scenes, Ellena calls out Vivaldi's name in a love trance. But none of these moments is presented from the same close view used to describe Vivaldi's desire for Ellena. It is only later, when Ellena first sees her mother, that the text offers a sustained account of her perspective.

21. This may explain why the Marchesa unknowingly wears a robe Ellena sewed (9).

22. Kristeva writes that "voice, hearing, and sight are the archaic dispositions where the earliest forms of discreteness emerge" (*Desire* 283); also see Silverman, *Acoustic Mirror* 80.

23. Ellena's and Olivia's unconscious familial recognition evokes the seventeenth- and eighteenth-century French dramatic convention known as "le cri du sang" or "la voix de la nature." For the history of representations of "an instinctive knowledge of consanguinity" between characters "who may never have seen each other," see Clifton Cherpack. Of particular relevance for both *The Italian* and *The Monk* is Cherpack's suggestion

that such recognition scenes often "depended upon confusion or conflict between the force of blood and the force of sexual love" (3).

24. I am indebted to Shawn Alexander for this insight. Also note that Antonia has "long fair hair, which descended in ringlets to her waist" (9)—like Milton's Eve, the sister who became the mother of mankind. Similarly Matilda, who looks like the Madonna, describes herself as a sister when recounting her passion for the Monk (59).

25. On the "ironic justice" of Ambrosio's violence against his mother see H. Anderson xiv.

26. On Radcliffe's inversion of Lewis's "enjoy[ment] and collu[sion] in the Promethean grossness of [Ambrosio's] crimes" see C. L. Johnson, *Equivocal Beings* 128.

27. Ruth Perry intriguingly suggests that the gothic novel's preoccupation with heterosexual incest is symptomatic of a rise in its actual incidence as kinship was increasingly defined by affinity rather than consanguinity; see Perry, "Incest."

Chapter 3

1. On this point, see B. Anderson.

2. On the rise of the science of population see Foucault 25–26, and Jordanova, "Interrogating the Concept" 382. For a fuller summary of the intersections among nationalism, colonialism, and the science of population, their effect on representations of maternity, and the influence of Thomas Malthus, see my introduction, *Inventing Maternity* 13–14.

3. "For complex reasons—including the spread of industrialism and urbanization, increases in immigration, and the cost of wars against France, especially over colonial territories—the numbers of poor people in England were rising, as were the debates about how to manage them" (Greenfield, introduction, *Inventing Maternity* 14).

4. Schiebinger suggests that Carolus Linnaeus's taxonomic coining of the term "mammalia" (based on milk-producing mammae) reflects the idealization of maternal breastfeeding throughout Europe (40–42, 69–70). For some of the many valuable discussions of eighteenth-century maternal breastfeeding, see the introductory chapter, n. 3.

5. Amusingly, Cadogan concludes his pamphlet with language ambiguous enough to suggest that he himself has breastfed a child: "I am a Father, and have already practised it with the most desirable Success" (34). For analysis of this passage see Kowaleski-Wallace 103.

6. On the history of the London Foundling Hospital see McClure. Nussbaum 27, and Bowers, *Politics* 10 discuss the Foundling Hospital and the economics of abandonment.

7. Also see Fildes, *Breasts* 102, 104, and Trumbach, *Rise* 202.
8. On Wollstonecraft and motherhood see Barker-Benfield, *Culture of Sensibility* 279–86; C. L. Johnson, "Mary Wollstonecraft"; C. Kaplan, "Pandora's Box" 158; Langbauer; Maurer; Perry, "Colonizing" 217; Poovey, *Proper Lady* 74–75.
9. For an exquisitely detailed examination of the problem see Staves.
10. Virginia Sapiro notes that for Wollstonecraft "maternal bonding, so often considered natural, is like other social feelings, shaped by the social conditions of the relationships" (155).
11. One negative contemporary review of the *Rights of Woman* in the *Critical Review* debunked Wollstonecraft for arguing that "there is no characteristic difference in sex" (Janes 296).
12. For a good corrective to this feminist critique see Anna Wilson's discussion of the historical context for Wollstonecraft's ideological development.
13. Wollstonecraft is openly concerned about male homosexuality; see her complaint that men in Italy and Portugal "attend the levees of equivocal beings, to sigh for more than female languor" (*VRW* 138); on Wollstonecraft's homophobia see C. L. Johnson, *Equivocal Beings* 11–12, 24, 47–48.
14. On Wollstonecraft's denunciation of female sexuality and erotic pleasure see C. Kaplan, "Wild Nights" 34–50 and "Pandora's Box," and Poovey, *Proper Lady* 74–75.
15. See C. Kaplan, "Pandora's Box" 158, and Poovey, *Proper Lady* 74–75.
16. On Wollstonecraft's critique of male desire see Poovey, *Proper Lady* 73, 74, and C. Kaplan, "Wild Nights" 43–46, 52, 54.
17. In the *Rights of Men* Wollstonecraft writes, "the tenderest mothers are often the most unhappy wives" (132).
18. Felicity Nussbaum notes that although Wollstonecraft does not explicitly contrast the African and English woman, "the implication is there" (93).
19. Wollstonecraft's depiction of the ease with which victims were incarcerated in insane asylums "by greedy relatives" is accurate; see Todd, *Mary Wollstonecraft* 427.
20. Todd offers an interesting account of Imlay's "intrusion" into the novel (*Mary Wollstonecraft* 431–32).
21. See Joan Scott's excellent account of how the tension between sameness and difference shaped feminist discourse from its inception (*Only Paradoxes to Offer* ix–xii and 1–18).
22. Gary Kelly, the editor of *Mary and the Wrongs of Woman,* points out that Venables's avoidance of violence hinders Maria's grounds for legal separation; the law required that a wife supply evidence of spousal abuse (*WW* 227n).

23. In one version of the ending it appears that Maria's brother was also involved in the kidnapping (*WW* 203).
24. In her valuable discussion of female reproduction and writing in *Wrongs*, Laurie Langbauer discusses the Minerva-Jove reference and the significance of "confinement."
25. "A father has no other power over his son's estate, than as his trustee or guardian, for though he may receive the profits during the child's minority, he must account for them, when he comes of age" (Blackstone 196). Maria's uncle does not even make Venables the guardian.
26. The detail is autobiographical: Wollstonecraft's eldest brother was the only one her mother nursed (Todd, *Mary Wollstonecraft* 4). In *Mary*, the heroine, like Maria, is "pain[ed]" by her mother's "partiality to her brother" (8). It is only when her brother dies and Mary becomes the heiress that her "mother began to think her of consequence" (12). Henry (who is a younger son) suffers the same kind of maternal neglect (34).
27. In his notes for the novel, Gary Kelly points out that Godwin amended this passage to indicate that since the case is tried in civil court and concerns only the damages for adultery, the judge can grant neither a separation (which would be handled by an ecclesiastical court) nor a divorce (which required an act of Parliament and was rarely allowed [*WW* 230–31n]). But Godwin's need to tamper with the text suggests that Wollstonecraft either was not concerned with these civil restrictions or meant to stress Maria's right to a separation (*WW* 196) and a divorce (*WW* 198) despite the judge's limitations.
28. In much of the analysis that follows, I am indebted to Claudia Johnson's "Mary Wollstonecraft," which discusses the rejection of heterosexuality in *Wrongs*.
29. The mother-daughter bond also displaces heterosexuality in *Mary*. Mary develops a "tenderness" and "compassion" for her neglectful mother that becomes the "governing propensity of her heart through life" (5), shaping her love for both Ann and Henry. Like Mary's mother, each of these characters becomes fatally ill, and in each case Mary nurses them. Before dying, Henry asks his own mother to "adopt" Mary (63). By mothering a man who resembles her mother, Mary finally secures one.
30. Janet Todd notes that Maria's history is marked both by a "circular and repetitive" movement that "binds her to male relationships" and by a "linear and developmental" movement "towards freedom and maturity" (*Women's Friendship* 211–12).
31. Wollstonecraft enjoyed and reviewed *The Italian*.
32. Haggerty argues that "the fragments suggest the force of narrative convention. Any . . . ending that did not accept the culturally sanctioned terms of closure would be mere fantasy" (119).
33. Wollstonecraft had no cause to worry about her custody of Fanny Imlay,

as mothers had legal custody of illegitimate children (*Great Britain Parliamentary Debates*, vols. 39–41, col. 1089). It may be significant, though, that she wrote the letter at a time when she was posing as Imlay's wife.

CHAPTER 4

1. For an overview of Malthus's *Essay* and its impact on perceptions of female fertility see my introduction, *Inventing Maternity* 13–14, and Anita Levy. Julie Costello considers Malthus's influence on Edgeworth; also see Jacobus 86–96.
2. Citing the *OED*, Colin and Jo Atkinson argue that "freak" does not refer to monstrosity or abnormality until the mid-nineteenth century (100); and Mitzi Meyers argues that "there was . . . a real Mrs. Freke" on whom the character is based (245n). But I would nevertheless suggest that the many references to monsters and deformity in *Belinda* raise the possibility that the text is one of the first to allude to "freak" in the modern sense.
3. L. Brown ("Romance") and M. W. Ferguson ("Juggling") each draw attention to this dialectic in *Oroonoko*. Similar theoretical formulations can be found in L. Brown, *Ends* 29–35, 199–200; Chaudhuri and Strobel; David 5, 77–117; Donaldson 1–31; Grewal and Kaplan 17–28; Hall 207; Nussbaum 1–7. For readings of Austen see Stewart and Moira Ferguson, "*Mansfield Park*."
4. See Kirkpatrick, "'Gentlemen'" and introduction, *Belinda;* Perera 15–34; and Moore, *Dangerous Intimacies* 75–108.
5. The peasant uprising, which began in May, was initially confined to Wexford, but in August a small group of French invaders incited the peasants in County Longford, where the Edgeworths lived. The invasion and rebellion were quickly suppressed, but Richard Edgeworth was subsequently accused of being a French spy (M. Butler, *Maria Edgeworth* 137–38).
6. England's war against France began in 1793 and continued with little intermission to 1815.
7. The term "miscegenation" was not current in the eighteenth century, but the concept had been established. See Margaret Ferguson, "News" 166–67. For general discussions of the relations among nation, sexuality, and race see Yuval-Davis and Anthias, and Williams and Chrisman 17, 193; for particular discussions of homosexuality see Parker et al. 6–7 and Mosse. Nussbaum examines the colonial implications of female homoeroticism (135–62).
8. In Pope's poem, Belinda's dressing table is covered with the spoils of empire; in addition to associating Lady Delacour's dressing ritual with

that described in the poem, *Belinda* alludes to other colonial products, such as a balsam discovered by a slave (75). Throughout, my reading of Pope's poem is influenced by L. Brown, *Pope* (esp. 13–14) and "Amazons" 126, and by Pollak, *Poetics* 77–107.

9. In 1812, Frances Burney wrote a horrifying account of the doctors who performed her mastectomy; anesthesia had not yet been invented. See Epstein, *Iron Pen* 53–83.

10. On the paternal family's supervision of childbirth in aristocratic households see J. S. Lewis 51–52.

11. Colin and Jo Atkinson suggest that Mrs. Freke marks Edgeworth's opposition to radical feminist thinkers like Wollstonecraft and Mary Hays (109). Similarly, Lisa Moore argues that through Harriet, Edgeworth "satirizes a whole cluster of proto-Romantic Jacobin ideas—feminism, domestic and political revolution, opposition to slavery, sexual freedom" ("'Something More Tender'" 505). I think Edgeworth's politics are more ambiguous. When she tries to kidnap Belinda in the name of the "Rights of Women" (229), Harriet can be read as a parody of Wollstonecraft. But the rationalist Henry Percival echoes Wollstonecraft in insisting that women "cultivate their minds" (233), and the account of his marriage to the well-educated Lady Anne reads like a passage from the *Rights of Woman*. She is "the chosen companion of her husband's understanding, as well as of his heart. . . . The partner of his warmest affections was also the partner of his most serious occupations" (216).

12. In this way, the transvestite figure differs little from the hermaphrodite, with whom she was linked in the cultural imagination. Juba calls Harriet a "*man-woman*" (219); in Charles Debierre's French treatise on hermaphroditism, hermaphrodites are described as "hommes-femmes" and "femme[s]-homme[s]" (qtd. in Epstein, "Either/Or" 122). See Moore ("'Something More Tender'" 508–9) on the significance of Juba's role as speaker here. In the eighteenth and nineteenth centuries hermaphrodites and female transvestites were sometimes subject to the same legal strictures. Both hermaphrodites who presented themselves as men but were judged to be "predominantly" female and biological women who cross-dressed could be legally charged with fraud (Epstein, "Either/Or" 124).

13. Castle discusses the homoerotic implications of "amazon" (*Apparitional Lesbian* 9). Meyers argues that readings (including my own) that suggest that Edgeworth's treatment of Harriet is "the mark of 'lesbian panic,'" . . . decontextualize literary strategies" (135, 245n).

14. Lady Delacour flirts with men, including the novel's hero, Clarence Hervey, but she is more emotionally involved with women. Clarence himself is described as "all things to all men—and to all women" (14), and in one scene he cross-dresses (75).

15. In addition to the genital connotations of "rod," the term was commonly associated with sexual flagellation by the mid-eighteenth century (Gibson 16).
16. Also see Moore, *Dangerous Intimacies* 97.
17. Lord Delacour later gains similar control over his uppity servant, exclaiming, "I'll show him I can be master, and will, in my own house" (262).
18. Despite his earlier dissipation, Clarence Hervey becomes such a pedantic spokesman of conduct-book virtues that Lady Delacour likens his letters to "Fordyce's Sermons for Young Women" (271).
19. Kowaleski-Wallace offers an excellent interpretation of the domestic significance of Lady Delacour's cure (110–11, 125–29). In the original sketch of *Belinda,* Lady Delacour's early death proves that there is no easy cure for her ambiguous body and failed maternity. For more on the differences between the sketch and the novel see my "'Abroad and at Home'" 214.
20. Hall describes England's mid-nineteenth-century tendency to root an English identity in assumptions about Jamaican difference (208, 209).
21. The connection between English women and slaves anticipates the one Moira Ferguson notes in *Mansfield Park* ("*Mansfield Park*"). I make a similar argument about *Mansfield Park* in "Fanny's Misreading" 318–19. For a general approach to the joint commodification of English women and slaves, see L. Brown, *Ends* 20–21.
22. Acquired from the French in 1763 and declared a separate colony the year that America began its revolution, Saint Vincent was subject to bouts of unrest, the most serious of which occurred when the French inspired the Caribs to revolt in 1795 (Burns 505–6, 570–72; Ward 38, 91).
23. Perera (31) and Kirkpatrick (Edgeworth, *Belinda* 495n; "'Gentlemen'" 334, 344–45) also discuss the problem of Mr. Vincent's race.
24. The depiction of Juba might be read in relation to that of Caesar, the slave featured in "The Grateful Negro" (1804), a story Edgeworth published shortly after *Belinda* that contrasts two Jamaican slave owners. The brutal Mr. Jefferies is distinguished from the good Mr. Edwards, who disapproves of slavery but believes "that the sudden emancipation of the negroes would . . . increase . . . their miseries." Mr. Edwards adopts a benevolent plan for his slaves' "amelioration" (195) consistent with the one Edgeworth's father applied to his Irish tenants (on Edgeworthstown see M. Butler, *Maria Edgeworth* 85–87, and Hurst 30–31). Caesar is so grateful to Mr. Edwards that he ultimately risks his life to save the planter in a slave revolt. "The Grateful Negro" was produced during a period when abolitionist legislation was defeated in England and there was a lull in antislavery activities (Blackburn 150; Moira Ferguson, *Subject* 249–50). Even William Wilberforce, the leading advocate of abolition

in Parliament, abandoned the annual abolition bill between 1799 and 1804 (Blackburn 150). Edgeworth's story criticizes both slavery and sudden abolition and suggests that benevolent paternalism reaps its own rewards.

25. In *Cato,* Juba is an apologist for Roman imperialism and is rewarded with the love of Cato's daughter. In the original edition of *Belinda,* Juba marries a white woman (discussed in text below). I thank Luis Gamez for suggesting the relevance of *Cato.*

26. In "curing" Juba of his belief in obeah, Belinda could be said to help "civilize" the colonial other, the role typically associated with the nineteenth-century domestic woman; see David, especially 111–17; Poovey, *Uneven Developments* 194–97.

27. For good discussions of obeah see Bush 74–77 and Patterson 265. Obeah is associated with slave resistance in "The Grateful Negro."

28. The 1772 Mansfield Decision, which some believed outlawed the owning of slaves in England, was notoriously confusing and ineffective.

29. Perera 30–32 discusses the importance of the poem. Mitzi Meyers offers a rich and informative account of Edgeworth's experience with Day and of her complex treatment of him in *Belinda.*

30. See also Shyllon 100. For other discussions of the threat of miscegenation in *Belinda,* see Kirkpatrick, introduction, *Belinda* xxii–xxiii, xxxi–xxxii, and "'Gentlemen.'"

31. See Long 265–66, Burns 551, and Stewart 92. Kirkpatrick discusses the relation between miscegenation and the management of colonial wealth in *Belinda* ("'Gentlemen'" 345–47). Lord Delacour is also a gambler, but his behavior does not raise the same colonial concerns, and it is brought under control as Lady Delacour recovers.

32. In *Castle Rackrent,* Thady describes the Jewish bride as "little better than a blackamoor" (76; see also 77). Felsenstein documents the widespread eighteenth-century English representation of the Jew as "the ultimate paradigm of the eternal Other," "whose unsettling presence serves to define the bounds that separate the native Englishman from the alien" (247, 3).

33. Virginia is not her original name. Clarence changed it to Virginia in homage to *Paul et Virginie,* a novel set in Mauritius (then a French colony). In *Paul et Virginie,* the heroine's sympathy for a brutalized slave collapses their differences; thus Paul wants to fight the slave's master on Virginia's behalf (Saint-Pierre 36–55, 91). Thomas Day, the author of *The Dying Negro,* tried and failed to raise a country bride. Edgeworth had personal reasons to be critical of Day, who had told her father not to allow her to publish her work (M. Butler, *Maria Edgeworth* 149; Meyers). Others have noted Edgeworth's disapproval of Clarence (Kowaleski-Wallace 100; Mellor 43–44; Shaffer 61–62; Spencer 161–62).

34. Even Clarence knows that gratitude is inappropriate for a potential wife, and he urges Virginia "not [to] consider me . . . your master" (399). As Meyers notes, Virginia's "grotesquely exaggerate[ed]" readiness "to immolate herself on the altar of gratitude" calls the "virtue" into question (112; see also 111).
35. In one advertisement, for instance, slaves named "Common Strop" and "Superior Strop" debate the product's merits (McKendrick et al. 157). The "rod of iron" with which Marriott controls Lady Delacour is relevant in this context. On Belinda's resistance to commodification, see MacFadyen 430.
36. In "The Grateful Negro," Jamaican slaves revolt when the master is brutal.

CHAPTER 5

1. Shortly after Wollstonecraft died, William Godwin published *Memoirs of the Author of a Vindication of the Rights of Woman* (1798), which disclosed the details of Wollstonecraft's premarital affairs and suicide attempts. Subsequently, "no woman novelist, even among the most progressive, wished to be discredited by association with" her (C. L. Johnson, *Jane Austen* xxiii; see also 19–21). On Opie's friendship with Godwin and Wollstonecraft see St. Clair, especially 164–65 and Todd, *Mary Wollstonecraft*, esp. 382; of Opie's growing disapproval of the couple see St. Clair 174, and Todd, *Mary Wollstonecraft* 421–22. Though scholars have noted Opie's invocation of Wollstonecraft, Todd interestingly suggests that the insane asylum in *Wrongs* partly derives from Wollstonecraft's talks with Opie, "who, as a morbid young girl, was obsessed with insanity" (*Mary Wollstonecraft* 427).
2. On the exclusivity of the family privileged by psychoanalysis see Wexler 159. Another problem, as Claudia Tate explains, is that psychoanalysis has conventionally "avoided examining the relationship of social oppression to family dysfunction and the blighted inner worlds of individuals. . . . Hence, there is hardly a leap between shifting the blame from the social trauma of chronic racism to pathologizing the black family, as the infamous *Moynihan Report* does" (16–17). Decades ago, Frantz Fanon pointed to the inadequacy of the familial model to describe black psychological experience: "A normal Negro child, having grown up within a normal family, will become abnormal on the slightest contact with the white world" (143).
3. Jean Walton's examination of the repression of racial information in early psychoanalytic case studies is excellent. On the emergence of

psychoanalysis in "historical relation to imperialism" see McClintock 74; also see B. Johnson 10–11.

4. Foucault suggests that the idealized mother necessarily generates her "negative image" (104).

5. Howard's attention to Savanna's maternal role and the novel's ultimately conservative effort to unite sentimental abolitionism and moral motherhood is excellent and highly relevant to my discussion. Also see Nussbaum 45. On nursemaids and nannies in the West Indies see Patterson 58–59, 62; on women's field work see Bush 36–38. These issues are discussed in more detail in the section entitled "The Mulatto."

6. Thus, by professing "her unbounded love for the great family of the world," Mrs. Mowbray can overlook the extent to which she allows "her own family to pine under the consciousness of neglect" (3).

7. Adeline resembles Richardson's Clarissa Harlowe in her emphatic literalism and preoccupation with the compatibility of theory and practice. In *Clarissa*, Anna Howe apologizes to the heroine for having temporarily doubted that "*theory and practice* were not the same thing with my beloved Clarissa Harlowe" (1150).

8. The passage echoes Opie's elegy to her own mother, "In Memory of My Mother" (1791, pub. 1834):

> I heard thee speak in accents kind,
>
> And promptly praise, or firmly chide;
>
> Again admir'd that vigorous mind
>
> Of power to charm, reprove, and guide.
>
> Hark! clearer still thy voice I hear!
>
> Again reproof, in accents mild,
>
> Seems whispering in my conscious ear,
>
> And pains, yet soothes, thy kneeling child!

Here the mother's words become her embodied replacement. Just as Mrs. Mowbray's books enter Adeline's heart, Opie is "joy'd to think some words of truth / sunk in my soul, and teach me still."

9. We can count Locke among the many who preceded Lacan in discussing the gap between word and thing. In *An Essay Concerning Human Understanding*, Locke warns that one "great *abuse of words is, the taking of them for things*. . . . [W]e should have a great many fewer disputes in the world, if words were taken for what they are, the signs of our ideas only, and not for things themselves" (442, 444).

10. In this Adeline resembles the melancholic child Kristeva describes, who

"becomes irredeemably sad before uttering his first words; this is because he has been irrevocably, desperately separated from the mother, a loss that causes him to try to find her again, along with other objects of love, first in the imagination, then in words" (*Black Sun* 6).

11. The heroine's insistence on the irrelevance of social norms is reminiscent of Wollstonecraft, who wrote Opie that "my conduct in life must be directed by my own judgment" (Brightwell 60).

12. Several times the narrative generalizes about the problem of women's bodily competition; see 18, 239, 245.

13. The curse marks another pointed reference to *Clarissa*. Clarissa's father curses her after she leaves his house and begins living with Lovelace, and Clarissa is tormented by his words for the short remainder of her life. As is typical of women's novels of the period, *Adeline Mowbray* alludes to the earlier novel to feminize it, changing the father's curse to a mother's curse. Also, whereas Clarissa never sees either of her parents again and is particularly pained by her alienation from her mother, Adeline and Mrs. Mowbray are reunited at the novel's end. Though obstructed in each novel, the mother-daughter relationship is ultimately not quite as bleak in *Adeline Mowbray*.

14. Like *Roxana*, *Adeline Mowbray* also introduces a Quaker woman (Mrs. Pemberton) toward the novel's end.

15. Margaret Homans's discussion of the historical affiliation of race with nature, essence, and ground influences my interpretation of Savanna's materiality; see her "'Racial Composition.'" Barbara Christian points out that "the mammy figure . . . in southern white literature" is "magnificently physical," and that it is exactly this physicality that the ideal white woman must expel in herself (2); the same could be said of Savanna and Adeline.

16. Toward the novel's end, for instance, Colonel Mordaunt and Mrs. Pemberton search for Adeline and Savanna, whom they view as externally analogous because of their differentiated skin: "a mulatto [and] a lady just recovered from the small-pox . . . were easily traced" (263). But they discover Adeline not by her bodily marks but her superior status when she alone is identified as "a poor sick young gentlewoman [who] . . . looks like a lady for certain" (267).

17. That critics can attend to the servant Freud repressed is another example of their using psychoanalytic theories to analyze psychoanalysis. For a provocative discussion of Freud's preoccupation with his own nanny and his repression of his feelings for her in designing his oedipal theory, see McClintock 87–95.

18. On the practice of delegating mixed-race slave women for child care see Christian 3–4, Patterson 61–62, and Prince 69. On the Ameri-

can iconization of the mammy see Christian 2–5 and Collins 70–73; for details about black women's domestic servitude in the post–Civil War American South see Jones 127–22. Because slavery did not exist in England proper, the mammy did not have the same institutional entrenchment there as in America. At the time of *Adeline Mowbray's* publication, the black female population was very small, and black women had difficulty securing domestic positions (Gerzina 75–76, 87). Nevertheless, there must have been a growing familiarity with the figure of the black nanny. In their slave narratives, for instance, both Mary Prince (76) and Harriet Jacobs (183) describe visiting England when working as nursemaids.

19. See McClintock 71–72, and Moglen 212–13.

20. Jennifer Brody makes a similar point about the effect of mixed-race female characters in Victorian literature (43).

21. This is generally true of the mulatto figure in literature, who, as Spillers puts it, was "created to provide a middle ground of latitude between 'black' and 'white'" ("Notes on an Alternative Model" 165).

22. Note the exchangeability of the characters; grammatically, "she was a mulatto" could refer to Adeline.

23. I am influenced by David's and Poovey's discussions of how, in the nineteenth century, women's charitable work was deployed in the service of empire; see David, especially 77–97, and Poovey, *Uneven Developments* 164–98.

24. See Howard's detailed discussion of the multiple meanings of the pineapple and of Opie's attention to "Britain's selfish and irresponsible consumption of the literal and metaphorical fruits of colonial lands" (359–62).

25. It is unclear whether Savannah was Indian or African, but one Briggs relative was anxious to avoid having her "bought or sold as a negro" (letter from William Briggs, August 23, 1749, cited in Brightwell 7–8). Howard also notes the autobiographical significance of Savanna.

26. This accords with the early modern stereotyping of black women as lascivious. See especially Bush 11–22, and Gilman's frequently cited article "Black Bodies, White Bodies."

27. The moment echoes the final fragment in *The Wrongs of Woman*, where Jemima brings Maria her daughter. Like *Roxana* before them, both novels suggest the need for servants physically to resolve the mother-daughter divide. But whereas Amy does so by killing the daughter, Jemima and Savanna reunite mother and child.

28. Once inducted into language, Editha articulates the endlessness of mother-daughter alienation. When the heroine tells her she will live in Mrs. Mowbray's beautiful house "when I am in my grave," the literal little girl innocently responds: "pray, mamma—pray be there soon!" (227).

Chapter 6

1. Freud did not invent the idea of the unconscious, which had already been evoked in poetry, philosophy, and nineteenth-century psychology (Austen herself uses the word in more than one novel), but he popularized it and gave it clinical definition (Mitchell 6 and Minsky 27). Juliet Mitchell's discussion of Freud's development of the unconscious remains very valuable (6–15). Rosalind Minsky makes the obvious but crucial point that "in spite of the criticisms of Freud's work, his theory of the unconscious and identity represents the monumental leap of the imagination from which all subsequent psychoanalytic theories have grown" (62; also see 26–27). Minsky's suggestion that in each major psychoanalytic school "the mother, explicitly or implicitly, stands at the centre of all identity and sexuality in the unconscious life of the child and adult" is especially relevant (21; 63 describes the loss of the mother). Also see E. Ann Kaplan, who writes that Freud's theory of the unconscious "produced the mother as the one through whom . . . the child, *become[s]* a subject" (*Motherhood* 8), and Mary Jacobus, who says that "the mother is at once the figure closeted in the unconscious and she who holds the door to it" (8). Although she does not directly discuss the unconscious, Patricia Spacks suggests that by the end of the eighteenth century, the novel form had invented the idea of "the energy of mind," a "sexualized, emotionalized transformation of intellect" that implies "a revolutionary conception of human psychology, not yet stated in . . . English philosophic or scientific discourse" (185). I would add that the intimation of the unconscious in *Emma* epitomizes the genre's role in revolutionizing human psychology and that this revolution depended on the creation of the preoedipal mother.

2. That other critics have already stressed the importance of maternal loss in *Emma* suggests the readiness with which the novel adapts to such an interpretation. See, for instance, Armstrong 154, and Restuccia's valuable "A Black Morning." I differ from Restuccia in viewing Emma's attempts to compensate for maternal absence as hopeless but not regressive; following Kristeva, Restuccia argues that Emma's inability "to master (the loss of) her mother" (458) is arrested and masochistic. For a contrasting examination of Emma's interest in "erotic domination" see Korba.

3. Susan Morgan also notes that while "Austen was never directly interested in villains . . . in all her other novels there is at least one man and one woman who are wicked" (81).

4. The concern with interior life is in keeping with Austen's much noted general rejection of external drama and attention to "the more difficult

and more subtle problem of how to understand those around us and ourselves" (Morgan 80).

5. *Emma* is commonly read as a conservative text, favoring old order economics. See, for instance, C. L. Johnson, *Jane Austen* 127, 130; and Tobin, "Aiding Impoverished Gentlewomen" 422 and "Moral and Political Economy" 229.

6. Though he does not discuss maternal absence in *Emma*, Paul Pickrel similarly suggests that each example of Emma's "snobbery" and socio-economic preoccupation actually disguises more pressing psychological concerns (300–301).

7. "Psychoanalysis has a normative ideological impact: it helps rationalize and naturalize the prevailing political and economic order by providing a psychological classification that makes institutionalized thought styles *in general* appear to be intimate aspects of 'my inner life' " (Winter 17; also see 52–53).

8. The only overt reference to colonialism occurs when Jane Fairfax likens the governess profession to the slave trade (300). Mrs. Elton's wealth is likely based in slavery, but the novel never states this directly; see Deforest. *Mansfield Park* is considerably more open in its discussion of Sir Thomas Bertram's Antiguan plantation.

9. It is commonplace for critics to suggest that in Austen's novels "political constructions are naturalized and therefore rendered invisible" (Finch and Bowen 2; also see Armstrong 158, 160; Moore, *Dangerous Intimacies* 110, 143; Tobin, "Aiding Impoverished Gentlewomen" 413). But there are also many studies that emphasize the political dynamics of Austen's novels; see especially Marilyn Butler's *Jane Austen and the War of Ideas* and Claudia Johnson's *Jane Austen: Women, Politics, and the Novel*, which reach different conclusions about Austen's ideological sympathies but similarly insist on the contemporary political resonance of her domestic details. Deirdre Lynch offers a highly original and convincing reading of the commercial complexities of Austen's psychological depth. Documenting Austen's "conscious" attention to "the mechanical part of novel writing, as well as the mechanical aspects of social life" (237), Lynch demonstrates "how Austen's novels position interiority at a relay point that articulates the personal with the mass produced" (210; see 207–49).

10. Elinor is, of course, prone to bouts of sensibility, epitomized when she listens to Willoughby's confession.

11. Morgan offers a particularly helpful explanation of the difference between *Clarissa*, which, for all "its emotional and psychological power . . . [is] a novel of principles" about a virtuous heroine (85), and *Emma*, in which the heroine is "too flawed and too modern to be a true heroine" (88). "In spite of Clarissa's difficulty in admitting her attraction to

Lovelace and her continual self-deception about that attraction, the action of the novel does not consist, even in part, of her movement to self-awareness. That simply is not what the novel is about" (85). "The true perfection of Clarissa has become the self-deception of Emma" (88).

12. Watt popularized this perspective in *The Rise of the Novel*. The problem of Watt's model and of the general scholarly tendency to chart the novel's origins in terms of Richardson and Fielding is the subject of much recent criticism; see especially Warner, "Formulating Fiction" and *Licensing Entertainment* 1–44. I preserve the formulation here because I find it particularly useful for appreciating Austen's narrative accomplishment.

13. Wayne Booth's estimation is also well known; see especially 253.

14. Austen is, if not the first English novelist to employ this technique, the first to do so consistently; see Cohn 108, Booth 245, and Watt 296–97. For other useful discussions of Austen's free indirect style see Finch and Bowen 4–8, 11; Flavin 51; Morgan 80; Pickrel 299, 302.

15. Marilyn Butler helpfully notes that Austen's "technical triumph is to . . . place the action almost wholly within the heroine's consciousness, to enlist . . . the reader's sympathy; and at the same time, largely through the medium of language, to invoke the reader's active suspicion of unaided thought" (*Jane Austen* 274; also see 264). Louise Flavin points out that of all Austen's heroines, Emma is most often represented in free indirect style (52). Though she does not discuss *Emma*, Eileen Gillooly notes "the affective closeness [Austen generally] sustains between her narrator and heroine, even when the latter is the object of narrative amusement" (80). See her book for a valuable analysis of the maternal role of narrative humor in Austen's novels and in a variety of nineteenth-century women's fiction.

16. For an excellent treatment of the problem of female reading in Austen see Uphaus.

17. Others have already observed the profusion of orphans; see, for instance, C. L. Johnson, *Jane Austen* 134, and Restuccia 452.

18. Offering an incisive reading of the problem posed by the ambiguous perspective here ("to whom did Emma 'seem' to unite these qualities?") Finch and Bowen suggest that the voice of *Emma* is that of the anonymous gossip, whose authority is "everywhere apparent but whose source is nowhere to be found" (6, 15). I would add that though the view is not rendered as Emma's own (see also Booth 257), it may include her perspective, or portions of it. After all, it is Emma who would know that she had only "an indistinct remembrance of her [mother's] caresses."

19. Critics often comment on the sequence of losses in *Emma;* see, for instance, Hirsch 58, and Restuccia 452.

20. Several studies address the problem of compulsory heterosexuality in

Emma and/or the novel's homoerotic implications; see C. L. Johnson, *Equivocal Beings* 192–94; Korba; Moore, *Dangerous Intimacies* 109–43; Perry, "Interrupted Friendships."

21. On Jane's fitness as heroine see Morgan 74. On the abundance of impoverished gentlewomen in the novel, see Tobin, "Aiding Impoverished Gentlewomen."

22. Tobin's "Moral and Political Economy" offers an excellent examination of Emma's peculiarly precarious socioeconomic position.

23. The resemblance between Emma and Mrs. Elton is commonly noted; see J. Brown 48, and Tobin, "Moral and Political Economy" 238–39.

24. Readers often note Emma's potential similarity to Miss Bates; see especially C. L. Johnson, *Jane Austen* 138–39. Emma tells Harriet that though she plans not to marry, "I shall not be a poor old maid" (85), but Knightley's comments suggest that if Emma remains single even she may one day sink "from the comforts she was born to." Such factors perhaps contribute to Emma's need to attack Miss Bates.

25. Claudia Johnson is eloquent on the insidiousness of gratitude; see *Jane Austen* 107–8.

26. On Miss Bates's social centrality see Flavin 50, 52, and J. Brown, who notes that "her small apartment joins the older gentry (the Woodhouses and Knightleys), the new rich (the Coles), and the lower-middle to lower-class townspeople and clerks" (55).

27. In this context Knightley's rebuke to Emma is especially telling. He reminds Emma that Miss Bates has known her "from an infant" and has "seen" her "grow up" (375). But unlike Emma, Miss Bates has a mother who has seen *her* grow up from infancy.

28. In addition to suggesting that the letters sounded by Emma's name spell "Ma," Restuccia makes the stunning point that Mrs. Woodhouse is "an uncanny name that fails to surface in the text" (460, 462).

29. This is easily seen as another example of the political mystification psychoanalysis and novels—Austen's in particular—tend to perform. As Finch and Bowen explain, Austen's "vision always involves such a moment of supreme ideological triumph" that disguises "the economic imperative [by bringing it] to bear on the very structure of desire" (2). Without denying such obfuscation, I mean to stress the historical significance of Austen's representation of maternity and the unconscious, which, however ideologically problematic, prefigure modern assumptions about identity with compelling precision.

30. Many feminist critics object to the marriage and deride Emma's concession to "the heterosexual narrative she has been represented as resisting all along" (Moore, *Dangerous Intimacies* 140); they describe Knightley as "authoritative and repressive" (Hirsch 63) and their relationship as "sadomasochistic" (Restuccia 466). Offering a more measured account,

Claudia Johnson describes Knightley as a "fantastically wishful creation of benign authority" (*Jane Austen* 141; see also 140, 142), which, to my mind, squares with his role as surrogate mother.

31. Minsky offers a similar assessment of Freud's understanding of female heterosexuality: "heterosexuality seems fundamentally to represent a return to the mother for both sexes" (69), offering "many women, despite the inequality implicit for them within its conscious meanings, the unconscious satisfaction of the very meaning it denies them in culture, desire for the mother" (71).

32. See Radway 119–56.

33. It solves broader socioeconomic problems as well by making Emma's money available for investment in Knightley's property. He is rich in land but not funds, as evidenced by his lack of a carriage. On the way the marriage "reconciles the competing claims of money and land" see Tobin, "Moral and Political Economy" 250, 254.

34. One might say the same of Shelley's *Frankenstein*. Though the creature technically has no mother, her absence is arguably the source of his suffering.

WORKS CITED

Abel, Elizabeth, Barbara Christian, and Helene Moglen. *Female Subjects in Black and White: Race, Psychoanalysis, Feminism.* Berkeley: Univ. of California Press, 1997.

Ackroyd, Peter. *Dickens.* New York: Harper Collins, 1990.

Addison, Joseph. *Cato. British Dramatists from Dryden to Sheridan.* Ed. George H. Nettleton. Boston: Houghton Mifflin, 1939. 477–503.

Allen, Dennis W. "Sexuality/Textuality in *Tristram Shandy.*" *Studies in English Literature* 25 (1985): 651–70.

Alliston, April. *Virtue's Faults: Correspondences in Eighteenth-Century British and French Women's Fiction.* Stanford: Stanford Univ. Press, 1996.

Anderson, Benedict. *Imagined Communities.* London and New York: Verso, 1991.

Anderson, Howard. Introduction. Lewis v–xxiv.

Aristotle. *Poetics.* Trans. Gerald F. Elsc. Ann Arbor: Univ. of Michigan Press, 1970.

Armstrong, Nancy. *Desire and Domestic Fiction: A Political History of the Novel.* New York: Oxford Univ. Press, 1987.

Atkinson, Colin B., and Jo Atkinson. "Maria Edgeworth, *Belinda*, and Women's Rights." *Eire Ireland* 19 (1984): 94–118.

Austen, Jane. *The Novels of Jane Austen.* 5 vols. Ed. R. W. Chapman. London: Oxford, 1971.

Backscheider, Paula R., ed. *Revising Women: Eighteenth-Century "Women's Fiction" and Social Engagement.* Baltimore: Johns Hopkins Univ. Press, 2000.

———. "The Novel's Gendered Space." *Revising Women* 1–30.

———. "The Rise of Gender as Political Category." *Revising Women* 31–57.

Ballaster, Ros. *Seductive Forms: Women's Amatory Fiction from 1684 to 1740.* Oxford: Clarendon Press, 1992.

Barker-Benfield, G. J. *The Culture of Sensibility: Sex and Society in Eighteenth-Century Britain.* Chicago: Univ. of Chicago Press, 1992.
———. "Mary Wollstonecraft: Eighteenth-Century Commonwealthwoman."
Journal of the History of Ideas 50 (1989): 95–115.
Bennett, Agnes Maria. *The Beggar Girl and Her Benefactors.* London: Minerva Press, 1797.
Blackburn, Robin. *The Overthrow of Colonial Slavery, 1776–1848.* London: Verso, 1988.
Blackstone, William. *Blackstone's Commentaries on the Law.* From the Abridged Edition of Wm. Hardcastle Browne. Ed. Bernard C. Gavit. Washington, D.C.: Washington Law Book Co., 1941.
Blakey, Dorothy. *The Minerva Press, 1790–1820.* Oxford: Bibliographical Society of the Univ. Press, 1939.
Bloch, Ruth H. "American Feminine Ideals in Transition: The Rise of the Moral Mother, 1785–1815." *Feminist Studies* 4 (1978): 101–26.
Bloom, Harold, ed. *Jane Austen's* Emma. New York: Chelsea, 1987.
Booth, Wayne. *The Rhetoric of Fiction.* Chicago: Univ. of Chicago Press, 1961.
Bowers, Toni. "'A Point of Conscience': Breastfeeding and Maternal Authority in *Pamela,* Part 2." Greenfield and Barash 138–58.
———. *The Politics of Motherhood: British Writing and Culture, 1680–1760.* New York: Cambridge Univ. Press, 1996.
Brightwell, Cecilia Lucy. *Memorials of the Life of Amelia Opie.* 2nd ed. London: Longman, Brown and Co., 1854.
Broadwell, Elizabeth P. "The Veil Image in Ann Radcliffe's *The Italian.*" *South Atlantic Bulletin* 40 (1975): 76–87.
Brody, Jennifer DeVere. *Impossible Purities: Blackness, Femininity, and Victorian Culture.* Durham: Duke Univ. Press, 1998.
Brown, Homer Obed. *Institutions of the English Novel: From Defoe to Scott.* Philadelphia: Univ. of Pennsylvania Press, 1997.
———. "Prologue: Why the Story of the Origin of the (English) Novel is an American Romance (If Not the Great American Novel)." Lynch and Warner 11–43.
Brown, Julia Pewitt. "Civilization and the Contentment of *Emma.*" Bloom 45–66.
Brown, Laura. *Alexander Pope.* Oxford: Basil Blackwell, 1985.
———. "Amazons and Africans: Gender, Race, and Empire in Daniel Defoe." Hendricks and Parker 118–37.
———. *Ends of Empire: Women and Ideology in Early Eighteenth-Century English Literature.* Ithaca: Cornell Univ. Press, 1993.
———. "The Romance of Empire: *Oroonoko* and the Trade in Slaves." *The New Eighteenth Century: Theory, Politics, English Literature.* Ed. Felicity Nussbaum and Laura Brown. New York: Methuen, 1987. 41–61.
Buchan, William. *Advice to Mothers on the Subject of Their Own Health; and on*

the Means of Promoting the Health, Strength, and Beauty of Their Offspring. Philadelphia: printed and sold by John Bioren, 1804.

Buhle, Mari Jo. *Feminism and Its Discontents: A Century of Struggle with Psychoanalysis.* Cambridge: Harvard Univ. Press, 1998.

Burney, Frances. "Dedication to Doctor Burney." *The Wanderer; or Female Difficulties.* London: Pandora Press, 1988. xvii–xxiii.

———. *Evelina, or the History of a Young Lady's Entrance into the World.* Ed. Edward A. Bloom. Oxford: Oxford Univ. Press, 1968.

Burns, Sir Alan. *History of the British West Indies.* London: George Allen & Unwin, 1965.

Burt, Alfred LeRoy. *The British Empire and Commonwealth from the American Revolution.* Boston: D. C. Heath and Co., 1956.

Bush, Barbara. *Slave Women in Caribbean Society, 1650–1838.* Bloomington: Indiana Univ. Press, 1990.

Butler, Judith. *Gender Trouble: Feminism and the Subversion of Identity.* New York: Routledge, 1990.

———. "Passing, Queering: Nella Larsen's Psychoanalytic Challenge." Abel et al. 266–84.

Butler, Marilyn. Introduction. *Castle Rackrent and Ennui.* By Maria Edgeworth. New York: Penguin, 1992.

———. *Jane Austen and the War of Ideas.* Oxford: Oxford Univ. Press, 1987.

———. *Maria Edgeworth: A Literary Biography.* Oxford: Clarendon Press, 1972.

Cadogan, William. *Essay upon Nursing, and the Management of Children from Their Birth to Three Years of Age.* London: printed for J. Roberts, 1749.

Campbell, Gina. "Bringing Belmont to Justice: Burney's Quest for Paternal Recognition in *Evelina.*" *Eighteenth-Century Fiction* 3 (1991): 321–40.

Campbell, Jill. "'The Exact Picture of his Mother': Recognizing Joseph Andrews." *ELH* 55 (1988): 643–64.

Cash, Arthur. "The Birth of Tristram Shandy: Sterne and Dr. Burton." *Studies in the Eighteenth Century.* Ed. R. F. Brissenden. Toronto: Univ. of Toronto Press, 1968. 133–54.

Castle, Terry J. "'Amy, Who Knew My Disease': A Psychosexual Pattern in Defoe's *Roxana.*" *ELH* 46 (1979): 81–96.

———. *The Apparitional Lesbian: Female Homosexuality and Modern Culture.* New York: Columbia Univ. Press, 1993.

Cervantes, Miguel de. *The Illustrious Kitchen-Maid. Exemplary Novels III.* Trans. Michael and Jonathan Thacker. Warminster, U.K.: Aris & Philips, 1992.

———. *The Little Gypsy Girl. Exemplary Novels I.* Trans. Michael and Jonathan Thacker. Warminster, U.K.: Aris & Philips, 1992.

Chaudhuri, Nupur, and Margaret Strobel, eds. *Western Women and Imperialism: Complicity and Resistance.* Bloomington: Indiana Univ. Press, 1992.

Cherpack, Clifton. *The Call of Blood in French Classical Tragedy.* Baltimore: Johns Hopkins Univ. Press, 1958.

Chodorow, Nancy. *The Reproduction of Mothering: Psychoanalysis and the Sociology of Gender.* Berkeley: Univ. of California Press, 1978.

Christian, Barbara. *Black Feminist Criticism: Perspectives on Black Women Writers.* New York: Pergamon Press, 1985.

Clément, Catherine. *The Lives and Legends of Jacques Lacan.* Trans. Arthur Goldhammer. New York: Columbia Univ. Press, 1983.

Cohn, Dorrit. *Transparent Minds: Narrative Modes for Presenting Consciousness in Fiction.* Princeton: Princeton Univ. Press, 1978.

Collins, Patricia Hill. *Black Feminist Thought: Knowledge, Consciousness, and the Politics of Empowerment.* Boston: Unwin Hyman, 1990.

Costello, Julie. "Maria Edgeworth and the Politics of Consumption: Eating, Breastfeeding, and the Irish Wet Nurse in *Ennui*." Greenfield and Barash 173–92.

Cott, Nancy F. *The Bonds of Womanhood: "Woman's Sphere" in New England, 1780–1835.* New Haven: Yale Univ. Press, 1977.

David, Deirdre. *Rule Britannia: Women, Empire and Victorian Writing.* Ithaca: Cornell Univ. Press, 1995.

Davidoff, Leonore, and Catherine Hall. *Family Fortunes: Men and Women of the English Middle Class, 1780–1850.* Chicago: Univ. of Chicago Press, 1987.

Davis, Lennard J. *Factual Fictions: The Origins of the English Novel.* New York: Columbia Univ. Press, 1983.

———. "Reconsidering Origins: How Novel Are Theories of the Novel?" *Eighteenth-Century Fiction* 12 (2000): 479–99.

Day, Thomas. *The Dying Negro, A Poetical Epistle, Supposed to be Written by a Black, (Who lately shot himself on board a vessel in the river Thames;) to his intended Wife.* London: W. Flexney, 1773.

Defoe, Daniel. *Roxana.* New York: Penguin, 1987.

Deforest, Mary. "Mrs. Elton and the Slave Trade." *Persuasions* (Dec. 1987): 11–13.

De Lauretis, Teresa. *Alice Doesn't: Feminism, Semiotics, Cinema.* Bloomington: Indiana Univ. Press, 1984.

———. *The Practice of Love: Lesbian Sexuality and Perverse Desire.* Bloomington: Indiana Univ. Press, 1994.

———. *Technologies of Gender: Essays on Theory, Film, and Fiction.* Bloomington: Indiana Univ. Press, 1987.

Demos, John. *Past, Present, and Personal: The Family and the Life Course in American History.* London: Oxford Univ. Press, 1986.

The Digest: Annotated British, Commonwealth and European Cases 28 (3). London: Butterworth, 1989.

Doane, Janice, and Devon Hodges. *From Klein to Kristeva: Psychoanalytic*

Feminism and the Search for the "Good Enough" Mother. Ann Arbor: Univ. of Michigan Press, 1995.

Doane, Mary Ann. "Film and the Masquerade: Theorizing the Female Spectator." *Issues in Feminist Film Criticism.* Ed. Patricia Erens. Bloomington: Indiana Univ. Press, 1990. 41–57.

Donaldson, Laura E. *Decolonizing Feminisms: Race, Gender, and Empire-Building.* Chapel Hill: Univ. of North Carolina Press, 1992.

Donoghue, Emma. *Passions Between Women: British Lesbian Culture, 1668–1801.* New York: Harper Collins, 1993.

Donovan, Josephine. *Women and the Rise of the Novel, 1405–1726.* New York: St. Martin's Press, 1999.

Doody, Margaret. "Beyond *Evelina:* The Individual Novel and the Community of Literature." *Eighteenth-Century Fiction* 3 (1991): 359–71.

———. *Frances Burney: The Life in the Works.* New Brunswick: Rutgers Univ. Press, 1988.

———. "Shandyism, Or, the Novel in Its Assy Shape: African Apuleius, *The Golden Ass,* and Prose Fiction." *Eighteenth-Century Fiction* 12 (2000): 435–58.

———. *The True Story of the Novel.* New Brunswick: Rutgers Univ. Press, 1996.

Dunne, Tom. *Maria Edgeworth and the Colonial Mind.* Cork: University Coll., 1984.

Edgeworth, Maria. *Belinda.* Ed. Kathryn J. Kirkpatrick. Oxford: Oxford Univ. Press, 1994.

———. *Castle Rackrent and Ennui.* Ed. Marilyn Butler. London: Penguin Books, 1992.

———. "The Grateful Negro." *Popular Tales.* London: J. Johnson, 1805. 193–240.

———. "Original Sketch of *Belinda:* 'Abroad and at Home.' " *Belinda.* Ed. Kathryn J. Kirkpatrick. Oxford: Oxford Univ. Press, 1994. 479–83.

Epstein, Julia. "Either/Or—Neither/Both: Sexual Ambiguity and the Ideology of Gender." *Genders* 7 (1990): 99–142.

———. *The Iron Pen: Frances Burney and the Politics of Women's Writing.* Madison: Univ. of Wisconsin Press, 1989.

Faderman, Lillian. *Surpassing the Love of Men: Romantic Friendship and Love Between Women from the Renaissance to the Present.* New York: William Morrow and Co., 1981.

Fanon, Frantz. *Black Skin, White Masks.* Trans. Charles Lam Markman. New York: Grove Press, 1967.

Fatherless Fanny. London: C & W Thompson, 1822.

Felsenstein, Frank. *Anti-Semitic Stereotypes: A Paradigm of Otherness in English Popular Culture, 1660–1830.* Baltimore: Johns Hopkins Univ. Press, 1995.

Ferguson, Margaret W. "Juggling the Categories of Race, Class and Gender: Aphra Behn's *Oroonoko.*" Hendricks and Parker 209–24.

——. "News from the New World: Miscegenous Romance in Aphra Behn's *Oroonoko* and *The Widow Ranter.*" *The Production of English Renaissance Culture.* Ed. David Lee Miller, Sharon O'Dair, Harold Weber. Ithaca: Cornell Univ. Press, 1994. 151–89.

Ferguson, Moira. "*Mansfield Park:* Slavery, Colonialism, and Gender." *Oxford Literary Review* 13 (1991): 118–39.

——. *Subject to Others: British Women Writers and Colonial Slavery, 1670– 1834.* New York: Routledge, 1992.

Fieldhouse, D. K. *The Colonial Empires: A Comparative Survey from the Eighteenth Century.* London: Weidenfeld and Nicholson, 1965.

Fielding, Henry. *Joseph Andrews.* Boston: Houghton Mifflin, 1961.

——. *Tom Jones.* New York: Penguin Books, 1987.

Fildes, Valerie. *Breasts, Bottles, and Babies: A History of Infant Feeding.* Edinburgh Univ. Press, 1986.

——. *Wet Nursing: A History from Antiquity to the Present.* Oxford: Basil Blackwell, 1988.

Fildes, Valerie, ed. *Women as Mothers in Pre-Industrial England.* London and New York: Routledge, 1990.

Finch, Casey, and Peter Bowen. " 'The Tittle-Tattle of Highbury': Gossip and the Free Indirect Style of *Emma.*" *Representations* 31 (1990): 1–18.

Fizer, Irene. "The Name of the Daughter: Identity and Incest in *Evelina.*" *Refiguring the Father: New Feminist Readings of Patriarchy.* Ed. Patricia Yaeger and Beth Kowaleski-Wallace. Carbondale: Southern Illinois Univ. Press, 1989. 78–107.

Flavin, Louise. "Free Indirect Discourse and the Clever Heroine of *Emma.*" *Persuasions* 13: 50–57.

Flint, Christopher. *Family Fictions: Narrative and Domestic Relations in Britain, 1688–1798.* Stanford: Stanford Univ. Press, 1998.

Foster, James. *History of the Pre-romantic Novel in England.* Modern Language Association, 1966.

Foucault, Michel. *The History of Sexuality, Volume I.* Trans. Robert Hurley. New York: Vintage Books, 1980.

Freud, Sigmund. "Analysis of a Phobia in a Five-Year-Old Boy." *The Sexual Enlightenment of Children.* Ed. Philip Rieff. New York: Collier Books, 1963. 47–183.

——. *Dora: An Analysis of a Case of Hysteria.* Ed. Philip Rieff. New York: Collier Books, 1963.

——. "Female Sexuality." *Sexuality and the Psychology of Love.* Ed. Philip Rieff. New York: Collier Books, 1963. 184–201.

——. "The Passing of the Oedipus-Complex." *Sexuality and the Psychology of Love.* 166–72.

ature and Interiority in *Mansfield Park.*" *Texas Studies in Literature and Language* 36 (1994): 306–27.

———. Introduction. Greenfield and Barash 1–33.

———. " 'Oh Dear Resemblance of Thy Murdered Mother': Female Authorship in *Evelina.*" *Eighteenth-Century Fiction* 3 (1991): 301–20.

———. "Veiled Desire: Mother-Daughter Love and Sexual Imagery in Ann Radcliffe's *The Italian.*" *The Eighteenth Century: Theory and Interpretation* 33 (1992): 73–89.

Greenfield, Susan C., and Carol Barash, eds. *Inventing Maternity: Politics, Science, and Literature, 1650–1865.* Lexington: Univ. Press of Kentucky, 1999.

Grewal, Inderpal, and Caren Kaplan, eds. *Scattered Hegemonies: Postmodernity and Transnational Feminist Practices.* Minneapolis: Univ. of Minnesota Press, 1994.

Hagan, John. "The Closure of *Emma.*" Bloom 45–66.

Hägg, Tomas. *The Novel in Antiquity.* Berkeley: Univ. of California Press, 1983.

Haggerty, George E. *Unnatural Affections: Women and Fiction in the Later Eighteenth Century.* Bloomington: Indiana Univ. Press, 1998.

Hall, Catherine. *White, Male and Middle Class: Explorations in Feminism and History.* New York: Routledge, 1992.

Hay, John A. "Rhetoric and Historiography: Tristram Shandy's First Nine Kalendar Months." *Studies in the Eighteenth Century.* Ed. R. F. Brissenden. Toronto: Univ. of Toronto Press, 1973. 73–91.

Helme, Elizabeth. *Louisa; or The Cottage on the Moor.* London: Kearsley, 1787.

Hendricks, Margo, and Patricia Parker, eds. *Women, "Race," and Writing in the Early Modern Period.* London: Routledge, 1994.

Hilbish, Florence. *Charlotte Smith, Poet and Novelist.* Philadelphia: Univ. of Pennsylvania Press, 1941.

Hirsch, Marianne. *The Mother/Daughter Plot: Narrative, Psychoanalysis, Feminism.* Bloomington: Indiana Univ. Press, 1989.

Hoffer, Peter C. and N. E. H. Hull. *Murdering Mothers: Infanticide in England and New England, 1558–1803.* New York: New York Univ. Press, 1981.

Homans, Margaret. *Bearing the Word: Language and Female Experience in Nineteenth-Century Women's Writing.* Chicago: Univ. of Chicago Press, 1986.

———. " 'Racial Composition': Metaphor and the Body in the Writing of Race." Abel et al. 77–101.

Howard, Carol. " 'The Story of the Pineapple': Sentimental Abolitionism and Moral Motherhood in Amelia Opie's *Adeline Mowbray.*" *Studies in the Novel* 30 (1998): 355–76.

Huet, Marie-Hélène. *Monstrous Imagination.* Cambridge: Harvard Univ. Press, 1993.

Hunter, J. Paul. *Before Novels: The Cultural Context of Eighteenth-Century Fiction*. New York: W. W. Norton, 1990.

———. "Clocks, Calendars, and Names: The Troubles of Tristram and the Aesthetics of Uncertainty." *Rhetorics of Order/Ordering Rhetorics in English Neoclassical Literature*. Ed. J. Douglas Canfield and J. Paul Hunter. Newark: Univ. of Delaware Press, 1989. 173–98.

Hurst, Michael. *Maria Edgeworth and the Public Scene: Intellect, Fine Feeling and Landlordism in the Age of Reform*. Coral Gables: Univ. of Miami Press, 1969.

Irigaray, Luce. *Speculum of the Other Woman*. Trans. Gillian C. Gill. Ithaca: Cornell Univ. Press, 1985.

———. *This Sex Which Is Not One*. Trans. Catherine Porter with Carolyn Burke. Ithaca: Cornell Univ. Press, 1985.

Jacobs, Harriet A. *Incidents in the Life of a Slave Girl*. Ed. Jean Fagan Yellin. Cambridge: Harvard Univ. Press, 1987.

Jacobus, Mary. *First Things: The Maternal Imaginary in Literature, Art, and Psychoanalysis*. New York: Routledge, 1995.

Janes, R. M. "On the Reception of Mary Wollstonecraft's *A Vindication of the Rights of Woman*." *Journal of the History of Ideas* 39 (1978): 293–302.

Johnson, Barbara. *The Feminist Difference: Literature, Psychoanalysis, Race, and Gender*. Cambridge: Harvard·Univ. Press, 1998.

Johnson, Claudia L. *Equivocal Beings: Politics, Gender, and Sentimentality in the 1790s; Wollstonecraft, Radcliffe, Burney, Austen*. Chicago: Univ. of Chicago Press, 1995.

———. *Jane Austen: Women, Politics, and the Novel*. Chicago: Univ. of Chicago Press, 1988.

———. "Mary Wollstonecraft: Styles of Radical Maternity." Greenfield and Barash 159–72.

Jones, Jacqueline. *Labor of Love, Labor of Sorrow: Black Women, Work and the Family From Slavery to the Present*. New York: Vintage, 1985.

Jordanova, Ludmilla. "Interrogating the Concept of Reproduction in the Eighteenth Century." *Conceiving the New World Order: The Global Politics of Reproduction*. Ed. Faye D. Ginsburg and Rayna Rapp. Berkeley: Univ. of California Press, 1995. 369–86.

———. *Sexual Visions: Images of Gender in Science and Medicine between the Eighteenth and Twentieth Centuries*. Madison: Univ. of Wisconsin Press, 1989.

Kaplan, Cora. "Pandora's Box: Subjectivity, Class and Sexuality in Socialist Feminist Criticism." *Making a Difference*. Ed. Gayle Greene and Coppélia Kahn. London: Methuen, 1985. 146–76.

———. "Wild Nights: Pleasure/Sexuality/Feminism." *Sea Changes: Essays on Culture and Feminism*. London: Verso, 1986. 31–56.

Kaplan, E. Ann. "Is the Gaze Male?" *Powers of Desire: The Politics of Sexuality*.

Ed. Ann Snitow, Christine Stansell, and Sharon Thompson. New York: Monthly Review Press, 1983. 309–27.

———. *Motherhood and Representation: The Mother in Popular Culture and Melodrama*. London: Routledge, 1992.

Keller, Eve. "Making Up for Losses: The Workings of Gender in William Harvey's *De Generatione animalium*." Greenfield and Barash 34–56.

Kerber, Linda K. *Women of the Republic: Intellect and Ideology in Revolutionary America*. Chapel Hill: Univ. of North Carolina Press, 1980.

King, Ross. "*Tristram Shandy* and the Wound of Language." *Studies in Philology* 92 (1995): 291–310.

Kirkpatrick, Kathryn J. "'Gentlemen Have Horrors Upon This Subject': West Indian Suitors in Maria Edgeworth's *Belinda*." *Eighteenth-Century Fiction* 5 (1993): 331–48.

———. Introduction. Maria Edgeworth, *Belinda*. Ed. Kathryn J. Kirkpatrick. Oxford: Oxford Univ. Press, 1994. ix–xxxii.

Korba, Susan M. "'Improper and Dangerous Distinctions': Female Relationships and Erotic Domination in *Emma*." *Studies in the Novel* 29 (1997): 139–63.

Kowaleski-Wallace, Elizabeth. *Their Fathers' Daughters: Hannah More, Maria Edgeworth, and Patriarchal Complicity*. New York: Oxford Univ. Press, 1991.

Kristeva, Julia. *Black Sun: Depression and Melancholia*. Trans. Leon S. Roudiez. New York: Columbia Univ. Press, 1989.

———. *Desire in Language: A Semiotic Approach to Literature and Art*. Ed. Leon S. Roudiez. Trans. Thomas Gora, Alice Jardine, and Leon S. Roudiez. New York: Columbia Univ. Press, 1980.

———. *Powers of Horror: An Essay on Abjection*. Trans. Leon S. Roudiez. New York: Columbia Univ. Press, 1982.

Lacan, Jacques. "The Function and Field of Speech and Language in Psychoanalysis." *Écrits: A Selection*. Trans. Alan Sheridan. New York: W. W. Norton, 1977. 30–113.

———. "On a Question Preliminary to any Possible Treatment of Psychosis." *Écrits*. 179–225.

Lamb, Jonathan. "Sterne and Irregular Oratory." *Cambridge Companion to the Eighteenth-Century Novel*. Ed. John Richetti. Cambridge: Cambridge Univ. Press, 1996. 153–74.

Landa, L. A. "The Shandean Homunculus: The Background of Sterne's 'Little Gentleman.'" *Restoration and Eighteenth-Century Literature: Essays in Honour of Alan Dugald McKillop*. Ed. Carroll Camden. Chicago: Univ. of Chicago Press, 1963. 44–68.

Langbauer, Laurie. "An Early Romance: Motherhood and Women's Writing in Mary Wollstonecraft's Novels." *Romanticism and Feminism*. Ed. Anne K. Mellor. Bloomington: Indiana Univ. Press, 1988. 208–19.

Lanser, Susan S. "Befriending the Body: Female Intimacies as Class Acts." *Eighteenth-Century Studies* 32 (1998–99): 179–98.

Laqueur, Thomas. *Making Sex: Body and Gender from the Greeks to Freud.* Cambridge: Harvard Univ. Press, 1990.

Laslett, Peter, Karla Oosterveen, and Richard M. Smith, eds. *Bastardy and Its Comparative History.* Cambridge: Harvard Univ. Press, 1980.

Lévi-Strauss, Claude. *The Elementary Structures of Kinship.* Ed. Rodney Needham. Trans. James Harle Bell, John Richard von Sturmer, and Rodney Needham. Boston: Beacon Press, 1969.

Levy, Anita. "Reproductive Urges: Literacy, Sexuality, and Eighteenth-Century Englishness." Greenfield and Barash 193–214.

Lewis, Judith Schneid. *In the Family Way: Childbearing in the British Aristocracy, 1760–1860.* New Brunswick: Rutgers Univ. Press, 1986.

Lewis, Matthew. *The Monk.* Ed. Howard Anderson. New York: Oxford Univ. Press, 1990.

Locke, John. *An Essay Concerning Human Understanding.* London: Penguin, 1997.

Long, Edward. *The History of Jamaica.* 3 vols. New York: Arno Press, 1972.

Lovell, Terry. *Consuming Fiction.* London: Verso, 1987.

Lynch, Deidre Shauna. *The Economy of Character: Novels, Market Culture, and the Business of Inner Meaning.* Chicago: Univ. of Chicago Press, 1998.

Lynch, Deidre, and William B. Warner, eds. *Cultural Institutions of the Novel.* Durham: Duke Univ. Press, 1996.

———. "Introduction: The Transport of the Novel." Lynch and Warner 1–10.

MacFadyen, Heather. "Lady Delacour's Library: Maria Edgeworth's *Belinda* and Fashionable Reading." *Nineteenth-Century Literature* 48 (1994): 423–39.

Maddox, James H. "On Defoe's *Roxana*." *ELH* 51 (1984): 669–91.

Maurer, Shawn Lisa. "The Female (as) Reader: Sex, Sensibility, and the Maternal in Wollstonecraft's Fictions." *Essays in Literature* 19 (1992): 36–54.

McClintock, Anne. *Imperial Leather: Race, Gender and Sexuality in the Colonial Conquest.* New York: Routledge, 1995.

McClure, Ruth K. *Coram's Children: The London Foundling Hospital in the Eighteenth Century.* New Haven: Yale Univ. Press, 1981.

McCrea, Brian. *Impotent Fathers: Patriarchy and Demographic Crisis in the Eighteenth-Century Novel.* Newark: Univ. of Delaware Press, 1998.

McKendrick, Neil, John Brewer, and J. H. Plumb. *The Birth of a Consumer Society: The Commercialization of Eighteenth-Century England.* Bloomington: Indiana Univ. Press, 1982.

McKeon, Michael. *The Origins of the English Novel, 1600–1740.* Baltimore: Johns Hopkins Univ. Press, 1987.

McNeil, David. "*Tristram Shandy:* The Grotesque View of War and the

Military Character." *Studies on Voltaire and the Eighteenth Century* 266 (1989): 411–32.

Mellor, Anne K. *Romanticism and Gender.* New York: Routledge, 1993.

Merchant, Carolyn. *The Death of Nature.* San Francisco: Harper, 1980.

Meyers, Mitzi. "My Art Belongs to Daddy? Thomas Day, Maria Edgeworth, and the Pre-Texts of *Belinda:* Women Writers and Patriarchal Authority." Backscheider, *Revising Women* 104–46.

Miles, Rosalind. *The Female Form: Women Writers and the Conquest of the Novel.* New York: Routledge, 1987.

Minsky, Rosalind. *Psychoanalysis and Gender: An Introductory Reader.* London: Routledge, 1996.

Mitchell, Juliet. *Psychoanalysis and Feminism: Freud, Reich, Laing and Women.* New York: Vintage Press, 1974.

Moglen, Helene. "Redeeming History: Toni Morrison's *Beloved.*" Abel et al. 201–22.

Moore, Lisa L. *Dangerous Intimacies: Toward a Sapphic History of the British Novel.* Durham and London: Duke Univ. Press, 1997.

———. "'Something More Tender Still Than Friendship': Romantic Friendship in Early-Nineteenth-Century England." *Feminist Studies* 18 (1992): 499–520.

Morgan, Susan. "*Emma* and the Charms of Imagination." Bloom 67–89.

Mosse, George L. *Nationalism and Sexuality: Respectability and Abnormal Sexuality in Modern Europe.* New York: Howard Fertig, 1985.

Needham, Joseph. *A History of Embryology.* New York: Arno Press, 1975.

Norton, Caroline. "A Plain Letter to the Lord Chancellor on the Infant Custody Bill." *Selected Writings of Caroline Norton.* Ed. James O. Hoge and Jane Marcus. Delmar, N.Y.: Scholars' Facsimiles and Reprints, 1978. 1–124.

Norton, Mary Beth. *Liberty's Daughters: The Revolutionary Experience of American Women, 1750–1800.* Boston: Little, Brown, 1980.

Nussbaum, Felicity. *Torrid Zones: Maternity, Sexuality, and Empire in Eighteenth-Century English Narratives.* Baltimore: Johns Hopkins Univ. Press, 1995.

Oakleaf, David. "The Name of the Father: Social Identity and the Ambition of *Evelina.*" *Eighteenth-Century Fiction* 3 (1991): 341–58.

Opie, Amelia Alderson. *Adeline Mowbray, or The Mother and Daughter.* London: Pandora, 1986.

———. "In Memory of My Mother." *Lays for the Dead* (1834). Brightwell 9–11.

Pagel, Walter. *William Harvey's Biological Ideas: Selected Aspects and Historical Background.* New York: Basel, 1967.

Parker, Andrew, Mary Russo, Doris Sommer, and Patricia Yaeger, eds. *Nationalisms and Sexualities.* London: Routledge, 1992.

Pateman, Carole. *The Sexual Contract.* Stanford: Stanford Univ. Press, 1988.

Patterson, Orlando. *The Sociology of Slavery: An Analysis of the Origins, Development and Structure of Negro Slave Society in Jamaica*. London: Cox and Wyman, 1967.

Pawl, Amy J. "'And What Other Name May I Claim?': Names and Their Owners in Frances Burney's *Evelina.*"*Eighteenth-Century Fiction* 3 (1991): 383–99.

Perera, Suvendrini. *Reaches of Empire: The English Novel from Edgeworth to Dickens*. New York: Columbia Univ. Press, 1991.

Perkin, Harold. *Origins of Modern English Society, 1780–1880*. London: Ark Paperbacks, 1985.

Perry, Ruth. "Colonizing the Breast: Sexuality and Maternity in Eighteenth-Century England." *Journal of the History of Sexuality* 2 (1991): 204–34.

———. "Incest as the Meaning of the Gothic Novel." *The Eighteenth Century: Theory and Interpretation* 39 (1998): 261–78.

———. "Interrupted Friendships in Jane Austen's *Emma*." *Tulsa Studies in Women's Literature* 5 (1986): 185–202.

———. *Women, Letters and the Novel*. New York: AMS Press, 1980.

———. "Words for Sex: The Verbal-Sexual Continuum in *Tristram Shandy*." *Studies in the Novel* 20 (1988): 27–42.

Peterson, William. *Malthus*. Cambridge: Harvard Univ. Press, 1979.

Pickrel, Paul. "Lionel Trilling and *Emma:* A Reconsideration." *Nineteenth-Century Fiction* 40 (1985): 297–311.

Pollak, Ellen. "Guarding the Succession of the (E)state: Guardian-Ward Incest and the Dangers of Representation in Delariviere Manley's *The New Atlantis.*" *The Eighteenth Century: Theory and Interpretation* 39 (1998): 220–37.

———. *The Poetics of Sexual Myth: Gender and Ideology in the Verse of Swift and Pope*. Chicago: Univ. of Chicago Press, 1985.

Pollock, Linda. *Forgotten Children: Parent-Child Relations, 1500–1900*. Cambridge: Cambridge Univ. Press, 1983.

Poovey, Mary. *The Proper Lady and the Woman Writer: Ideology as Style in the Works of Mary Wollstonecraft, Mary Shelley, and Jane Austen*. Chicago: Univ. of Chicago Press, 1984.

———. *Uneven Developments: The Ideological Work of Gender in Mid-Victorian England*. Chicago: Univ. of Chicago Press, 1988.

Pope, Alexander. *The Rape of the Lock*. Ed. J. S. Cunningham. Oxford: Oxford Univ. Press, 1966.

Prince, Mary. *The History of Mary Prince, A West Indian Slave*. Ed. Moira Ferguson. Ann Arbor: Univ. of Michigan Press, 1993.

Radcliffe, Ann. *The Italian*. Ed. Frederick Garber. Oxford: Oxford Univ. Press, 1981.

Radway, Janice. *Reading the Romance: Women, Patriarchy and Popular Literature*. Chapel Hill: Univ. of North Carolina Press, 1984.

Reconsidering the Rise of the Novel. Eighteenth-Century Fiction 12 (2000).

Reeves, John K. "The Mother of *Fatherless Fanny.*" *ELH* 9 (1942): 224–33.

Restuccia, Frances L. "A Black Morning: Kristevan Melancholia in Jane Austen's *Emma.*" *American Imago* 51 (1994): 447–69.

Rich, Adrienne. "Compulsory Heterosexuality and Lesbian Existence." *Signs* 5 (1980): 631–60.

Richardson, Ronald Kent. *Moral Imperium: Afro-Caribbeans and the Transformation of British Rule, 1776–1838.* New York: Greenwood Press, 1987.

Richardson, Samuel. *Clarissa; or the History of a Young Lady.* New York: Penguin, 1985.

———. *Pamela.* Boston: Houghton Mifflin, 1971.

Richetti, John. *The English Novel in History, 1700–1780.* London and New York: Routledge, 1999.

———. "The Family, Sex, and Marriage in Defoe's *Moll Flanders* and *Roxana.*" *Studies in the Literary Imagination* 15 (1982): 19–35.

———. Introduction: Twenty Years On. *Popular Fiction Before Richardson: Narrative Patterns, 1700–1739.* New York: Oxford Univ. Press, 1992. xi–xxix.

Roche, Regina Maria. *The Children of the Abbey.* London: Minerva Press, 1797.

Rogers, Deborah D. "Eighteenth-Century Literary Depictions of Childbirth in the Historical Context of Mutilation and Mortality: The Case of *Pamela.*" *Centennial Review* 37 (1993): 305–24.

———. Introduction. *The Critical Response to Ann Radcliffe.* New York: Greenwood Press, 1994.

Roof, Judith. *A Lure of Knowledge: Lesbian Sexuality and Theory.* New York: Columbia Univ. Press, 1991.

Rose, Jacqueline. Introduction-II. *Feminine Sexuality: Jacques Lacan and the Ècole Freudienne.* Ed. Juliet Mitchell and Jacqueline Rose. New York and London: W. W. Norton, 1985. 27–57.

———. *Sexuality in the Field of Vision.* London: Verso, 1986.

Rousseau, Jean-Jacques. *Émile.* Trans. Barbara Foxley. London: J. M. Dent & Sons, 1989.

Rubin, Gayle. "The Traffic in Women: Notes on the 'Political Economy' of Sex." *Toward an Anthropology of Women.* Ed. Rayna R. Reiter. New York: Monthly Review Press, 1975. 157–210.

Saeger, James. "'Why Bastard? Wherefore Base?': Representing Bastardy in Early Modern England." Diss. Univ. of Pennsylvania, 1996.

Saint-Pierre, J. H. Bernardin de. *Paul et Virginie.* Trans. Helen Maria Williams. Oxford: Woodstock Books, 1989.

Sapiro, Virginia. *A Vindication of Political Virtue: The Political Theory of Mary Wollstonecraft.* Chicago: Univ. of Chicago Press, 1992.

Schiebinger, Londa. *Nature's Body: Gender in the Making of Modern Science.* Boston: Beacon Press, 1993.

Scholten, Catherine M. *Childbearing in American Society, 1650–1850.* New York: New York Univ. Press, 1985.

Scott, Joan Wallach. *Gender and the Politics of History.* New York: Columbia Univ. Press, 1988.

———. *Only Paradoxes to Offer: French Feminists and the Rights of Man.* Cambridge: Harvard Univ. Press, 1996.

Sedgwick, Eve Kosofsky. *Between Men: English Literature and Male Homosocial Desire.* New York: Columbia Univ. Press, 1985.

———. *The Coherence of Gothic Conventions.* New York: Methuen, 1980.

Shaffer, Julie. "Not Subordinate: Empowering Women in the Marriage-Plot—The Novels of Frances Burney, Maria Edgeworth, and Jane Austen." *Criticism* 34 (1992): 51–73.

Shakespeare, William. *Pericles. The Riverside Shakespeare.* Ed. G. Blakemore Evans. Boston: Houghton Mifflin, 1974. 1479–1511.

———. *The Winter's Tale. Riverside Shakespeare.* 1569–1605.

Sharpe, Jenny. *Allegories of Empire: The Figure of Woman in the Colonial Text.* Minneapolis: Univ. of Minnesota Press, 1993.

Shorter, Edward. *The Making of the Modern Family.* New York: Basic Books, 1975.

Shyllon, Folarin. *Black People in Britain, 1555–1833.* London: Oxford Univ. Press, 1977.

Silverman, Kaja. *The Acoustic Mirror: The Female Voice in Psychoanalysis and Cinema.* Bloomington: Indiana Univ. Press, 1988.

———. *The Subject of Semiotics.* New York: Oxford Univ. Press, 1983.

Siskin, Clifford. "Epilogue: The Rise of Novelism." Lynch and Warner 423–40.

Smith, Charlotte. *Celestina.* Dublin: R. Cross, 1791.

Smith-Rosenberg, Carroll. "The Female World of Love and Ritual: Relations Between Women in Nineteenth-Century America." *A Heritage of Her Own.* Ed. Nancy F. Cott and Elizabeth H. Pleck. New York: Simon and Schuster, 1979. 311–42.

Spacks, Patricia Meyer. *Desire and Truth: Functions of Plot in Eighteenth-Century English Novels.* Chicago: Univ. of Chicago Press, 1990.

Spencer, Jane. *The Rise of the Woman Novelist.* New York: Basil Blackwell, 1986.

Spender, Dale. *Mothers of the Novel.* London: Methuen, 1986.

Spillers, Hortense. "'All the Things You Could Be by Now, If Sigmund Freud's Wife Was Your Mother': Psychoanalysis and Race." Abel et al. 135–58.

———. "Notes on an Alternative Model—Neither/Nor." *The Difference Within.* Ed. Elizabeth Meese and Alice Parker. Philadelphia: John Benjamins, 1989.

Sprengnether, Madelon. *The Spectral Mother: Freud, Feminism, and Psycho-analysis.* Ithaca: Cornell Univ. Press, 1990.

Staves, Susan. *Married Women's Separate Property in England, 1660–1833.* Cambridge: Harvard Univ. Press, 1990.

St. Clair, William. *The Godwins and the Shelleys: A Biography of a Family.* New York: W. W. Norton, 1989.

Sterne, Laurence. *The Life and Opinions of Tristram Shandy.* New York: Penguin, 1983.

Stevenson, John Allen. "Sterne: Comedian and Experimental Novelist." *Columbia History of the British Novel.* Ed. John Richetti. New York: Columbia Univ. Press, 1994. 154–80.

Stewart, Maaja A. *Domestic Realities and Imperial Fictions: Jane Austen's Novels in Eighteenth-Century Context.* Athens: Univ. of Georgia Press, 1993.

Stone, Lawrence. *The Family, Sex and Marriage in England, 1500–1800.* New York: Harper and Row, 1977.

———. *Road to Divorce: England 1530–1987.* Oxford: Oxford Univ. Press, 1990.

Straub, Kristina. *Divided Fictions: Fanny Burney and Feminine Strategy.* Lexington: Univ. Press of Kentucky, 1987.

Sypher, Wylie. "The West-Indian as a 'Character' in the Eighteenth Century." *Studies in Philology* 36 (1939): 503–20.

Tate, Claudia. *Psychoanalysis and Black Novels: Desire and the Protocols of Race.* New York: Oxford Univ. Press, 1998.

Teichman, Jenny. *Illegitimacy: An Examination of Bastardy.* Ithaca: Cornell Univ. Press, 1982.

Thackeray, William. *Vanity Fair.* New York: Oxford Univ. Press, 1983.

Theriot, Nancy M. *Mothers and Daughters in Nineteenth-Century America: The Biosocial Construction of Femininity.* Lexington: Univ. Press of Kentucky, 1996.

Thurer, Shari. *Myths of Motherhood: How Culture Reinvents the Good Mother.* Boston: Houghton Mifflin, 1994.

Tobin, Beth Fowkes. "Aiding Impoverished Gentlewomen: Power and Class in *Emma.*" *Criticism* 30 (1988): 413–30.

———. "The Moral and Political Economy of Property in Austen's *Emma.*" *Eighteenth-Century Fiction* 2 (1990): 229–54.

Todd, Janet. *Mary Wollstonecraft: A Revolutionary Life.* London: Weidenfeld and Nicolson, 2000.

———. *The Sign of Angellica: Women, Writing and Fiction, 1660–1800.* New York: Columbia Univ. Press, 1989.

———. *Women's Friendship in Literature.* New York: Columbia Univ. Press, 1980.

Tompkins, J. M. S. *The Popular Novel in England, 1770–1800.* Lincoln: Univ. of Nebraska Press, 1967.

————. "The Psychogenesis of a Case of Homosexuality in a Woman." *Sexuality and the Psychology of Love.* 123–49.

————. "Some Psychological Consequences of the Anatomical Distinction Between the Sexes." *Sexuality and the Psychology of Love.* 173–83.

Gallagher, Catherine. *Nobody's Story: The Vanishing Acts of Women Writers in the Marketplace, 1670–1820.* Berkeley: Univ. of California Press, 1994.

Gallop, Jane. *The Daughter's Seduction: Feminism and Psychoanalysis.* Ithaca: Cornell Univ. Press, 1982.

Garber, Frederick. Introduction. Ann Radcliffe, *The Italian.* Ed. Frederick Garber. Oxford: Oxford Univ. Press, 1981. vii–xv.

Garner, Shirley Nelson, Claire Kahane, and Madelon Sprengnether. Introduction. *The (M)other Tongue: Essays in Feminist Psychoanalytic Interpretation.* Ithaca: Cornell Univ. Press, 1985. 15–29.

Garside, Peter and Rainer Schöwerling, eds. *The English Novel 1770–1829: A Bibliographical Survey of Prose Fiction Published in the British Isles.* Vol. II. Oxford: Oxford Univ. Press, 2000.

Gasking, Elizabeth B. *Investigations into Generation, 1651–1828.* Baltimore: Johns Hopkins Univ. Press, 1967.

Gelpi, Barbara Charlesworth. *Shelley's Goddess: Maternity, Language, Subjectivity.* New York: Oxford Univ. Press, 1992.

————. "Significant Exposure: The Turn-of-the-Century Breast." *Nineteenth-Century Contexts* 20 (1997): 125–45.

George, Dorothy M. *London Life in the Eighteenth Century.* Chicago: Academy Chicago, 1984.

Gerzina, Gretchen. *Black England: Life Before Emancipation.* New Brunswick: Rutgers Univ. Press, 1995.

Gibson, Ian. *The English Vice: Beating, Sex, and Shame in Victorian England and After.* London: Duckworth, 1978.

Gillis, John R. *For Better, For Worse: British Marriages, 1600 to the Present.* New York: Oxford Univ. Press, 1985.

————. *A World of Their Own Making: Myth, Ritual, and the Quest for Family Values.* New York: Basic Books, 1996.

Gillooly, Eileen. *Smile of Discontent: Humor, Gender, and Nineteenth-Century British Fiction.* Chicago: Univ. of Chicago Press, 1999.

Gilman, Sander L. "Black Bodies, White Bodies: Toward an Iconography of Female Sexuality in Late Nineteenth-Century Art, Medicine, and Literature." *"Race," Writing, and Difference.* Ed. Henry Louis Gates, Jr. Chicago: Univ. of Chicago Press, 1985. 223–61.

Great Britain Parliamentary Debates (Hansard) Series 3. Vols. 39–50.

Greenfield, Susan C. "'Abroad and at Home': Sexual Ambiguity, Miscegenation, and Colonial Boundaries in Edgeworth's *Belinda*." *PMLA* 112 (1997): 214–28.

————. "Fanny's Misreading and the Misreading of Fanny: Women, Liter-

Trenkner, Sophie. *The Greek Novella in the Classical Period.* Cambridge: Cambridge Univ. Press, 1958.

Trumbach, Randolph. "London's Sapphists: From Three Sexes to Four Genders in the Making of Modern Culture." *Body Guards: The Cultural Politics of Gender Ambiguity.* Ed. Julia Epstein and Kristina Straub. New York: Routledge, 1991. 112–41.

———. *The Rise of the Egalitarian Family: Aristocratic Kinship and Domestic Relations in Eighteenth-Century England.* New York: Academic Press, 1978.

Turner, Cheryl. *Living by the Pen: Women Writers in the Eighteenth Century.* London: Routledge, 1992.

Uphaus, Robert W. "Jane Austen and Female Reading." *Studies in the Novel* 19 (1987): 334–45.

Vickery, Amanda. *The Gentleman's Daughter: Women's Lives in Georgian England.* New Haven: Yale Univ. Press, 1998.

Walpole, Horace. *The Castle of Otranto.* London: Oxford Univ. Press, 1964.

———. *The Mysterious Mother. Five Romantic Plays, 1768– 1821.* Ed. Paul Baines and Edward Burns. Oxford: Oxford Univ. Press, 2000. 1–70.

Walton, Jean. "Re-Placing Race in (White) Psychoanalytic Discourse: Founding Narratives of Feminism." Abel et al. 223–51.

Ward, J. R. *British West Indian Slavery, 1750–1834.* Oxford: Clarendon Press, 1988.

Wardle, Ralph M., ed. *Collected Letters of Mary Wollstonecraft.* Ithaca: Cornell Univ. Press, 1979.

Warner, William. "Formulating Fiction: Romancing the General Reader in Early Modern Britain." Lynch and Warner 279–305.

———. *Licensing Entertainment: The Elevation of Novel Reading in Britain, 1684–1750.* Berkeley: Univ. of California Press, 1998.

Watt, Ian. *The Rise of the Novel: Studies in Defoe, Richardson and Fielding.* Berkeley: Univ. of California Press, 1957.

Wexler, Laura. "Seeing Sentiment: Photography, Race, and the Innocent Eye." Abel et al. 159–86.

Whitford, Margaret. "Rereading Irigaray." *Between Feminism and Psychoanalysis.* Ed. Teresa Brennan. London: Routledge, 1989. 106–26.

Wiegman, Robyn. "Economies of the Body: Gendered Sites in *Robinson Crusoe* and *Roxana.*" *Criticism* 31 (1989): 33–51.

Williams, Patrick, and Laura Chrisman, eds. *Colonial Discourse and Post-Colonial Theory.* New York: Columbia Univ. Press, 1994.

Wilson, Anna. "Mary Wollstonecraft and the Search for the Radical Woman." *Genders* 6 (1989): 88–101.

Winter, Sarah. *Freud and the Institution of Psychoanalytic Knowledge.* Stanford: Stanford Univ. Press, 1999.

Wollstonecraft, Mary. *Mary and The Wrongs of Woman.* Ed. Gary Kelly. Oxford: Oxford Univ. Press, 1983.

————. *Thoughts on the Education of Daughters.* London: 1787.

————. *A Vindication of the Rights of Men, in a letter to the Right Honourable Edmund Burke.* Delmar: Scholars' Facsimiles and Reprints, 1975.

————. *A Vindication of the Rights of Woman.* Ed. Carol H. Poston. New York: W. W. Norton, 1988.

Yalom, Marilyn. *A History of the Breast.* New York: Knopf, 1997.

Yuval-Davis, Nira, and Floya Anthias, eds. *Woman-Nation-State.* London: MacMillan, 1989.

INDEX

Lightning Source UK Ltd.
Milton Keynes UK
UKHW021041170920
370030UK00010B/2633